**Regional
Growth and
Industrial
Location**

Regional Growth and Industrial Location

An Empirical Viewpoint

Leonard F. Wheat
Economist, Economic
Development Administration
U.S. Department of Commerce

Lexington Books
D.C. Heath and Company
Lexington, Massachusetts
Toronto   London

338.0973
W 556

Library of Congress Cataloging in Publication Data

Wheat, Leonard F
    Regional growth and industrial location.

    1. Industries, Location of—United States. 2. United States-Manufac-
tures. 3. Economic development. I. Title.
HC110.D5W46   338'.0973   73-3089
    ISBN 0-669-87031-5

Published simultaneously in Canada.

Printed in the United States of America.

International Standard Book Number: 0-669-87031-5

Library of Congress Catalog Card Number: 73-3089

To Janis

Contents

List of Tables

Preface

This study was born of a sense of frustration. Faced with a professional need for knowledge of the identity and relative importance of the influences responsible for regional differences in manufacturing growth in the United States, I found the relevant literature to be severely limited in its ability to provide answers.

A basic problem is that the literature has a strong theoretical bias. Most students of regional growth and industrial location are primarily concerned with theory and with model-building. Assumptions and hypotheses tend to take the place of facts; fortuitous relationships, useful for predicting, take the place of causal relationships. The relative overemphasis on theory is so severe, in fact, that model-builders often ignore what little empirical knowledge there is—such as findings suggesting that climate may play a very important role in industrial location.

Empirical studies have been undertaken, of course, including some of excellent quality. But they leave many questions unanswered. The unanswered questions result from a variety of limitations in the earlier studies. Although a few studies have flaws that cast doubt on their conclusions or render them ambiguous, this isn't the main problem. Problems of scope, for example, are far more serious. A study may focus on a particular industry or a particular locational factor. Alternatively, it may deal only with a particular geographic region, sometimes just a single state. Another problem is orientation. Some studies deal with local influences rather than broad regional influences. Others are oriented toward forecasting rather than explanation. Still another problem is that the studies that *have* sought broad explanations of manufacturing growth in the United States have tended to be descriptive and historical in their approach. Their conclusions are somewhat impressionistic, reflecting only limited statistical analysis.

These limitations leave the economist and the economic geographer with a dearth of factual knowledge about the economic relationships governing regional growth—knowledge of the sort that comes from quantitative studies designed to test hypotheses. David Smith can thus observe in his 1971 textbook, *Industrial Location: An Economic Geographical Analysis* (New York: John Wiley & Sons), that "there is a substantial body of abstract theory already in existence, and capable of extension, which has not been sufficiently tested in the arena of empirical inquiry" (p. 22). He adds—quite accurately—that industrial location is "a field of inquiry still in its infancy" (ibid.).

With this study, I hope to make a modest contribution to reducing the gap between fact and theory. The study is quantitative. It embraces all manufacturing, all regions. In it I take seven hypotheses (and many more subhypotheses) dealing with regional manufacturing growth and subject them to detailed testing. I examine both growth and its hypothetical causes from many angles, looking at a wide assortment of variables. The findings reflect extensive efforts to statistically control influences other than those being tested in particular experiments. Whatever its errors of method or interpretation, the study perhaps qualifies as one of the more rigorous and comprehensive attempts thus far undertaken to test hypotheses in this field. If it does nothing more than inspire others to develop and apply better tests, it will have served a useful purpose.

Regional
Growth and
Industrial
Location

1

Introduction

This is a study of the forces influencing regional growth in the United States. It seeks to identify and evaluate the relative importance of factors that cause one region to grow faster than another. States are the basic units examined; local influences affecting the distribution of industry within states are not considered. The study uses manufacturing employment to measure growth. Changes in manufacturing employment are analyzed in relation to a broad spectrum of explanatory hypotheses.

Study Objectives

Over the past two decades or so, regional economics has become a field of greatly expanded interest among economists and geographers. Geographically localized unemployment in Appalachia and other coal-mining regions, in the Upper Great Lakes (iron ore depletion), and in New England (where the textile industry moved out) has sparked the new interest; low income and other manifestations of underdevelopment in the South have also contributed. The economic woes of these regions have led policy-makers and planners to search for methods of stimulating economic growth. And this has naturally brought the causes of growth into the spotlight.

When one speaks of regional economic growth, thoughts quickly turn to manufacturing. To be sure, increases in employment and income can be achieved, in theory anyhow, in other sectors—agriculture, mining, finance, and tourism, for example. (Retailing and services are deliberately omitted, since they are not export sectors and can expand only to the extent that increased purchasing power is generated by other activities.) Yet as a practical matter, the best opportunities for economic development usually lie with manufacturing. Some observers would probably dispute this last statement, and it doesn't apply to all states; but it is certainly true that manufacturing gets the most attention.

Manufacturing growth is thus of basic concern for regional growth. We need to know what causes manufacturing to grow faster or slower in different regions. (A *region* can be defined as a large geographical area ordinarily encompassing a group of states or parts thereof.) Although most of the factors affecting manufacturing growth have been catalogued, major knowledge gaps remain. At least one factor identified in the present study as an important locational influence— the threshold influence—has received scarcely any attention in the context of

1

domestic economic development. (However, it has been considered in relation to developing nations and, within the United States, cities.) Climate is usually ranked as an also-ran but is gaining increased respect. What is its true impact? Most perplexing of all is the question of markets. Markets is widely regarded as the number one locational factor. But a recent study, one of the two most comprehensive to date of manufacturing growth in the United States, sharply disputes the significance of markets. [1]

By learning more about the forces behind manufacturing growth, we can provide a firmer foundation for public policy. A clear set of applications need not be claimed to justify the effort; indeed, the relevance of basic research in any field to concrete problems is often unforeseeable in the absence of foreknowledge of not only the problems but the specific operational questions that will arise. Nevertheless, concrete applications can be given. A developmental highway system is now being built in Appalachia at a cost of over $2 billion. It is predicated largely on the idea of exploiting market orientation by bringing factory and market closer together. This raises the obvious question of how much industry is truly market-oriented. Other federal programs are designed to develop depressed local areas. Related research on the effect of local attractions on area growth requires knowledge and control of regional factors that might bias the findings. Other applications could be cited, but these are sufficient to illustrate the point, namely, that the economist needs better knowledge of the regional forces influencing manufacturing growth.

Regional Growth Patterns

The hypotheses, findings, and conclusions of the study will be clearer if the regional growth patterns being explored are understood. Table 1-1 describes these growth patterns. [2] The table shows manufacturing growth for each of the four main regions of the United States, as delineated by the Bureau of the Census. In the lower part of the table, each region is broken into two subregions. For the West, an alternate breakdown is also shown. To allow comparison of growth with economic development, the table shows manufacturing employment per capita for each region and subregion. This is followed by the three growth measures used in this study—absolute, per capita, and percentage growth in manufacturing employment. All regional figures are the *averages* of the state figures for the states included; these are not aggregate regional figures. (Aggregate regional figures are unduly influenced by the more populous states, especially where California is concerned.)

The table is structured in a way that calls attention to important locational influences. The comparative industrialization column relates to the market influence; it allows growth to be compared with the ratio of supply (manufacturing employment) to demand (population), which is a good way of measuring the

Table 1-1
1947–63 Manufacturing Employment Growth, by Region and Subregion
(Average State Values)

	Number of States	1950 Manufac'ng Employ- ment Per Capita[a]	Absolute Growth (÷1000)	Per Thousand Capita Growth	Percentage Growth
National Average	48	0.080	54.7	18.2	45.2
Census Regions					
Northeast	9	0.143	7.9	-0.9	-0.2
North Central	12	0.085	32.4	10.6	21.1
South	16	0.066	73.0	26.5	50.7
West	11	0.041	90.7	30.1	100.9
Subregions					
New England	6	0.145	-8.3	-4.6	-2.5
Middle Atlantic	3	0.138	40.4	6.4	4.4
E. North Central	5	0.141	32.0	6.9	5.2
W. North Central	7	0.045	32.6	13.3	32.4
South Atlantic	8	0.084	74.6	32.6	50.9
South Central	8	0.049	71.3	20.4	50.4
Northwest	5	0.044	27.8	18.8	44.5
Far Southwest	6	0.038	143.2	39.4	147.8
Alternate West Subregions					
Mountain	8	0.029	17.9	25.2	113.2
Pacific	3	0.072	284.8	43.0	67.9

[a]1950 manufacturing employment was obtained by interpolation, using the 1947 and 1963 Census of Manufactures figures; it is not a population census figure. The denominator, 1950 population, *is* a population census figure.

strength of markets. By separating northern from southern regions, the table also provides a preview of climate's influence. Labor is identified through the delineation of the South as a separate region; it is the only region with an appreciable labor advantage (low wages, weak unions, surplus labor). In the West, the alternate subregional scheme at the bottom of the table is designed to reveal the role of a threshold influence affecting most of the Mountain states. (The Mountain subregion includes the five most underdeveloped states in the country—Montana, Idaho, Wyoming, New Mexico, and Nevada.)

The comparative industrialization column reveals that the regions become progressively less industrialized as we proceed from Northeast to North Central to South to West. Correspondingly, *all three* growth measures show progressively faster growth as we proceed from Northeast to North Central to South to West. It is especially remarkable that even absolute growth, which is heavily influenced by population, follows the pattern. In other words, there is at the regional level

a perfect rank relationship between industrialization and growth; the less industrialized a region (the lower the supply of manufactured goods is relative to
demand), the faster it grows.

The market influence is also suggested by the subregional breakdown.
Within each region, the least industrialized subregion generally grows faster.
Exceptions found in the South and under the Alternate West breakdown can be
explained by the phenomenal growth of industry in Florida—this inflates the
South Atlantic averages—and by the failure of certain Mountain states to have
crossed a developmental threshold leading to faster growth. Another exception
arises when we compare the South's two subregions with the West North Central
and Northwest subregions: the northern subregions are less developed yet show
slower growth. But this evidence is less a denial of the market influence than an
affirmation of the climate and labor influences.

The influence of climate—slow growth in the regions with cold winters,
fast growth in the warmer regions—is suggested by a comparison of the northern
and southern regions. Let us first consider the four main regions, but with the
West subdivided into the Northwest and Far Southwest to make five regions. The
three northern regions (Northeast, North Central, and Northwest) all show
slower growth in every column than the two southern regions (South and Far
Southwest). If we turn to the eight subregions, five are northern and three are
southern. Significantly, the five slowest-growing subregions are the five northern
subregions, no matter which measure of growth is employed.

Labor is harder to preview, for (as will become evident later) it is heavily
overshadowed by markets and climate. But the South, the only region with an
appreciable labor advantage, is in the upper half of the class. So are both of its
subregions. True, the West has no labor advantage yet shows faster growth than
the South. But this merely suggests that the market influence outweighs labor:
the West has better markets.

The threshold influence, referring to the hypothetical adverse effect of too
much underdevelopment, is also suggested by the table. To anticipate later
analyses, five western states that lack major metropolitan areas—Montana, Idaho,
Wyoming, New Mexico, and Nevada—fall into a subthreshold category. Their
extreme underdevelopment reflects in the Mountain region's industry ratio of
.029 manufacturing employees per capita, lowest in the nation. This means a
wide gap between supply and demand, and it should put the Mountain states in
front growthwise. But, although they do lead in percentage growth (low employment bases inflate their percentage growth rates), the Mountain states lag
behind the more industrialized Pacific states in absolute and per capita growth.

The reader interested in a more detailed look at the points just discussed
will find the statistics repeated for individual states in table 1–2. This table also
presents the raw material from which the regional averages in table 1–1 were
computed.

Table 1-2

1947-63 Manufacturing Employment Growth, by Subregion and State (Average State Values Shown for Subregions)

	1950 Manufac'ng Employment Per Capita	Absolute Growth (÷1000)	Per Thousand Capita Growth	Per-centage Growth
New England	*0.145*	*-8.3*	*-4.6*	*-2.5*
Maine	0.109	-0.2	-0.2	-0.2
New Hampshire	0.144	9.4	17.5	12.5
Vermont	0.092	-1.1	-3.0	-3.3
Massachusetts	0.151	-44.0	-9.4	-6.1
Rhode Island	0.178	-33.4	-4.2	-2.3
Connecticut	0.197	19.5	9.6	4.9
Middle Atlantic	*0.138*	*40.4*	*6.4*	*4.4*
New York	0.121	79.9	5.3	4.5
New Jersey	0.156	90.2	18.6	12.2
Pennsylvania	0.136	-48.8	-4.6	-3.4
E. North Central	*0.141*	*32.0*	*6.9*	*5.2*
Ohio	0.151	45.3	5.6	3.8
Indiana	0.142	61.6	15.6	11.2
Michigan	0.153	-14.4	-2.2	-1.5
Illinois	0.137	24.7	2.8	2.1
Wisconsin	0.124	43.1	12.5	10.3
W. North Central	*0.045*	*32.6*	*13.3*	*32.4*
Minnesota	0.065	64.4	21.6	35.3
Iowa	0.056	37.8	14.4	26.9
Missouri	0.086	64.1	16.2	19.6
North Dakota	0.009	1.3	2.0	24.9
South Dakota	0.017	3.0	4.5	28.9
Nebraska	0.038	17.9	13.4	38.0
Kansas	0.043	39.7	20.8	53.1
South Atlantic	*0.084*	*74.6*	*32.6*	*50.9*
Delaware	0.123	23.7	74.3	68.1
Maryland	0.100	35.0	14.9	15.3
Virginia	0.070	85.6	25.7	39.5
West Virginia	0.063	-10.3	-5.1	-8.8
North Carolina	0.101	149.2	37.7	39.1
South Carolina	0.096	72.9	34.4	38.6
Georgia	0.078	104.1	30.2	41.6
Florida	0.038	136.8	49.3	173.9
South Central	*0.049*	*71.3*	*20.4*	*50.4*
Kentucky	0.047	50.9	17.2	39.3
Tennessee	0.074	116.8	35.5	52.5
Alabama	0.070	37.6	12.2	18.2
Mississippi	0.040	51.2	23.4	66.1
Arkansas	0.039	47.9	25.0	72.7
Louisiana	0.050	7.0	2.6	5.3
Oklahoma	0.028	42.3	18.9	76.2
Texas	0.044	216.7	28.1	73.0

Table 1-2 (continued)

	1950 Manufac'ng Employment Per Capita	Absolute Growth (÷1000)	Per Thousand Capita Growth	Per- centage Growth
Northwest	0.044	27.8	18.8	44.5
Montana	0.028	4.4	7.4	27.8
Idaho	0.033	13.6	23.0	80.3
Wyoming	0.020	1.2	4.0	21.2
Washington	0.067	80.1	33.6	55.5
Oregon	0.074	39.6	26.0	37.5
Far Southwest	0.038	143.2	39.4	147.8
Colorado	0.046	39.7	29.9	73.3
New Mexico	0.012	8.6	12.6	128.9
Utah	0.043	29.0	42.0	118.4
Arizona	0.030	42.9	57.1	302.0
Nevada	0.021	4.1	25.6	153.8
California	0.076	734.7	69.4	110.7

Recent Empirical Studies

Various studies completed since World War II give us an empirical basis for supposing that the forces just introduced—markets, climate, labor, and thresholds—contribute to the disparities in regional growth. These studies also provide several other locational hypotheses, for example, the resource and agglomeration hypotheses. And they provide insights and evidence with which the interpretations and conclusions of the present study can be checked and compared. Six major studies deserve mention: (1) a 1949 investigation by McLaughlin and Robock, (2) a 1959 study by Thompson and Mattila, (3) a 1960 study undertaken by the Harvard Graduate School of Public Administration and reported on separately by Chinitz and Vernon and by Lichtenberg, (4) a 1960 study by Perloff, Dunn, Lampard, and Muth, (5) a 1962 inquiry by Fuchs, and (6) a 1966 report prepared for the Appalachian Regional Commission by the Fantus Company. A few lesser studies also merit brief attention.

The McLaughlin-Robock Study

The earliest of the major studies is that of Glenn E. McLaughlin and Stefan Robock.[3] Their research was confined to a group of thirteen southern states (Virginia through Oklahoma and Texas). The authors used the interview technique in looking at eighty-eight plants established in the South after World War II. These represented all major industry groups except tobacco. Each company official was encouraged to tell his story his own way. Then he was queried about any omitted items from a locational factor checklist.

The authors find that business almost always selects its locations in two steps. First it selects a general region; then it selects a location within the region. The general region is one that secures the most important advantage—a regional market, a source of raw materials, or a source of cheap labor. Other requirements are then met by finding a suitable location within the region. Depending on how the general region is selected, a plant is (1) market-oriented, (2) materials-oriented, or (3) labor-oriented.

Markets was easily the leading determinant of location: 45 percent of the plants surveyed were market-oriented. Moreover, about one-fourth of the market-oriented plants but less than one-sixth of the materials-oriented and none of the labor-oriented ones employed over 1,000 workers; so if impact is measured by employment, markets accounted for over half of the new industry. The market-oriented firms were mostly existing firms seeking to tap an expanding southern market by establishing branch plants; only two of the plants represented new firms. Sometimes growth in the southern market meant that, for the first time, a plant of economical scale could be established. The branch plants were placed near their markets in order to cut transport costs or because their products were perishable. Both consumer markets (e.g., food, automobiles) and industrial markets (e.g., paper products) were involved.

Raw materials ranked second: materials and energy resources attracted 30 percent of the plants. Plants were materials-oriented when (a) the raw materials were perishable or otherwise not freely transportable or (b) freight was an important element of the final cost and raw materials were more costly to transport than the finished product. With over two-fifths of the South covered by forests, abundant pulpwood attracted several paper and paper products firms. Oil and natural gas deposits induced chemical plants to locate in the western part of the region. Agricultural products, hydroelectric power, sulphur, and phosphorus also served as magnets.

Labor ranked third, accounting for 25 percent of the new plants. The South has the lowest wages, the lowest degree of unionization, and the most surplus labor of any region. Firms seeking attractive labor conditions have therefore gravitated to this region. Here the South's abundant surplus labor should not be underrated as an attraction: an adequate supply of labor was often sought as a means of reducing turnover, weakening the competitive bidding-up of wages, and allowing marginal workers to be weeded out. For labor-oriented firms, transportation was usually a small part of the delivered cost of the product; the market attraction was weak. Textiles, apparel, shoes, and machinery were the principal labor-oriented industries.

Some plants primarily oriented to one of the three main factors were secondarily influenced by another. A phosphorus plant chose a southern source of phosphorus ore over a Northwest source (the only nonsouthern alternative) to be closer to the biggest markets. Labor-oriented textile plants went to the northern part of the South to be closer to northeastern markets. Natural gas supplies sometimes induced market-oriented companies to deviate from central points within their marketing regions. Market-oriented and materials-oriented firms were seldom concerned about wages, but they often checked the labor histories of various communities before selecting a specific site.

McLaughlin and Robock discuss several other factors, but most are community influences or have strong market overtones. Transportation, for example, is primarily a reason for locating close to markets (but can also involve raw materials). One additional factor deserves attention, however. This is climate. Some firms locating in the South expected to save on construction and heating costs, avoid winter shipping delays, or otherwise capitalize on the South's warm climate. One company chose a southern location in preference to one in upper New York because it was feared that the second-choice location might have excessive absenteeism during the winter.

The Thompson-Mattila Study

The prior study most nearly resembling the present one in methodology was prepared by Wilbur Thompson and John Mattila.[4] It is geared to predicting state manufacturing growth. It develops multiple regression equations for this purpose. But most of the study deals with statistical by-products, namely, correlations between manufacturing growth and predictive variables. There are two growth (dependent) variables: 1947–54 absolute growth in manufacturing employment and 1947–54 percentage growth. The authors correlate each growth variable with sixteen predictive variables (not counting some specific-industry variables), most of which are converted from absolutes to ratios or rates for analyzing percentage growth. Since Thompson and Mattila are primarily concerned with forecasting, they use some variables that predict but do not necessarily explain. The authors are quite aware that these may be "more a reflection of some fortunate blend of favorable economic characteristics" than actual determinants of growth.[5]

Most of the significant findings point to the market influence. The strongest relationship is between manufacturing growth and prior growth in consumer demand. Absolute growth (1947–54) shows correlations of +.90 and +.86 with prior (1940–47) absolute increases in population and income; percentage growth has a +.62 correlation with prior percentage increase in income. Prior growth, of course, represents not just increased demand but a whole complex of forces that influenced growth in one period and carried over into the next. But two considerations suggest that prior growth in demand emphasizes markets. First, it has higher correlations than a modified prior growth variable that is clearly a better proxy for miscellaneous attractions but a poorer measure of demand: prior growth in *manufacturing employment* has a +.73 correlation with absolute growth, compared to the +.90 achieved by prior growth in population. Second, correlations for individual industries known to be attracted to labor and raw materials are relatively low, as they should be if prior growth in population and income describes markets.

A +.84 correlation between the number of college-trained people and absolute growth reiterates that strong consumer demand spurs growth. Intended as a proxy for skills and training, the college variable seems really to be a proxy for population and (especially) income. Similarly, a +.31 correlation between percent college-educated and percentage growth seems to describe the effect of high per capita income, or high relative demand.

Two industry variables, likewise intended for other purposes, also deserve market interpretations. First, 1947 manufacturing employment (absolute) has a +.65 correlation with absolute growth; and, second, manufacturing employment as a percentage of total employment has a −.66 correlation with percentage growth. In the first case, manufacturing employment is almost certainly a proxy for population and income (not tested): high demand, high growth. Thus in the present study, manufacturing employment lags well behind population in its positive correlation with absolute growth (just as it lags behind the college variable, which leads +.84 to +.65, here) and develops a strongly negative partial correlation (−.87) when income is held constant. Furthermore, if the +.65 reading really meant that growth occurs at existing locations (the hypothesis the authors were testing), the correlation between relative employment in manufacturing and relative growth would also be positive—instead of −.66. The −.66 reading says that the least industrialized states, where supply is low relative to demand, grew fastest.[6]

Two labor variables, average hourly earnings in manufacturing (1949) and union membership as a percentage of nonagricultural employment (1947), are examined. For all manufacturing combined, their correlations with absolute and percentage growth are generally positive (the wrong sign). But this is less a denial of labor influences than an affirmation that high incomes attracts industry. Thus the correlations for particular industries recognized as labor-oriented (e.g., apparel, leather and leather products) still come out negative: high wages and strong unions = low growth.

The only other findings of interest come from two tax variables: state and local taxes as a percentage of personal income, and state and local nonagricultural business taxes per employee. Neither is significantly correlated with absolute or percentage growth in any industry or for all industries combined—provided we do not count some positive correlations (the wrong sign). Taxes do not seem to be a significant influence.

The New York Metropolitan Region Study

In 1956 the Harvard Graduate School of Public Administration was asked to undertake a three-year study of the New York metropolitan region. Raymond Vernon directed the study. In order to grasp the influences at work in the region, the study team investigated factors shaping the growth of the nation as a whole. The relevant findings are summarized in two places: (1) a *Harvard Business Review* article by Benjamin Chinitz and Vernon [7] and (2) a book by Robert Lichtenberg. [8] Using a historical-descriptive approach, the authors develop important insights and evidence bearing on industrial location.

The Chinitz-Vernon Article. Chinitz and Vernon begin by noting that the South and West have been growing faster than the rest of the country since 1899. This means that industry is decentralizing—becoming more evenly distributed in relation to population. Examining 119 industries for the period 1939–54, the authors compare population distribution with manufacturing employment distribution. In 90 of the 119 industries, manufacturing distribution more closely resembled population distribution in 1954 than in 1939.

The main force behind this decentralization is transportation, that is, the desire to cut transport costs by locating close to the market. Transport costs weigh heavily in the cost structures of the decentralizing industries. At the same time, the advent of highways and trucking has radically altered transport costs. Compared to rail transport, trucking offers low short-haul costs: truckers have lower terminal costs to spread over short hauls. Short-haul shippers—firms moving goods up to 300 to 500 miles—also benefit from average terminal time savings of forty-eight hours, which means proportionately high time savings on short hauls. Thus, whereas manufacturers had little to gain from decentralization in the pretrucking days, regional plants now yield substantial transport savings.

Meanwhile, the competing nonmarket attractions have weakened. The resource influence has been hurt by (*a*) the lengthening chain of production linking raw materials to end products and (*b*) depletion of the best forests and mines, which has resulted in a more even distribution of resources. Interregional wage gaps have also narrowed, lessening the attraction of low wages. And external economies (e.g., sheet metal shops and trucking depots) once found only in certain areas are now more widely available.

The Lichtenberg Book. Using information from economic histories, economic geographies, industry studies, observed locational patterns, and interviews, Lichtenberg classifies manufacturing according to five dominant locational factors. He finds that, based on 1954 manufacturing employment, 51 percent of the nation's industry is transport-sensitive, 15 percent seeks external economies, 14 percent is governed by inertia (historical factors), 8 percent emphasizes labor costs and supply, and 12 percent is unclassifiable. The transport-sensitive industry subdivides into 43 percent oriented to markets and 8 percent oriented to raw materials.

New York vividly illustrates the role of transportation, particularly in relation to markets. Located far from the national market center of gravity, New York has only 27 percent of its manufacturing employment in transport-sensitive industries, compared to the 51 percent nationwide figure. About half of New York's 27 percent—13 percent—is in industries serving local or regional markets. The rest is in industries where widely separated firms compete. These national market industries show strong tendencies toward decentralization. In each of three periods—1929-39, 1939-47, and 1947-54—New York's growth in these industries was (a) less than the industry's national average if New York's share of industry employment exceeded its share of national population and (b) more than the national average when New York fell below its prorata share of industry employment. Thus even the nationally competitive industries were becoming regionalized.

New York also illustrates the role of other influences. Many external economies—rentable space, commercial services, skilled worker pools, unique wholesaling facilities, and so on—are found in New York. Correspondingly, 39 percent of New York's manufacturing employment—compared to 15 percent of the nation's—is in industries seeking external economies. The region has hardly any raw materials and very little materials-oriented industry; what there is depends on New York's port facilities (transportation), which provide such raw materials as copper and petroleum for refining and sugar for candy. Due to high wages, New York has just 1 percent—the national figure is 5 percent—of its manufacturing in industries oriented to unskilled labor; Puerto Rican in-migration is New York's main source of this labor. However, the region has abundant skilled labor and has 7 percent of its employment in skilled labor industries, compared to 3 percent for the nation. In short, New York's proportion of employment (a) exceeds the national proportion in categories where New York has the appropriate attraction and (b) falls below the national proportion where New York lacks the attraction.

The Perloff Study

The broadest and most useful study to date dealing with manufacturing location is that of Harvey Perloff, Edgar Dunn, Eric Lampard, and Richard Muth.[9] This study was designed and directed by Perloff and will hereafter be called the Perloff study. It reviews the overall growth of the economy since 1870, carrying some analyses as far forward as 1957 and stressing the 1939-54 period. Like the New York study, it is basically historical-descriptive in nature, but there is some hypothesis testing. Judgments about locational influences rest on historical trends, shift-share analysis coupled with investigation of the causes of shifts in particular industries (many specialized studies are brought to bear), and a few correlations.

Prepared for Resources for the Future, the study adopts a resource perspective: industries are described as falling along a continuum ranging from resource orientation through production for intermediate (industrial) markets to final (consumer) market orientation. In the analysis, intermediate markets become linked with external economies; the two influences jointly constitute the agglomeration attraction, which is an industry-attracts-industry influence believed to operate in industrialized areas. Influences such as labor and climate, which fall outside the chain-of-production framework, get little attention, although the authors do examine them in connection with specific industries and sometimes treat labor as a resource.

Over the years industry has shifted steadily from resource to market orientation: industries selling to other industries now produce almost 40 percent of all output, and most consumer industries have only remote connections to raw materials. Thus by 1950 markets "operated as the dominant locational force in the economy." [10] "Filling-in" growth in the South and West has increased the importance of markets. California, the prime mover in the spectacular growth of the Far West, passed a "market threshold" beyond which internal and external scale economies became operative;[11] remoteness from the Manufacturing Belt aided this development. Westward shifts in final markets have pulled intermediate markets along.

As evidence of the market attraction, the authors present rank correlations between employment in specific industries and population (forty-eight states). Industries generally regarded as market-oriented show the highest correlations; for example, printing and publishing reads +.93. But industries regarded as labor-oriented or resource-oriented have relatively low correlations—+.58 for lumber, +.63 for textiles, +.66 for leather and leather products, +.69 for petroleum and coal products, and so on.[12] Since a particular industry cannot easily exert a strong influence on population, causality would seem to run mainly from population (markets) to manufacturing employment.

By implication if not in so many words, the authors rank agglomeration second to markets in importance. But the discussion embodies some confusion about how agglomeration is defined (when spoken of as a cause rather than as an effect), and this weakens the appraisal. The authors sometimes treat agglomeration and the Manufacturing Belt's high consumer demand as separate attractions,[13] but at other times the national market advantages of Manufacturing Belt locations are made part of the agglomeration attraction.[14] This and heavy stress on intermediate markets vis-à-vis external economies make agglomeration hard to differentiate from markets. Furthermore, although regional agglomeration in the Manufacturing Belt is central to the discussion (it explains the Manufacturing Belt's continued dominance), emerging local (metropolitan area) agglomerations outside the Manufacturing Belt get considerable play. Is agglomeration truly a regional influence today? Or does it merely influence location within regions?

The study's main thrust is in the direction of a Manufacturing Belt concept of agglomeration. The authors seek a balanced explanation of growth—balanced in giving "full attention" to both the rapid gains of the West and the "remarkably small loss in relative standing" of the northeastern Manufacturing Belt.[15] Agglomeration thus becomes the offset to markets, which directs growth to the South and West. And the chief evidence of agglomeration is that "after more than a half-century of 'filling in' and probing of new wealth and new opportunities across the vast continent, the Manufacturing Belt . . . in 1957 contained 46% of the total population of the nation, 53% of the total income, and 64% of the total manufacturing employment."[16] The respective figures for 1900 were 49%, 61% and 74%. This stability and the findings of several industry studies suggest that "the existing agglomeration pattern has a great deal to do with decisions currently made by producers as to the appropriate location of new or added production facilities."[17]

Other influences are not ranked, but resources gets the most attention. In specific industries resources still exert a strong locational pull. Examples are refining and petrochemicals in the Southwest; other chemicals in various places; lumber products in the Southeast and West; pulp and paper in the South; canning, preserving, and freezing in several areas; and tobacco in the Upper South. The pull of resources on these industries is reflected in relatively low correlations between population and industry employment.

Despite these examples, the resource attraction has become weak. This conclusion is supported by a comparison of two groups of industries: (a) first-stage resource users, which use resources for over 10 percent of their inputs, and (b) second-stage users, which use first-stage products for over 10 percent of their inputs. For the forty-eight states, first-stage user employment has a rank correlation of +.68 with resource employment but a +.92 correlation with population; second-stage employment has a +.58 correlation with resource employment and a +.94 correlation with population.[18] That is, even the first-stage users are tied more to markets than to resources, and the resource pull weakens as resource use becomes more indirect. "As the major part of manufacturing activity is even further removed from resource association than these groups, natural resources do not appear to bind manufacturing very closely in location in any over-all sense."[19]

Labor, climate, and industry mix are covered briefly. Analyses of individual industries credit labor with attracting textiles, apparel, and shoe manufacturing to the South (but furniture, sometimes viewed as partly oriented to labor, is judged to be market-oriented). The fast-growing aircraft industry has located in California and other warm states partly because of climate; and market-oriented industries have grown rapidly in two of the fastest-growing states, California and Florida, in response to climate-related population growth. Industry mix, however, fails to score: the authors correlate two industry mix variables—employment and employment growth in nine fast-growing industries as percentages of employment and employment growth in all industries—and find them to be negatively correlated with total and per capita increase in manufacturing employment (1939-54).

The Fuchs Study

One major study challenges the rest by holding that markets is not an important determinant of manufacturing location. This is Victor Fuchs' study.[20] It uses a shift-share technique that focuses on manufacturing growth in the period 1929-54; supplementary analyses cover 1947-54. Fuchs' general approach entails measuring interregional shifts in manufacturing, pinning these down to the industries primarily responsible, and then explaining what happened in these industries. Judgments about the relative importance of different influences rest on (a) the factors affecting the industries with the biggest shifts, as suggested by a review of available literature, (b) an industry-wide correlation analysis relating comparative growth to several explanatory variables, (c) other statistical analyses, and (d) theory.

The shifts studied indicate rapid growth in the South and West (especially the West), moderate growth in the North Central region (above average in the western part, below average in the eastern part), and a comparative loss in the Northeast. "The most important factors influencing these changes in the location of industry appear to have been climate, labor, and the availability of raw materials."[21] Fuchs estimates that one-third of all employment shifts between census regions were due to resources (including climate) and raw materials; that "almost" another one-third resulted from abundant, low-cost, nonunion labor in the South; and that the remaining one-third was variously caused by changes in demand or could not be assigned to identifiable influences.[22] The one-third credited to resources depends "heavily" on treating climate as a resource; so if climate and raw materials are separated as in the above quotation, labor ranks first. "Heavily" implies that climate ranks second, ahead of raw materials, which is apparently third. Since markets is not even close enough to deserve mention in the summary quotation, one infers that Fuchs would assign markets less than one-sixth (raw materials) and probably closer to one-tenth of the credit.

Labor's first-place rank is supported by a finding that four labor-oriented industries—textiles, apparel, footwear, and furniture—contributed heavily to the South's gains and the Northeast's losses.[23] Also, a special analysis shows that growth in low-wage and labor-intensive industries is better correlated with wages and unionization than is growth in other industries—which supports the idea that the first industries are attracted by favorable labor conditions.

Finally, wages and unionization have significant industry-wide correlations of
-.35 and -.38 with 1929-54 comparative growth (percent) in manufacturing
value added; and unionization joins population density (-.51) and temperature
deviation from 65 degrees (-.53) in the best three-variable multiple regression
equation. [24]

Climate's importance is suggested by its great influence on the location of
aircraft manufacturing, a leading growth industry and the most important
contributor to upward shifts in California and the Southwest. Climate has also
influenced migration and the location of military bases, thereby supporting
the growth of market-oriented industries. The -.53 industry-wide correlation
between temperature deviation from the "ideal" (65 degrees) and percentage
shift is exceeded only by the -.57 correlation for manufacturing employment per
capita (used as a market variable) and -.57 for patents per capita (evidently
acting as a proxy for per capita manufacturing). (Intercorrelations between
growth measures are not counted.)

Raw materials gains its high ranking from findings that raw materials lay
behind some important upward shifts—chemicals in the South, lumbering on the
West Coast, pulp and paper in the South and West, and canned and frozen foods
in the South. The industry-wide correlations omit raw materials because "it is
not feasible to assign a simple measure of raw material availability to each state
which would meaningfully describe the diverse products of forests, fields, and
mines that form the basis of much manufacturing activity." [25]

So far, so good. But when Fuchs gets to markets, analytical errors abound.
His conclusion that markets is a minor influence is based largely on three
considerations, none of which withstand scrutiny. The principal consideration
is a comparison of 29 industries held to be oriented to local markets with 192
described as "non-market-oriented" (all others). [26] Fuchs shows that the
"market-oriented" group contributed little to comparative shifts and that growth
in these industries is no better correlated with growth in population and income
than is growth in the "non-market-oriented" group. The obvious flaw in this
analysis is its substitution of the narrow concept of local markets for the usual
local-or-regional concept. Ice, ice cream, soft drinks, newspapers, concrete—these
are not the only type of market-oriented firm. Market orientation typically
relates to a region, often covering many states; and Fuchs' "non-market-oriented"
group is actually riddled with industries that feature branch plants serving
regional markets. To say that these industries are not market-oriented simply
begs the question.

Fuchs next argues that the "catching up" hypothesis—industry catching up
with markets in less developed states—fails to explain why certain underdeveloped northern states (e.g., the Dakotas, Montana, Wyoming) grew less than some
generally more developed southern ones (e.g., Kansas, Texas, California). In the
paragraph preceding this argument, in another context, he invokes *ceteris
paribus*;[27] with his impressionistic argument he forgets all about it. Specifi-

cally, he overlooks the fact that the northern states (1) have unfavorable climates and (2) may be burdened by excessive underdevelopment, or the failure to have crossed a threshold leading to external economies and to markets adequate to permit economies of scale.

Fuchs' third reason for discounting markets is that his industry-wide correlations, as he reads them, deny a market influence. He is not impressed by the -.57 correlation between manufacturing employment per capita (correctly described as a market variable) and growth. Instead he focuses on an insignificant partial correlation shown by this variable when population density, temperature deviation, and unionization are jointly held constant. But, following the -.57 simple correlation, the insignificant partial can only mean that manufacturing employment per capita is duplicated by one or more of the variables held constant. Actually, it is duplicated by two: population density and unionization, both of which decrease with decreasing industrialization. Fuchs' basic error is failure to see that population density (-.51) is essentially a proxy for manufacturing employment per capita (-.57). (His data show a +.76 intercorrelation between them; my own data show an even better one of +.85 after correction for curvilinear correlation, not to mention a +.98 intercorrelation between the log of population density and the log of manufacturing employment density.)[28] Fuchs chooses to treat population density as a measure of land area available for factories. But this is exceedingly far-fetched: factory space may be hard to find near a given city, but it is hardly so scarce or expensive in high-density states that industry must look toward low-density states for plant sites.

Two also-rans in Fuchs' analysis are industry mix and taxes. Although the shift-share technique used by Fuchs assumes that a state's mix of fast-growing and slow-growing industry substantially affects its growth, a "comparative industrial structure" variable shows a totally insignificant correlation of +.003 with comparative growth in manufacturing. Reviewing four tax studies, Fuchs finds general agreement that state and local tax differences among states have little impact.

The Fantus Study

The last major study deserving attention was conducted in 1966 for the Appalachian Regional Commission by the Fantus Company, a leading plant location consulting firm. In its report, [29] Fantus drew on its own experience and expertise. Extensive use was made of information in Fantus' files, most of it obtained during the course of several thousand plant location searches. In addition, Fantus made personal calls on plants and headquarters offices of firms located inside and outside of Appalachia. The study consists of twenty-five substudies examining industries believed to have significant growth potential in Appalachia.

A table in the summary report lists a number of locational factors, local and regional, found to be significant. We can ignore the local factors (except for one), the most important of which is an adequate local labor supply. The regional factors are (1) transportation, (2) proximity to customers, (3) state manpower training assistance, (4) labor cost advantage, (5) low-cost electric power, (6) urban orientation, and (7) proximity to raw materials. Transportation, as used in this context, is partly a local factor (facilities) but mainly regional (cost of distributing over a region); power is largely a regional matter; urban orientation is mostly a local factor but has a bearing on the attractiveness of sparsely developed regions. Each factor is judged, relative to each of the twenty-five industries, as being of (a) critical importance, (b) primary importance, (c) importance, or (d) minor or no importance.

Fantus refrains from scoring or otherwise attempting to synthesize the ratings, because *"cruciality in one industry seldom has equivalence with cruciality in another."* [30] But I think the consultant is being unnecessarily conservative on this point, making it difficult to compare the competing factors. True, this is not a representative sample of industry—it is geared to Appalachia—and the industries are not equally important. If we keep these reservations in mind, however, it is reasonable and helpful to employ a 3-2-1-0 scoring system for the four "importance" categories—critical, primary, moderate, and minor. Table 1-3 is the result. The number of industries for which each factor was of critical importance appears next to the weighted score for each factor.

Markets is clearly the most important regional influence among the industries studied: transport services, transport costs, and proximity to customers—three aspects of the market attraction—rank one, two, three. Transportation can

Table 1-3
The Fantus Study: Industrial Location Factor Scores

Location Factor	Weighted Score	Critical Importance Industries
Transportation:		
Services	53	8
Costs	41	8
Proximity to customers	46	8
State manpower training assistance	31	2
Labor cost advantage	24	2
Low cost electric power	24	2
Urban orientation	24	1
Proximity to raw materials	11	2

Source: Based on Fantus report, *The Appalachian Location Research Studies Program: Summary Report and Recommendations* (New York, December 1966), table 3, pp. 12–13.

also involve raw materials, of course, but the report indicates that outbound transportation is usually what matters: most firms wish to minimize the time and cost of shipping goods to market. According to Fantus, the high ranking for proximity to customers indicates the desire of many firms to establish deeper market penetration: regional branch plants offer greater market access than a central plant or regional warehouses.

Two labor factors, state manpower training assistance and labor cost advantage, come next. Note that, even taken individually, both rank well ahead of raw materials. Since no other study mentions training, it may count more among the unskilled workers of Appalachia than for the country as a whole. The relevant labor costs include not just wages but fringe benefits, work rules (unions), turnover, and absenteeism. The two industries for which labor costs are rated "crucial" are textiles and apparel.

Electric power and raw materials can be combined under the heading of resources. Fantus states that energy is seldom a critical item. The two "crucial" industries are chlor-alkali (chlorine and caustic soda) and primary aluminum. Although Appalachia has impressive timber and energy resources, "it is difficult to establish any crucial relationship between these resources and the needs of manufacturing industries which now operate in the region or are likely candidates for new operations."[31] Pulp and paper and certain agricultural products are exceptions.

Urban orientation, primarily a local rather than a regional factor, is included in the table because of its relationship to two factors examined in the present study—thresholds and the urban attraction. The Fantus concept of urban orientation is nothing very specific but designates a desire of some industries to locate within, in the suburbs of, or close to a city of some minimal size. The "crucial" industry is office machinery; other urban-oriented industries are paper boxes and shipping containers, plastics for packaging, nonferrous metal operations, and instruments and controls—industries variously attracted to intermediate markets and urban amenities (e.g., trim neighborhoods, recreational facilities, and good schools).

Other Studies

Many other studies bearing on manufacturing location are available, but most have little to contribute to a broad understanding of regional influences: they emphasize community factors, or they are too narrow in scope, or they have serious methodological and conceptual problems, or they are basically theoretical. But seven of the lesser studies are sufficiently important to be mentioned.

The first of these is a 1963 questionnaire survey conducted by James McCarthy for the American Trucking Associations.[32] McCarthy queried 4,140 firms that had recently established new plants or expanded existing facilities. Usable responses came from 1,363 companies. The questionnaire listed thirteen locational factors, five of which were to be checked. Only two factors—"proximity to markets" and "availability of raw materials"—were predominantly regional. For these two, markets won over raw materials by a 59 percent to 32 percent response margin. When the responses were classified by industry (SIC two-digit groups), markets led raw materials in 17½ (one tie) of the 19 SIC manufacturing groups. Markets and raw materials were equal in the textile industry, and raw materials was ahead in the lumber industry. Even in paper and paper products, chemical and allied products, and furniture and fixtures— industries with some resource orientation—markets was well ahead.

The next study is empirical only in the loose sense that it offers a few hard facts and attempts to interpret them; it is really not a study at all. Yet Edward Ullman's analysis of climate's role in regional growth is too significant to ignore:[33] Ullman was the first to give adequate attention to climate as a crucial factor influencing the location of population and industry, and even today no other analyst except Fuchs has accepted climate as a dominant influence. Ullman's thesis is that, for the first time in world history, pleasant living conditions are becoming the spark behind population shifts. Regional amenities—primarily climate—have directly and indirectly boosted industrial growth. The most important population change between 1940 and 1950, other than the flight to the suburbs, was the rapid growth of California, Arizona, and Florida. Post-1952 moves favored New Mexico and Texas as well. Growth in these states appears to be mainly the result of comfortable climates. Climate has directly attracted some manufacturing, whose executives are as much concerned as anyone else about finding a nice place to live. And, indirectly, climate has stimulated the growth of market-oriented industries.

A third study, Edwin Cohn, Jr.'s in-depth investigation of industry in the Pacific Northwest,[34] has useful insights into the roles of power resources and developmental thresholds. Cohn's conclusions are based on 158 interviews with manufacturing executives and other knowledgeable individuals and on an examination of literature and statistics concerning the region. A desire to study the effect of abundant cheap hydroelectric power as a locational attraction was largely responsible for Cohn's selection of the Pacific Northwest (roughly the Columbia River basin) for study. The relevant finding is that power has had little effect in shaping the region's growth. Only a limited class of manufacturing, the electro-process industries, has been attracted. These industries, moreover, create little employment—their ratio of electric power to manpower is too high— and they draw few related industries.[35] Elsewhere, without using the term "threshold," Cohn suggests that the region is handicapped by failure to have reached a level of development where growth becomes self-sustaining.[36]

A study by George Borts and Jerome Stein is useful for its findings about industry mix. The authors correlate actual growth rates for the forty-eight states during four periods (1919–29, 1929–47, 1948–53, and 1948–57) with hypothetical growth rates that would have arisen if each industry in a state had grown as fast as the industry did nationally. "Except for the period 1948–53, there was no significant association between the actual and hypothetical growth rates. Interstate differences in growth rates of manufacturing production worker employment do *not* arise because states have different compositions of industries. These differences arise because, in the industries they contain, states grow at rates different from the national average in those same industries."[37]

This finding is repeated by Robert Bretzfelder. Although Bretzfelder studies income growth, his findings are relevant to manufacturing: twenty-two of thirty-eight income components analyzed represent manufacturing. Bretzfelder looks at the eight U.S. economic regions delineated by the Commerce Department's Bureau of Economic Analysis. For each he compares the 1959–69 growth rate for total income with the "component-mix effect," which measures the difference between the region's income structure and the nation's. Two of three regions with above-average growth have disadvantageous component mixes; three of five regions with below-average growth have advantageous mixes. Thus, what little correlation there is between regional growth and component mix is negative. The explanation is that individual industries grow faster or slower in particular regions than nationally: all three fast-growing regions have a positive "regional-share effect" (their specific-industry growth rates generally exceed the industry national averages), and all five slow-growing regions have a negative "regional-share effect."[38]

The last two studies look at the effect of tax differentials. These studies, one by the Advisory Commission on Intergovernmental Relations [39] (ACIR) and the other by William Williams,[40] supplement the Thompson-Mattila findings and Fuchs' literature survey in defending the conclusion that taxes are not a significant locational influence. The ACIR study uses a pairs procedure that divides the nation into eight regions and then compares the states with the highest and lowest 1950–65 manufacturing employment growth rates within each region (eight pairs). The conclusion is that, because tax neutralization policies leave very small tax differentials between neighboring states, there is no clear relationship between business taxes and manufacturing growth rates within regions. Williams compares production costs for average establishments in specific two-digit and four-digit (SIC code) industries before and after taxes. He finds that state and local taxes constitute only 1 or 2 percent of the value of shipments and that taxes have very little effect on the cost rankings of individual states for specific industries.

2 Hypotheses and Methodology

The studies reviewed in chapter 1 give us many hypotheses seeking to explain why one region grows faster than another. These hypotheses form the subject matter of the present study. This chapter identifies and develops the hypotheses to be tested, rejecting some that the earlier studies have already discredited. It then describes the methodology used in testing the selected hypotheses and considers problems of attribution.

Manufacturing Growth Hypotheses

Rough consensus as to the relative importance of the hypothetical locational influences emerges from the studies surveyed. There is almost universal agreement—Fuchs is the exception—that markets (sometimes viewed as transportation) is the leading factor in regional manufacturing growth. Labor and resources rank second and third, generally in that order; just about everyone considers them significant. Agglomeration and climate rank fourth and fifth, having somewhat less support. Agglomeration achieves its position largely on the basis of emphasis it gets in the Perloff study, but it also has indirect support from the high rating given to external economies in the New York study. Climate gets most of its support from the Fuchs study and Ullman's analysis. A threshold influence is at least alluded to in the Perloff and Cohn studies and can claim some emprical support; it ranks sixth in the consensus. Urban orientation, the only other factor supported by evidence (chiefly the Fantus study) ranks seventh. The seven ranked factors translate into seven hypotheses. Rearranged here to group together four that call for measures of industrial or urban development, the hypotheses concern (1) markets, including underdevelopment, (2) agglomeration, (3) thresholds, (4) urbanization, (5) labor, (6) resources, and (7) climate. Two other hypotheses, namely, the industry mix and tax hypotheses, have been discredited repeatedly; they do not inspire further testing.

Markets

The first hypothesis, dealing with markets, can be broken into two sub-hypotheses. The first deals with markets per se; the second looks at markets from the standpoint of underdevelopment, speculating that the least developed regions (where markets are strongest) are "catching up."

21

Markets per se. The leading hypothesis is that industry seeks to locate near its markets. Branch plants and other regional plants are established that bring the factory closer to the consumer. The object is to minimize the time and cost required to transport goods to market. As the New York study points out, regional plants have short-haul transport requirements that can be met by trucking, which offers two-day terminal time savings over rail transport and is generally cheaper for distances of up to several hundred miles. Shifts toward regional production are encouraged by the growth of hinterland markets, more and more of which are reaching sizes that allow economies of scale to be realized by regional plants in particular industries.

The market attraction has several facets amenable to measurement. First, where absolute growth in manufacturing is concerned, a very obvious facet is the absolute size of the market. The size of the market determines the *current* demand for manufactured goods; it also influences *future* growth in demand, because absolute growth in population is heavily influenced by the population base. The absolute size of the market—absolute demand—can be measured by population (number of consumers), urban population (number of above-average-income consumers), or personal income (total purchasing power).

The relative size of the market also counts. Relative size has a demand aspect, a supply aspect, and a supply-demand ratio aspect. On the demand side, relative demand is essentially the same as per capita income: if two states are equal in population and other respects, the one where income is highest relative to population should attract the most industry. Since per capita income is higher in urban states, rural-urban variables are potentially good proxies for relative demand. On the supply side, those markets that have relatively little manufacturing are the most attractive: competition tends to be weak, and comparatively large shares of the goods consumed must be imported from outside—with transport costs tacked on. The most direct measure of relative supply is manufacturing employment (or value added) per capita; manufacturing density can also be used. Manufacturing employment per capita can also be viewed as a supply-demand ratio—which brings us to the third aspect of relative size. Theoretically at least, the best measures of relative size are supply-demand ratios that combine relative supply with relative demand. The ratio of manufacturing employment to income is an example.

A third facet of markets is spatial isolation, or remoteness from the Manufacturing Belt. The distance concept invites confusion because economists ordinarily speak of isolation as a handicap. A firm located far from the major eastern markets may find it difficult to compete in them. But what is a handicap from the standpoint of a plant producing for nationwide distribution is an advantage for one serving a regional market. Most manufacturing is still concentrated in the Manufacturing Belt. The farther a state is from northeastern manufacturing centers, the more protected local industry is from outside competition: distance becomes a time-cost protective tariff. Distance from the

Manufacturing Belt (or any arbitrary northeastern point) is therefore a potential measure of market strength.

Underdevelopment.   Another way to express the market hypothesis is to hypothesize that underdevelopment stimulates growth. This hypothesis is rather vague, however, until the term "underdevelopment" is defined. Underdevelopment has a fairly clear meaning in the context of underdeveloped countries, but underdeveloped states are something else. An underdeveloped state might be one which has (1) low per capita income, in which case we are talking about the South, (2) a low degree of urbanization, in which case we are dealing with southern plus some midwestern and western states, (3) low developmental density, in which case we are talking about central and western states, or (4) a low ratio of industry to population, in which case we are again discussing the central and western states—mostly the latter.

The concept that will receive primary emphasis is the one embodied in the "filling in" (Perloff) hypothesis, also called "catching up" (Fuchs). This concept says that the more sparsely populated, sparsely industrialized states are growing fastest. The third and fourth types of underdevelopment both fit the description. But since manufacturing employment per capita has already been subsumed . under markets per se, we shall concentrate in the density aspect of underdevelopment. Developmental density can be measured not only by population density but by income density, manufacturing employment density, farm population density, and similar variables. All of these, it will soon become clear, are highly intercorrelated with various supply-demand ratios—which is why underdevelopment is being treated as an alternative way of looking at markets. "Filling in" implies markets: it implies that the industrial void is being filled in where supply is low relative to demand.

The rural-urban concept of underdevelopment will get secondary attention. This concept is substantively different from a low ratio of manufacturing to population. The most rural states are not the underindustrialized western states: an arid climate, mountainous terrain, and high altitudes (shorter growing season) militate against agriculture in large areas of the West. It is in the South, which is relatively industrialized, that urbanization is lowest. What we shall consider is the possibility that growth is influenced by market expansion attributable to accelerated urbanization in rural states.

Agglomeration

The second broad hypothesis is that agglomeration economies found where industry is clustered stimulate growth. Stated otherwise, the hypothesis is that industry attracts industry. Such an attraction is believed to result from the combined effect of two subattractions, intermediate markets and external economies. Intermediate markets (intermediate between raw materials and consumer markets) are industrial markets, where companies buy from and sell to each other. Suppliers can save on transportation and achieve the advantage of face-to-face contact by locating close to potential customers; consumer industries can save on input costs by locating close to suppliers. The external economies, in turn, are savings realized outside of the productive process by locating where other industries are. These include transport facilities and services (e.g., freight forwarding), business services (e.g., advertising), and skilled labor.

This description might seem reasonably clear, but conceptual problems remain. As we saw in connection with the Perloff study's treatment of agglomeration, it can be construed as a regional influence attracting industry to the Manufacturing Belt or as an essentially local influence directing any region's industry to major metropolitan areas. A second problem arises from the likelihood that intermediate markets are strongest not where the total amount of industry is greatest but where the amount of recently established industry is greatest. If recently established industry is greatest where consumer markets are strongest (in the South and West), is it helpful or practicable to distinguish between intermediate and consumer markets? Finally, when it comes to external economies, they seem to depend as much on population agglomerations as on industrial agglomerations; transport facilities are an example. Is urbanization better than industrialization as a measure of agglomeration attractions?

These problems will be resolved through a multiple approach to agglomeration. First, in deference to the Perloff study's great emphasis on agglomeration attractions in the Manufacturing Belt, variables that define the Manufacturing Belt and measure its industry will be used. This will allow us to inquire whether industry is attracting industry to the Manufacturing Belt. Second, to whatever extent intermediate markets follow consumer markets, they will be treated as an indirect expression of consumer markets and counted under the market influence. This is as much a necessity as a choice: if manufacturing growth in supplier industries is influenced by consumer markets, this growth will be reflected in correlations between manufacturing growth and market variables. Third, in order to maximize the chances of recording external economies available outside (as well as inside) the Manufacturing Belt, both industry and urbanization variables will be used.

Thresholds

The threshold hypothesis is related to agglomeration—both involve intermediate markets and external economies—but differs in two respects. First, agglomeration focuses on a limited number of highly developed states (the Manufacturing Belt states primarily), whereas the idea of thresholds deals with a limited number of highly underdeveloped states. Second, agglomeration is an industry-attracts-industry influence, whereas thresholds is something broader. The threshold hypothesis holds that, although underdevelopment is generally stimulating to growth, too much underdevelopment weakens the stimulus. More specifically, and here the hypothesis is actually being refined on the basis of findings, growth is held to be impeded in states where (a) developmental density is low and (b) there is no major metropolitan area.

At least five factors could contribute to a threshold influence. Three involve markets. If a regional market (e.g., one state, or two or three adjacent ones) is too underpopulated, particular industries will be unable to realize necessary economies of scale through regional production.[1] If an under-developed state is part of a relatively large marketing region, say, five or more states, it is unlikely to hold the region's population (market) center of gravity: a regional plant can usually minimize its distribution costs by locating in or near a major metropolitan area. As a third market factor, ultra-underdeveloped states lack strong intermediate markets: the industrial consumers are clustered in large metropolitan areas in other states.

The other two factors impeding growth in the most underdeveloped states are weak external economies and lack of urban amenities. Attractions described as external economies are now widely available, but there are still gaps.[2] Shortages of skilled labor are apt to be especially troublesome in states without large cities.[3] Even when unskilled labor is all that is needed, many firms cannot go below a certain labor market size and still meet their hiring ratios: a state with four or five cities of adequate size has more chances of landing a plant than a state with just one or two such cities. Air service, though available, may be limited to feeder service; direct or one-stop connections with company headquarters in the East may be lacking. Beyond external economies, there is the noneconomic matter of some executives not wanting to live in places that lack certain residential, commercial, cultural, and social amenities that they desire—amenities that may call for a metropolitan area. Professional and mana-gerial talent a firm may hope to attract has the same tastes to be satisfied.

Urban Attraction

The next hypothesis is related to thresholds but imposes a handicap on states that may have (and in fact generally have) crossed the developmental threshold, assuming that development is described in terms of density. It is also related to one of the underdevelopment hypotheses, the one holding that rural states grow faster, but is really its opposite. The new hypothesis—the urban attraction hypothesis—holds that the most urbanized states *within a region* grow fastest. The hypothesis assumes that per capita income, industrialization, labor factors, and thresholds are held constant. These other factors must be controlled to minimize conceptual overlap between the urban attraction and other influences.

The "within a region" qualification seeks to differentiate between the urban attraction and agglomeration. When a Manufacturing Belt concept of agglomeration is used, agglomeration and urbanization overlap heavily: most of the highly urbanized states are in the Manufacturing Belt, and all of the Manufacturing Belt states are urban (at least 58 percent urban in 1950). But we are not now concerned that the Manufacturing Belt may have a special attraction; that is another matter. What now concerns us is the idea that new plants locating in the developing regions show a preference for the most urbanized states within those regions.

Why might the relatively urbanized states be preferred? The possibilities include market factors and external economies. Rural states in the South have a high incidence of poverty, which could cut sharply into the demand for manufactured goods—to a degree that per capita income would not necessarily reflect. It is also possible—indeed likely—that the urban states, through their metropolitan areas, have greater absolute and relative increases in consumer demand. Again, the urban states are more likely to contain the regional market centers of gravity. Finally, they have the agglomeration attractions: intermediate markets and external economies. Obviously, all of this could be classified as markets or agglomeration. However, because it is impossible to tell which factors are dominant or even operative, it is expedient to combine disparate elements.

Labor

A very popular hypothesis is that labor attractions—low wages, weak unions, and surplus labor—stimulate manufacturing growth, most notably in the South. Regarding wages, some industries are "labor-intensive." Wages account for a relatively high proportion of the cost of finished goods in these industries. Just as transport-sensitive industries seek to minimize transport costs by locating near the market, labor-intensive industries gravitate toward cheap labor. As observed in chapter 1, the principal industries with wage sensitivity are textiles, apparel, and leather goods.

Industry's aversion to unions requires little elaboration. The threat of strikes and other work stoppages, disputes about "management prerogatives," and the efficacy of unions in raising wages make a union anything from a nuisance to an abomination in the eyes of most companies (not that firms necessarily seek to avoid unions). Since the effect of unions on wages is only part of the picture, there is no reason to suppose that any effect of unions on manufacturing growth is necessarily covered by wages. Moreover, in some parts of the West, unions are weak while wages are relatively high (because of the West's high price-wage structure).

Labor supply is closely related to wages and unionization. Where there is abundant surplus labor, the law of supply and demand dictates a low wage level; this is one reason for the low wage structure in the South. (But there are also deeper reasons having to do with the South's history of slavery—unpaid labor—and with the tenant farmer-sharecropper system.) Unions likewise tend to be weak in situations where union activists can easily be fired and replaced; typically they are also weak in agricultural areas, where most surplus labor is generated, because rural society tends to be hostile toward unions. However, quite apart from wages and unions, a tight labor market imposes its own costs: there are recruitment and turnover problems; and selection standards must be lowered, leading to lower productivity and higher absenteeism.

Natural Resources

Natural resources rank with markets and labor among the influences that have received the most attention in the literature. As used in this study, *resources* is essentially a synonym for raw materials, including agricultural products. Like the market-oriented industries, most resource-oriented industries choose their locations because transport costs weigh heavily in the cost of finished goods. But now the raw materials are more expensive to ship than the finished goods. Sometimes this is because the raw materials are perishable and cannot be shipped long distances. Fruits and vegetables are examples. Other raw materials undergo a weight loss in processing, making the finished product lighter than what went into it: pulpwood loses 60 to 65 percent of its weight when converted into paper.

Nontransportation considerations may also influence firms to locate near resources. Some resources are relatively immobile. Water is a case in point. Many industries, as in the case of chemicals, use water in massive quantities for processing or cooling. These must locate near a supply of water. (Water is partly a local and partly a regional factor: there are regions, particularly in the West, where locations with abundant water are scarce or nonexistent.) Also, natural gas is not available in many locations in sufficient supply for use as a raw material; so some industry locates in gas-producing areas.

There is reason to believe that the resource influence is fairly weak and growing weaker. Many of the richest supplies have been depleted, resulting in more uniform distribution. Different states have different resources, which tend to offset one another; unlike labor advantages, resource advantages are not concentrated in one region. Then too, the multistage production found in the modern economy means that relatively few industries are direct users of natural resources. Some of those that do use resources use more than one, which makes it impossible to locate close to all and may effectively neutralize the attraction. Still, despite these limitations on the resource pull, it is virtually certain that resource imbalances contribute something to geographic disparities in manufacturing growth.

Climate

The climate hypothesis is that a cold climate inhibits growth and a warm climate stimulates growth. Why should climate affect growth? In the North, harsh winters are a negative influence. Plant construction and operating costs are higher (foundation requirements, winter construction costs, heating costs, and so on). Blizzards and ice choke roads and airports, causing transport breakdowns. Snow and cold weather restrict outdoor operations and storage; certain products risk damage through freezing. Winter absenteeism adds to labor costs. Perhaps even more important, northern states can be unpleasant places in which to live for persons raised in warmer regions and unaccustomed to severe cold. Some business executives would probably reject northern locations for personal reasons. Likewise, northern climates restrict in-migration and encourage out-migration among retirees. Population growth may stagnate; demand grows slowly if at all.

The southern states, in contrast, offer year-round transport security. Outdoor activity is feasible; this seems to be quite important for at least one high-growth industry—the aircraft industry. Military bases and aerospace installations, attracted by the warm climate, spur the growth of markets. In Florida, Arizona, and California—three of the fastest-growing states—markets have been further enhanced by the in-migration of retirees and (Florida) by wealthy winter vacationers. Climate thus operates through the market mechanism by boosting consumer demand. A final consideration, not to be underestimated, is that air conditioning breakthroughs have fairly recently weakened what may have been a formidable barrier to southern industrialization: torrid summers. Markets that may formerly have been neglected because of unpleasant summer living and working conditions are now wide open. Is industry racing to catch up?

A subordinate hypothesis is that climate interacts with—is an inhibitor or catalyst toward—other influences. Cold winters may well inhibit the exploitation of northern markets; mild winters provide secondary incentives for exploiting markets in the lower states and, through migration, appear to actually contribute to rapid expansion in these markets. These possibilities invite us to test climate-weighted market variables. Wages is another influence with interaction possibilities. A few nonsouthern states, most notably Maine and North Dakota, have wage scales rivaling those of many states in the South. But why go to North Dakota and freeze when plenty of southern locations are available?

Rejected Hypotheses

Considerations of practicality limit the number of hypotheses that can be tested under the methodology being used. Two prominent hypotheses that were rejected for testing deal with industry mix and taxes.

The industry mix hypothesis holds that states tend to grow faster when they begin with relatively high proportions of industry that is fast-growing nationally. A tacit assumption is that much growth takes place either through expansion of existing plants or through the attraction of new plants to old locations, perhaps because of resource advantages. Findings in the Perloff study, the Fuchs study, the Borts-Stein study, and the Bretzfelder study challenge this assumption. These studies test industry mix variables without uncovering evidence of an influence. Meanwhile, the New York study finds that the New York region is growing fastest in those industries in which it has less than its population-prorated share of national employment and slowest in other industries. The study also finds that, throughout the United States, most industries are growing slowest in states with more than their population-prorated shares of the industries. Now, an above-prorata share is not quite the same as a high proportion of an industry, but it can easily amount to the same thing. States with high proportions of fast-growing industries may thus really have *un*favorable industrial structures: their growth may be concentrated where supply is deficient—in the slow-growing industries.

The tax hypothesis holds that low taxes hold down costs and thereby attract industry. This is perhaps the most tested of all locational hypotheses. And the results of prior testing do not encourage further tests. The McLaughlin-Robock interviews develop scant evidence of a tax influence. Thompson and Mattila test two tax variables without finding significant correlations, either industry-wide or for specific industries. The New York and Perloff studies, which rely heavily on secondary materials dealing with particular industries, fail to conclude that taxes are an important influence. Fuchs surveys four tax studies and finds agreement that taxes have little effect. The Fantus study, drawing heavily on practical experience, cannot provide so much as an honorable mention for taxes. Finally, the tax study by the Advisory Commission on Intergovernmental Relations and that by Williams reject the tax hypothesis.

Methodology

The study uses data for the forty-eight contiguous states to measure regional growth patterns and regional influences. Three growth variables— absolute, per capita, and percentage growth in manufacturing employment, 1947–63—are examined. Correlations between these and a wide range of explanatory variables are used to test the selected hypotheses. The methodology first uses simple correlations to identify the dominant influences and to refine the variables measuring them; then it proceeds to partial correlations showing latent influences not visible until the dominant ones (and sometimes other hidden ones) are held constant; and finally it looks at multiple correlations, which indicate which combinations of variables best explain the interregional differences in manufacturing growth.

Dependent Variables

Either an employment measure or a value measure can be used to record manufacturing growth. Total manufacturing employment, as opposed to production workers only, is the best employment measure when growth is viewed from the standpoint of benefits; value added by manufacture is generally regarded as the best value measure. Total manufacturing employment and value added are so closely related that a choice between them has little practical significance: there is a + .996 intercorrelation between them (state totals) for 1947. But since concern about growth rates usually stems from concern about employment and unemployment, the employment measure is slightly more appropriate. This study therefore uses manufacturing employment to measure growth.

Measuring growth requires not only a unit of measure but a growth period. The growth period for this study is 1947 to 1963. This period was selected with a view toward keeping it (*a*) as nearly current as possible in terms of the termination date, (*b*) recent enough in its beginning date to avoid distortions caused by wartime dislocations and the depression, and (*c*) sufficiently long-run to eliminate short-run anomalies in growth patterns. The first criterion dictated the 1963 termination date, that being the date of the most recent census of manufactures published at the time this study was begun.[4] The second criterion suggested the 1947 starting date, 1947 being the year of the first postwar manufacturing census. The sixteen-year interval between 1947 and 1963 adequately serves the third criterion.

Employment growth for the 1947–63 period could be described in several ways. The most obvious are absolute growth, per capita growth, and percentage growth. All three are used in this study. Shift-share measures could have been used instead. These are useful in certain applications but have no particular advantage that would justify their use in this study.

The three dependent (growth) variables were computed as follows:

1. Absolute Growth = 1963 E – 1947 E
2. Per capita Growth = Absolute Growth/1950 P
3. Percentage Growth = Absolute Growth/1947 E

In these formulas and throughout this study, P stands for population and E for *manufacturing* employment.

The main reason for using three measures of growth instead of just one is that different measures behave differently. Consequently, any particular measure could mislead in describing the significance of locational influences. For example, Nevada ranks third in percentage growth, fifteenth in per capita growth, and thirty-eighth in absolute growth. New Jersey ranks thirty-fourth in percentage growth, twenty-second in per capita growth, and seventh in absolute growth. By using all three measures, one gets a well-rounded picture. Each measure provides somewhat different findings. At the same time, where the three are in substantial agreement about the importance of a certain influence, the finding is more reliable than if just one measure were observed. Also, using three variables minimizes the chances that a significant relationship will be overlooked.

Independent Variables: Structural Types

Correlations between each of the three dependent (growth) variables and hundreds of independent (explanatory) variables were computed in order to test the hypotheses. The next section of this chapter, dealing with substantive types of independent variables, describes these variables from the standpoint of these hypotheses. Before we take up substantive types, however, we need to consider some computational matters. All but thirteen of the hundreds of variables tested were generated internally by a computer; they are ratios, roots, and other mathematical forms derived from the original group. Since most of the variables thus generated cannot be obtained directly from published sources, a description of their derivation is in order.

Original Variables. The computational input included the three growth variables (but only one at a time) and the original thirteen explanatory variables. These thirteen original variables, their abbreviations (used throughout this study in text and tables), and their sources are as follows:

Abbre-viation	Variable	Source
P	Population, 1950	SA, p. 12
Y	Personal Income, 1950	SA, p. 330
E	Manufacturing Employment, 1947	Census Mfg.
VA	Value Added by Manufacture, 1947	Census Mfg.
F	Farm Population, 1950	SA, p. 16
M	Land Area in Square Miles	SA, p. 171
CP/P	Urban (City) Population Percentage, 1950	SA, p. 16
A	Average Acres per Farm, 1954	SA, p. 617
T	January Mean Temperature, Principal City	SA, p. 182
Lat	Latitude, Center of State	U.S. Map
Lg	Longitude, Center of State	U.S. Map
W	Average Hourly Wages in Manufacturing, 1960	SA, p. 240
U	Unionization, Adjusted for Industry Mix, 1953	Fuchs, pp. 354–55

The source abbreviations used above, in order of presentation, refer to (*a*) the *Statistical Abstract of the United States, 1966*, (*b*) the *1963 Census of Manufactures, Volume III: Area Statistics*, pp. 86–94, (*c*) the Bureau of Public Roads' official *Federal-Aid Highways Map of the United States*, 1965 edition, and (*d*) Victor Fuchs, *Changes in the Location of Manufacturing in the United States Since 1929* (New Haven: Yale University Press, 1962). In CP/P (urban population percentage), the letter C (City) is used in lieu of U (Urban) because U is reserved for unionization; but C does not literally mean city: the census definition of urban places, which includes some unincorporated places and urban fringe areas, is being used. The 1960 figure for average hourly wages was selected primarily because it was conveniently available. However, it is actually more relevant to the latter half of the 1947–63 growth period than the 1950 figure is. Table 2-1 gives the values for each original variable.

Derived Variables. Most variables used in the study were derived from the original variables. The computer program [5] included a transgeneration routine allowing any variable to be related to any other or to a constant though addition, subtraction, multiplication, or division. The routine could also create dummy variables placing each state into one of two groups, the "have's" (valued at one) and the "have not's" (valued at zero), depending on whether a certain variable was above or below a specified value. And it could provide any root or power, the log or antilog, and the reciprocal of any variable. The routine could proceed through several steps to develop a desired mathematical function. Transgeneration was used to create hundreds of basically new, mathematically adjusted, and weighted variables.

The basically new variables are of five types: (1) *Derived absolutes* are absolute variables obtained by computation. The study uses only three: urban population (CP), or CP/P × P; total hourly manufacturing earnings, or E × W; and total union membership, or E × U. (2) *Reversed variables* are variables subtracted from a constant, for example, 50 – Lat. Since reversal does not affect a variable's correlation with any other variable, except to change the sign (e.g., negative becomes positive), it is useful only where a variable is going to be used as a multiplier. (3) *Products* (other than derived absolutes) are variables obtained by multiplying one variable by another. Thus longitude was multiplied by reversed latitude to get a distance-from-Northeast variable, (50 – Lat) (Lg – 65), where the constant subracted from Lg increases its weight in the formula. (4) *Ratios* and *percentages* are variables created by division. Examples are per capita income (Y/P), population density (P/M), and farm population percentage (F/P). (5) *Dummy variables*, as used in this study, assign a value of either one or zero to each state, depending on whether or not a certain criterion is met. Some are created directly by using a specified cutoff value for a certain variable; others require several steps to compute.

Table 2–1
Original Independent Variables

	Population (000s)	Personal Income (000,000s)	Mfg. Employment (000s)	Mfg. Value Added (000,000s)	Farm Population (000s)	Square Miles (000s)
Maine	914	$ 1,086	100	$ 430	122	33.2
New Hampshire	533	703	75	307	47	9.3
Vermont	378	434	35	150	81	9.6
Massachusetts	4,691	7,676	718	3,356	80	8.3
Rhode Island	792	1,275	147	659	10	1.2
Connecticut	2,007	3,776	400	1,897	63	5.0
New York	14,830	27,813	1,773	9,656	578	49.6
New Jersey	4,835	8,936	739	4,186	105	7.8
Pennsylvania	10,498	16,183	1,442	6,926	705	45.3
Ohio	7,947	12,947	1,194	6,358	853	41.2
Indiana	3,934	6,003	548	2,970	667	36.3
Michigan	6,372	10,887	975	5,200	695	58.2
Illinois	8,712	15,949	1,186	6,683	763	56.4
Wisconsin	3,435	5,070	419	2,263	725	56.2
Minnesota	2,982	4,225	182	1,021	740	84.1
Iowa	2,621	3,926	140	671	783	56.3
Missouri	3,955	5,672	327	1,621	863	69.7
North Dakota	620	782	5	29	254	70.7
South Dakota	653	813	10	51	254	77.0
Nebraska	1,326	1,977	47	261	391	77.2
Kansas	1,905	2,766	75	461	444	82.3
Delaware	318	676	35	183	34	2.1
Maryland	2,343	3,773	229	1,139	183	10.6
Virginia	3,319	4,069	217	1,051	732	40.8
West Virginia	2,006	2,136	127	664	411	24.2
North Carolina	4,062	4,193	381	1,646	1,377	52.7
South Carolina	2,117	1,886	189	794	701	31.1
Georgia	3,445	3,545	250	1,016	962	58.9
Florida	2,771	3,601	79	350	233	58.6
Kentucky	2,945	2,926	130	743	974	40.4
Tennessee	3,292	3,315	222	961	1,016	42.2

Table 2-1 (continued)

	Popu-lation (000s)	Personal Income (000,000s)	Mfg. Employ-ment (000s)	Mfg. Value Added (000,000s)	Farm Popu-lation (000s)	Square Miles (000s)
Alabama	3,062	$ 2,689	206	$ 877	960	51.6
Mississippi	2,179	1,642	77	302	1,097	47.7
Arkansas	1,910	1,606	66	268	802	53.1
Louisiana	2,684	3,020	132	694	567	48.5
Oklahoma	2,233	2,549	55	341	553	69.9
Texas	7,711	10,488	297	1,727	1,292	267.3
Montana	591	962	16	91	136	147.1
Idaho	589	763	17	110	165	83.6
Wyoming	291	484	6	35	57	97.9
Washington	2,379	3,992	144	874	274	68.2
Oregon	1,521	2,428	106	675	228	97.0
Colorado	1,325	1,971	54	287	198	104.2
New Mexico	681	810	7	32	132	121.7
Utah	689	910	25	128	81	84.9
Arizona	750	1,005	14	84	77	113.9
Nevada	160	327	3	17	13	110.5
California	10,586	19,760	664	3,995	568	158.7

	Popu-lation % Urban	Average Acres per Farm	January Mean Temper-ature	Lati-tude	Longi-tude	Average Hourly Mfg. Wages	Relative Unioni-zation
Maine	51.7	155	22°	44.0°	69°	$1.77	75.4
New Hampshire	57.5	140	21	43.0	72	1.77	81.7
Vermont	36.4	208	16	43.5	73	1.85	66.8
Massachusetts	84.4	83	30	42.3	72	2.09	101.3
Rhode Island	84.3	77	29	41.7	71	1.88	89.2
Connecticut	77.6	89	26	41.7	73	2.32	74.6
New York	85.5	143	27	42.5	75	2.31	111.7
New Jersey	86.6	73	35	40.5	74	2.37	101.7
Pennsylvania	70.5	102	31	40.5	77	2.31	112.1

Ohio	70.2	113	31	40.5	83	2.60	109.2
Indiana	59.9	125	29	40.0	86	2.51	114.0
Michigan	70.7	119	25	43.0	85	2.75	121.3
Illinois	77.6	173	26	40.0	89	2.45	118.5
Wisconsin	57.9	147	21	44.0	89	2.37	116.8
Minnesota	54.5	195	12	45.0	94	2.36	122.5
Iowa	47.7	177	20	42.0	93	2.35	85.0
Missouri	61.5	170	32	38.5	92	2.24	126.0
North Dakota	26.6	676	10	47.0	100	1.97	58.0
South Dakota	33.2	719	15	44.0	100	2.02	55.8
Nebraska	46.9	471	22	41.5	99	2.08	73.5
Kansas	52.1	416	32	38.8	98	2.36	76.4
Delaware	62.6	129	33	39.0	76	2.31	52.7
Maryland	69.0	120	35	39.0	77	2.26	73.7
Virginia	47.0	108	40	37.5	78	1.77	60.0
West Virginia	34.6	107	37	38.5	80	2.41	114.5
North Carolina	33.7	68	42	35.5	79	1.54	30.2
South Carolina	36.7	89	47	34.0	81	1.57	32.0
Georgia	45.3	145	45	33.0	83	1.66	51.9
Florida	65.5	316	61	28.0	82	1.86	58.7
Kentucky	36.8	93	35	37.5	85	2.13	71.8
Tennessee	44.1	87	41	35.8	86	1.84	73.1
Alabama	43.8	118	53	33.0	87	1.92	82.4
Mississippi	27.9	96	48	32.5	90	1.52	54.0
Arkansas	33.0	124	41	34.8	92	1.56	87.0
Louisiana	54.8	103	55	31.0	92	2.12	63.9
Oklahoma	51.0	300	37	35.5	97	2.10	51.8
Texas	62.7	498	47	32.0	98	2.17	53.4
Montana	43.7	1,859	22	46.7	110	2.45	143.3
Idaho	42.9	371	29	43.5	115	2.25	69.6
Wyoming	49.8	3,069	25	42.8	107	2.54	79.0
Washington	63.2	271	32	47.0	121	2.63	190.4
Oregon	53.9	387	38	44.5	121	2.55	157.3
Colorado	62.7	942	29	39.2	105	2.42	92.7
New Mexico	50.2	2,347	35	34.8	106	2.08	46.0
Utah	65.3	537	27	40.0	112	2.46	92.0
Arizona	55.5	4,483	50	33.8	112	2.46	84.7
Nevada	57.2	2,881	30	38.0	117	2.75	92.7
California	80.7	307	52	35.5	119	2.62	119.8

Mathematically adjusted variables provided corrections for curvilinear correlation. Relationships between paired variables are often nonlinear: as one variable increases, the other increases (or decreases if the correlation is negative) by more or less than the same proportion. (When percentage growth is correlated with the *log* of manufacturing employment density, the correlation jumps from −.37 to −.57; growth penalties attached to increases in density are less than proportional to the increases.) All variables used in the study were therefore tested for curvilinear correlation with growth. Initial tests used squares, square roots, and reciprocals of the independent variables to see if their correlations could be improved. Favorable results led to experimentation with stronger corrections, such as cubes and logs. If this didn't help, weaker corrections were tried. (One of the key variables for predicting absolute growth is $E^{1.5}$.) Different corrections were sometimes used for different partial and multiple correlation contexts: curvilinearity can change when something is held constant.

Weighted variables, obtained by multiplication or division, were used to inquire whether two influences interact (i.e., whether one "conditions" another). The weighted variables used in this study are certain variables multiplied by (or divided into) temperature, latitude, longitude, or a dummy. An example is $T \times Y/E$, a temperature-weighted demand-supply ratio that asks whether the market attraction is enhanced in warm states and weakened in states with harsh winters. Dummy multipliers render a variable inoperative in the absence of some condition. $MB \times E/M$ (where MB is a dummy valued at one for the Manufacturing Belt states and at zero elsewhere) is equal to $1 \times E/M = E/M$ in the Manufacturing Belt and $0 \times E/M = 0$ elsewhere. It tests the idea that industrial agglomerations are attractive, but only when Manufacturing Belt levels of industrial density are reached.

The weighted variables often use constants and exponents to alter the relative weights of the variables being weighted. A variable's weight is, in substance, the ability of a high value for the variable to offset a low value for another variable being multiplied. This ability depends on the ratio of the variable's maximum value to its minimum value: a variable with a 2:1 maximum-minimum ratio has less influence in a weighting scheme than one with an 11:1 ratio. A variable's weight is increased either by subtracting a constant or by raising it to a power (or both); raising to a power simultaneously adjusts for curvilinear correlation. Longitude, which has a natural range (rounded here for simplicity) of from 120 in Washington to 70 in Maine, has roughly a 2:1 maximum-minimum ratio; but this becomes 55:5, or 11:1, when Lg − 65 substitutes for Lg: (50 − Lat) (Lg − 65) gives more weight to Lg than does (50 − Lat)Lg. Cubing the longitude variable will now raise its ratio from 11:1 to 1331:1, giving it still more weight. This is no academic example: the best overall spatial isolation variable in the study is $(50 - Lat)(Lg - 65)^3$.

Independent Variables: Substantive Types

We have been viewing the independent variables from the standpoint of structural (computational) types; now it is time to look at them from the standpoint of the locational hypotheses set forth at the beginning of the chapter. For each hypothesis, anywhere from a few to a large number of test variables were devised.

Markets: Absolute Variables. The market hypothesis, we saw earlier, has several facets: absolute demand, the supply-demand relationship (including relative demand and relative supply), spatial isolation, and underdevelopment. When absolute growth is the dependent variable, absolute demand and the supply-demand relationship are crucial. And they must be measured with absolute variables.

Three variables were used to measure absolute demand:

P   CP   Y

The first of these, P (population), is basic: total demand depends more than anything else on the number of people whose wants must be satisfied. The third variable, Y (income), is based on P—it is equivalent to population adjusted for variations in per capita income—but counts dollars rather than heads. Theoretically, this should make it the best measure of demand: total purchasing power depends on both the number of people and their wealth. CP (urban population) is a compromise between P and Y. It counts heads but only the wealthy heads, which recognizes that urban residents have generally higher incomes.

The supply side of markets is best measured by the absolute amount of manufacturing when absolute growth is the dependent variable. Two variables describe absolute supply:

E   VA

E (manufacturing employment) uses the number of people producing goods to measure production; VA (value added) looks at the value added by manufacture to the value of the inputs used to produce the finished goods.[6] Unfortunately, both measures are so highly intercorrelated with population and income that they function as proxies for demand until demand is held constant. What they are really useful for, therefore, is measuring the *relationship* between supply and demand. This relationship is examined either by looking at supply with demand held constant, or by looking at demand with supply held constant (e.g., at E with P constant or at P with E constant).

Markets: Relative Supply and Demand. The two relative dependent variables—per capita and percentage growth—take relative measures of supply and demand. Relative demand in the sense of total purchasing power related to population can be measured by per capita income and by several rural-urban variables that sometimes function as proxies for per capita income. The variables:

$$Y/P \qquad CP/P \qquad F/P \qquad CP/F \qquad F/CP$$

Y/P (per capita income) is in theory the purest measure of relative demand, but it is not always the best in practice. CP/P (urban population percentage), F/P (farm population percentage), and the two farm-urban population ratios are imperfect measures of relative income; but they compensate by reflecting population clustering. States with large cities, where demand is spatially concentrated, may be more attractive to industry than per capita income shows.

Relative supply is measured by a series of supply-demand ratios. These relate the two absolute supply variables (E and VA) to the three absolute demand variables (P, CP and Y). Six ratios result:

$$E/P \qquad E/CP \qquad E/Y \qquad VA/P \qquad VA/CP \qquad VA/Y$$

E/P (manufacturing employment per capita) and VA/P (value added per capita) are the best measures of industrialization, if a superficial distinction between relative industrialization and the supply-demand relationship is permitted. But since P measures not only population per se but demand, E/P and VA/P are supply-demand ratios as well. The two income ratios, E/Y and VA/Y, are theoretically the best overall supply-demand ratios. The urban population ratios, E/CP and VA/CP, are very much like the income ratios but again register the attraction of large cities. (In some partial correlation situations, E/CP and VA/CP behave differently from the other four ratios, suggesting that rural-urban characteristics are taking control.)

Markets: Spatial Isolation. The spatial isolation facet of markets arises from the transportation "tariff" that protects plants locating in the South and West—especially the West—from competition from Manufacturing Belt factories. Degrees latitude (north-south) and longitude (east-west) are convenient measures of distance from the Manufacturing Belt. Latitude, however, is also a proxy for climate when used alone; only longitude will be considered in unweighted form. Three longitude variables are used in this study:

$$Lg \qquad\qquad West \qquad\qquad Central-West$$

Lg is longitude itself; it increases east to west. West is a dummy variable valued at one for the eleven westernmost states (Montana, Idaho, Wyoming, Colorado,

Utah, New Mexico, Arizona, Nevada, Washington, Oregon, California) and at zero in all the others. Central-West is a dummy valued at one for the twenty-two states located west of the Mississippi River.

Latitude-longitude variables, or contour variables, are also used. These variables describe the combined effect of north-south and east-west isolation. Secondarily, they describe industrial development contour lines: economic geographers know that industrialization can be described on a map by a series of concentric contour lines rippling out from the Northeast, with secondary ripples moving east from Los Angeles and San Francisco. To obtain contour variables, latitude was first reversed—subtracted from 50 and other constants—so it would increase north to south. Constants were also used to alter longitude's weight. Five measures of latitude and five of longitude—twenty-five combinations—were selected for preliminary testing. Here are two representative contour variables:

$$(60 - Lat)(Lg - 65) \qquad\qquad (48 - Lat)(Lg - 68)$$

Different combinations give different weights to latitude and longitude. The heaviest weights used belong to $48 - Lat$ and $Lg - 68$.

Markets: Underdevelopment.   The discussion of the market hypothesis indicated that two concepts of underdevelopment would be examined, low developmental density and low degree of urbanization. Density is population or any other economic measure per square mile, but it can also be described by proxy. Seven density measures, including one proxy, are used in this study:

$$P/M \qquad CP/M \qquad Y/M \qquad E/M \qquad VA/M \qquad F/M \qquad A$$

These measures are, respectively, population density, urban population density, income density, manufacturing employment density, value-added density, farm population density, and average acres per farm. The last variable is a proxy for farm population density: F/M is low where A is high. All seven, in turn, are essentially proxies for relative industrialization, or the supply-demand relationship; although they also reflect the spatial isolation facet of markets (low density in the West).

The rural-urban concept of underdevelopment can be tested by means of the four rural-urban variables listed previously in connection with relative demand: CP/P, F/P, CP/F, and F/CP. The hypothesis is that the rural states are experiencing faster urbanization, hence faster expansion in consumer demand and consequently faster industrialization. Of course, this contradicts the earlier hypothesis that the urban states have stronger demand patterns and faster industrial growth. But either hypothesis is plausible, and there is no reason why the same variables cannot be used to test both. (Which, if either, is correct can be ascertained from the signs on the correlations.) As a matter of fact, these same variables will be used in connection with the urban attraction hypothesis, coming up shortly.

Agglomeration. Leaving markets, we come to the industry-attracts-industry hypothesis—agglomeration. Agglomeration is in a very real sense the opposite of markets: the market hypothesis calls for faster growth in the least industrialized states, but the agglomeration hypothesis calls for faster growth in the most industrialized ones. Since both hypotheses deal with industrialization, it is possible to use some of the same variables to test both. Two of the relative supply variables, E/P and VA/P, are especially appropriate; and two of the density variables, E/M and VA/M, are equally suitable. If these variables are to register agglomeration, however, they must show positive correlations rather than the negative ones that the market hypothesis calls for.

The Perloff study places heavy emphasis on agglomeration economies in the thirteen-state Manufacturing Belt (Massachusetts, Rhode Island, Connecticut, New York, New Jersey, Pennsylvania, Delaware, Maryland, Ohio, Michigan, Indiana, Illinois, and Wisconsin). It is therefore advisable to supplement the above variables with additional ones that likewise stress the Manufacturing Belt. To do this we shall utilize two dummy variables and a related series of dummy-weighted variables:

NE	MB × E	MB × E/M	MB × E/P
MB	MB × VA	MB × VA/M	MB × (E/M)^2

NE is a dummy variable representing (valued at one in) sixteen Northeast states—the Manufacturing Belt states plus northern New England. MB is a dummy representing the Manufacturing Belt. The dummy-weighted variables multiply manufacturing indicators by one or zero, which means that industry is assumed to exert no attraction (is valued at zero) in states outside the Manufacturing Belt. MB × (E/M)^2 was thrown in to test the possibility that agglomeration's pull is disproportionately strong in the biggest industrial agglomerations: squaring a variable gives exaggerated weight to the extremely high cases. Some NE-weighted variables were also tested in connection with absolute and per capita growth, but these gave correlations almost identical to those of their MB counterparts and will receive minimal attention.

New variables were also created to test a broader concept of agglomeration. The broader concept allows for agglomeration economies in states outside the Manufacturing Belt that have reached or are approaching Manufacturing Belt levels of development. Five dummy variables represented agglomeration in the broad sense:

E > 145,000	E/P > 7%	CP/P > 57.7%
VA > $1 billion	E/P > 6%	

The E dummy, which cuts off immediately below Rhode Island, identifies twenty-two states: twelve Manufacturing Belt states (all but Delaware—E = 34,738) plus Virginia, North Carolina, South Carolina, Georgia, Tennessee, Alabama, Minnesota, Missouri, Texas, and California. The VA dummy identifies eighteen states: eleven from the Manufacturing Belt (all but Rhode Island and Delaware) plus Virginia, North Carolina, Georgia, Minnesota, Missouri, Texas, and California. The E/P > 7% dummy identifies twenty-one states: the thirteen Manufacturing Belt states plus Maine, New Hampshire, Vermont, Virginia, North Carolina, South Carolina, Georgia, and Missouri. The E/P > 6% dummy identifies twenty-eight states: the twenty-one just mentioned plus West Virginia, Tennessee, Alabama, Minnesota, Washington, Oregon, and California. The CP/P dummy, which cuts off immediately below the lowest urban percentage found in the Manufacturing Belt (Wisconsin), identifies twenty states: the thirteen from the Manufacturing Belt plus Florida, Missouri, Texas, Colorado, Utah, Washington, and California.

Thresholds. The threshold hypothesis, which says that extreme under-development impedes growth, was tested primarily with density variables. The most important of these were density reciprocals:

$$1/(P/M) \quad 1/(Y/M) \quad 1/(E/M) \quad 1/(VA/M) \quad 1/(CP/M) \quad 1/(F/M)$$

These variables (except for the last, which isn't very effective) work because of a mathematical quirk sometimes exhibited by reciprocals. If a variable ranges from extremely high to extremely low values, the reciprocal may not effectively distinguish among degrees of highness (which become degrees of lowness in the reciprocal): all high cases become one over a very high number, or approximately zero. But the reciprocal can distinguish among the low cases (the highest reciprocals) and can also distinguish between the two extremes. The upshot of this is that $1/(P/M)$ can easily distinguish between Wyoming and Utah but not between New York and Alabama: it can pick out the most underdeveloped states and differentiate among them according to extent of underdevelopment.

Some preliminary findings pointed to a threshold influence operating in the five western states that lack major metropolitan areas: Montana, Idaho, Wyoming, New Mexico, and Nevada. This led to the creation of some dummy and dummy-weighted variables. The following are representative:

West	West-Rural	West-Metro
West × 1/(P/M)	West-Rural × 1/(P/M)	West-Rural × 1/E
West × 1/(E/M)	West-Rural × 1/(E/M)	West-Rural × 1/VA

West, West-Rural, and West-Metro are dummies respectively valued at one in the eleven western states, the above-mentioned five least developed western states, and the six western states with major metropolitan areas. The dummy-weighted reciprocals give the highest values to the least developed states. We are looking for negative correlations for the West-Rural dummy and all weighted reciprocals. The West-Metro dummy should be positively correlated with growth, assuming that the West-Metro states do not have a threshold handicap. The West dummy could lean either way.

To further test the threshold hypothesis, three nonreciprocal density variables were weighted by the West dummy, as follows:

$$\text{West} \times \text{P/M} \qquad\qquad \text{West} \times \text{CP/M} \qquad\qquad \text{West} \times \text{E/M}$$

These variables start with the knowledge that, for the nation as a whole, density is negatively correlated with growth: high density, low growth. They inquire whether this relationship is reversed in the West, so that the correlation becomes positive: low density, low growth. Note that these variables give the least developed western states slightly higher values than the central and eastern states (valued at zero) but lower values than the most developed western states.

Urban Attraction. The urban attraction hypothesis, which looks for a residual attraction in urban states after per capita income and thresholds have been accounted for, uses the rural-urban variables presented earlier:

$$\text{CP/P} \qquad \text{F/P} \qquad \text{CP/F} \qquad \text{F/CP} \qquad \text{CP/P} > 57.7\%$$

Since these variables have been suggested for a variety of contexts, there might seem to be a problem of determining what they represent. But there is no serious problem. If the variables with CP in the numerator are positive, for example, the idea that states which are underdeveloped in the rural-urban sense have faster growth is not supported. And, since the urban attraction hypothesis requires that per capita income be held constant, these variables cannot function as proxies for per capita income when this hypothesis is being tested.

There are two minor problems. The first is that when the rural-urban variables are being used to measure relative demand (when per capita income is *not* held constant), the hypothetical urban attraction and the narrower consumer demand attraction are intermingled. One cannot be sure of the extent to which external economies, urban amenities, or something of that sort (as opposed to demand factors) are responsible for any rapid growth noted in urban states. A second problem is that urbanization could be a proxy for agglomeration economies: after all, the CP/P dummy was created to test for agglomeration. This problem cannot be completely resolved but can partly be met by observing which states achieve improved predictions when rural-urban variables are used in regression equations. If most of the improvement is in Manufacturing Belt states, agglomeration is indicated. If, on the other hand, the Manufacturing

Belt states are not the urban states that benefit, agglomeration in the Manufacturing Belt sense of the term can be discounted. Agglomeration economies may still be involved, but a wider set of influences will seem likely.

Labor. The labor hypothesis deals broadly with three related factors: wages, unionization, and labor supply (or surplus labor). Two wage variables are used in the study, one relative and one absolute:

$$W \qquad\qquad\qquad E \times W$$

W is average hourly earnings in manufacturing, one of the thirteen original variables. $E \times W$, or manufacturing employment times hourly wages, is total wage payments per hour. This latter variable was designed for use with absolute growth, where it seemed likely that the influence of wages would be proportional not only to the wage level but to the growth potential of a state. But because W varies within a narrow range (has a low maximum-minimum ratio) while E fluctuates widely, E dominated the formula: $E \times W$ gave almost the same simple and partial r's as E alone. This problem might have been mitigated by reweighting E and W, but it was evident that even an improved version of $E \times W$ would still be ambiguous. Therefore, although simple correlations for $E \times W$ will be shown, the variable was abandoned early in the experiments.

A comparable pair of variables was used to measure unionization:

$$U \qquad\qquad\qquad E \times U$$

The basic variable, U (unionization), comes from figures compiled for the National Bureau of Economic Research and published in the Fuchs study. It is the ratio of a state's actual union membership to a hypothetical membership which would obtain if each industry in the state had the same percentage of workers unionized as were unionized nationwide in that industry. The variable is based on 1953 levels of unionization. The absolute version, $E \times U$, presented the same problems as $E \times W$ and was abandoned at an early stage for the same reason.

We have already seen the most of the surplus labor in the country comes from agriculture, where advancing technology is displacing farm workers. This makes farm variables the best place to start looking for a measure of labor supply. Several farm variables, including A (average acres per farm) and F/P (farm population percentage), were tested. But only two types proved effective:

$$F^k \qquad\qquad\qquad (F/M)^k$$

In these variables, the exponent k is a constant. The best version of F (farm population) was generally $F^{1.5}$; sometimes F^2 gave a higher partial correlation.

The best F/M (farm population density) variables were $(F/M)^4$, $(F/M)^3$, and $(F/M)^2$. Absolute growth generally favored the first, per capita growth the second, and percentage growth the second and third. The exponents on these variables have the effect of magnifying the importance of high values: variations within the high set of states (the states with surplus labor) have the most influence in the correlation. Various tests used to confirm that surplus labor is actually what these variables describe will be discussed later.

Resources and Climate. The remaining hypotheses—resources and climate—employ a severely limited selection of variables. Satisfactory resource variables are not available and would be difficult to construct. The best possibility would be to total the employment in various resource sectors and relate this to population or square miles. But this would involve serious problems of how to weight the sectors and, in any case, time and clerical constraints prevented such an approach. The best that could be done was to use M (square miles) as a crude measure of resources. Here the theory is that resources tend to be evenly distributed, so that the larger states will generally have more. However, M did not prove to be a useful variable, and the conclusions about the resource influence are based on indirect analyses, explained later.

Climate was perhaps the easiest influence to measure. The study used two climate variables:

$$T \qquad\qquad\qquad\qquad\qquad 50 - Lat$$

T is January mean temperature for a state's principal city. Weighted averages were used in a few states with more than one large city, but only in California did this affect T by more than one or two degrees. The other variable, 50 - Lat (latitude), was recorded to the nearest half degree for the center of each state or, in a few instances, for a compromise location between the center and the principal city. As already explained, Lat was subtracted from 50 so that it would increase north to south and could be used as a multiplier for longitude. Reversing the variable changes the sign but does not otherwise affect the correlation. Probably the main difference between T and 50 - Lat in terms of substance is that 50 - Lat gives more emphasis to southern locations: T is influenced by the warming effect of the Gulf Stream and the Japanese Current in coastal states and by altitude in some of the western states.

Interaction Variables. Temperature-weighted and distance-weighted variables are a final pair of substantive types. These test the idea that different influences interact in such a way that their joint effect is greater than the sum of their independent effects.

The temperature-weighted variables are the more important. Some preliminary experiments used both T and 50 - Lat as weights with several market variables. The weighted variables using T gave generally higher correlations; so subsequent experiments concentrated on it. Weighting experiments showed that T works best when its weight is increased by subtracting the constant 9, which is the largest constant that can be subtracted without creating zero or negative values; hence T – 9 became the standard variable for temperature weighting. The main effect of subtracting 9 is to impose heavier climate penalties on the Dakotas and Minnesota.

Many different market and wage variables were weighted by T – 9. Variables positively correlated with growth were multiplied; negatively correlated ones were divided into T – 9. The latter procedure in effect converts the negatively correlated variables into reciprocals, making them positive, and then multiplies: $(T - 9) (E/M) = (T - 9) \times 1/(E/M)$. A few of the best weighted variables were refined by trial-and-error methods until the optimal combination of weights and adjustments for curvilinearity was reached. A complete list of all temperature-weighted variables would be redundant at this point, but a representative selection can be given. Here are some positively correlated variables weighted by temperature:

$$(T - 9)^2 Y \qquad (T - 9) \times Y/P \qquad (T - 9) \times Y/E$$

$$(T - 9) (Lg - 65) \quad (T - 9)^{1.5} \times (Y^{0.8}/P) \quad (T - 9)^{2.5} \times [(Y/M)^{0.65}/(E/M)]$$

This is a similar group of negatively correlated (before weighting) variables:

$$(T - 9)/(E/M) \qquad\qquad (T - 9)/(F/M) \qquad\qquad (T - 9)/W$$

$$(T - 9)^2/\sqrt{E/M} \qquad\qquad (T - 9)^2/\sqrt{F/M} \qquad\qquad (T - 9)^2/W^2$$

Most of the distance-weighted variables used Lg or a more heavily weighted version of it, either Lg – 50 or Lg – 65. A few experiments used the West dummy (the eleven western states) on the theory that variations in distance within the West are not as crucial as the basic east-west distinction. And some other weighted variables used a latitude-longitude contour variable, $(50 - Lat) (Lg - 65)$, as a weight. Only the market variables were weighted by distance, because theoretical considerations did not support its use with labor and other variables. Some representative distance-weighted variables are these:

$$(Lg - 65)P \qquad\qquad West \times Y \qquad\qquad (50 - Lat)(Lg - 65) \times Y/E$$

Experimental Procedure

The analysis employed a computer program capable of providing (1) an eighty-variable correlation matrix—a table showing the correlation of every variable with every other—and (2) stepwise computations showing partial and multiple correlations at each of any designated number of steps, hence for any desired combination of variables. This program adds independent variables to a combination (control group) one at a time. At each step a printout shows the multiple correlation (R) between the variables in the combination and the dependent variable (growth). It also shows the partial correlations between the remaining independent variables and growth when the variables in the combination are jointly held constant. The procedure can be carried out to any reasonable number of steps. Five steps gives five Rs and five sets of partial correlations.

The same procedure was followed for each growth variable, although the actual experiments differed considerably because of the different characteristics of the three growth variables. In each case the analysis began with simple correlations (nothing held constant). Successive matrixes tested each variable for curvilinear correlation and worked out the best adjustments for weighted and unweighted variables. (The "best" adjustment is the one that maximizes the simple correlation; it is not necessarily best for partial and multiple correlation purposes.)

Once the best adjustments had been worked out, the partial correlation experiments began. These utilized a control-delete capability in the program. Either the computer or the analyst can select the variable to be added (held constant) at each step of the stepwise regression analysis; the computer selects the variable with the highest simple or partial correlation. A starting matrix was constructed that included all thirteen original variables, the basic forms of all derived variables, the best adjusted versions of any original or derived variable that could be substantially improved through an adjustment (minor improvements sufficed for significant variables), and basic and adjusted versions of the more promising weighted variables. Almost all of these variables—all but some near-duplicates of others—were then successively held constant to see what partial correlations developed. The experiments gradually worked up to six or more variables held constant. New variables were created and added to the matrix, others revised, and still others dropped during the course of the experiments. The overall effort was geared to finding out (a) which variables had latent significance or could be made more significant, (b) which other variables had to be held constant to reveal this significance, and (c) which adjustments for curvilinearity for the experimental and control variables yielded the highest partial correlations.

The multiple correlation experiments began with a large number of six-step regressions. Many of these had just the first variable (step one) specified; others used two or three preselected variables. These runs and the many preceding ones from the partial correlation experiments gave a good indication of which variables were important. They also provided a series of best, second-best, and third best Rs for two to six steps. These best Rs were then improved through trial-and-error methods involving the modification or replacement of particular variables. Many new variables were created and tested during this process. And there was considerable feedback from one growth variable's experiments to another's (particularly between per capita and percentage growth). The experiments did not stop with the best six-variable Rs for the dependent variables but proceeded to ten or twelve variables. (In this era of the computer, simplicity is not the virtue it once was; so no effort was made to severely limit the number of variables, and neither was there an attempt to keep the variables simple.) Naturally, only significant variables were included in the "best" combinations as finally determined for different numbers of steps.

Attribution and Estimation

There is a well-known typology of lies—lies, damn lies, and statistics—that implores every investigator using statistics to be cautious in his inferences. I certainly have no desire to mislead or to be accused of extravagant interpretations or judgments. The following remarks are therefore offered to clarify the basis for causal inferences and for estimated contributions by locational influences to variations in regional growth.

The Attribution Problem

Practically everyone familiar with correlation analysis knows that correlation does not prove causality. But some commentators, rightly concerned that correlations can be abused and misinterpreted, overstate the point: they in effect deny that correlations constitute useful evidence of causality. Because this attitude is far from rare, it must be stressed here that correlations can provide solid support for causal hypotheses.

The causal inferences made in this study are based on considerably more than one or two correlations in support of an inference. A causal inference begins with a theoretical relationship between two variables: industry seeks the market in order to minimize transportation costs, industry seeks low wages in order to hold down production costs. The theoretical bases for most of the inferences made in this study are well developed in the literature; the study supplements and expands previous theory. Another consideration is that alternative explanations for a significant correlation can often be ruled out as implausible. Why should we entertain the possibility that rapid growth causes a warm climate? How could fast growth drive wages down?

Beyond theory, we have the findings of prior studies offering different methodologies, different evidence. Interviews and questionnaires, authoritative descriptions of company or industry behavior, observed locational patterns for particular industries, and earlier statistical studies all lend support to causal hypotheses. The present study provides corroborative evidence derived from three different measures of growth. Not just the simple correlations but literally thousands of partial and multiple correlations have been examined. The possibility that one variable seeming to have independent significance actually represents another has been checked against evidence provided by (a) intercorrelations between independent variables, (b) observations of whether certain variables move up and down together in their partial r's under varying controls, (c) additional partial r's holding first one and then the other of two variables constant in different situations to see if the companion variable drops toward zero, (d) comparisons of the relative magnitudes of two partials to see which variable is in command, if the two seem to be linked, and (e) feedback results obtained from similar experiments using alternative measures of growth. Analyses of residuals and tests with dummy variables have also been used in checking causal interpretations.

Relative Importance Estimates

It is unrealistic to try to say precisely what percentage of the variation in growth is attributable to this or that influence. But it is possible to develop maximum and minimum percentages describing the approximate range within which a contribution seems to fall and to rough out a central tendency within that range. This can be done by examining simple, partial, and multiple correlations. Simple correlations provide r^2 (coefficient of determination), which is read as a percentage—the percentage of the variation in the dependent variable (growth) that is statistically explained by the independent variable being examined. Partial and stepwise multiple correlations show a variable's potential or actual contribution to R^2 (coefficient of multiple determination) when differing combinations of other variables are held constant.

A given variable will statistically explain different percentages of growth in different contexts. Much depends on whether favorable and unfavorable intercorrelations have been controlled (by holding intercorrelated variables constant) so that other influences do not reinforce or counteract the influence described by the variable being observed. For example, the favorable effect of low wages can be obscured by the unfavorable effect of low income (weak demand) when per capita income is not held constant. Duplication is a related problem: a climate variable held constant will partly duplicate a wage variable, and one market variable may involve substantial duplication of another. It is erroneous to assume, though, that cumulative duplication of one variable by others held constant is the rule. The variables (or influences) controlled are just as likely to offset as to duplicate the one being observed. The general rule in this study was that the explanatory power of an uncontrolled variable increased as additional variables *describing other influences* were held constant.

Because of the overlap problem, the estimating procedure did not focus on any particular simple or partial correlation or contribution to R^2; it looked at significant variables in a wide variety of contexts. These contexts included numerous multiple correlation combinations. Particular variables were entered in many different orders in given combinations—resulting in different contributions to R^2. Extremely small contributions judged to result from immature partials were ignored. Extremely large contributions were ignored or judgmentally reduced if they (a) were based on obvious proxy relationships or (b) borrowed extensively from interfering variables forced to play setup roles. (Where two variables tend to neutralize each other, almost all of their joint contribution to R^2 will be made by the one entering a combination last.)

The estimates developed in this study place considerable weight on a few large multiple correlation combinations that explain most of the variation in growth. Most influences are represented by more than one variable in these combinations: the best ten-variable combination for absolute growth has five market variables (two weighted by climate). All variables in a family were considered in assessing an influence's importance, as judged by any particular combination. And, to repeat, these variables were tested in many different entry orders within the combination.

The use of climate-weighted variables made a market-climate control total advisable as a first step in estimating markets and climate. Thus markets and climate were first estimated to jointly explain 80 to 90 percent, or around 85 percent, of percentage growth. The total was divided between markets and climate according to the ratio of (a) the R^2 for a basic set of unweighted market variables to (b) the r^2 for the best climate variable (which could not be helped by additional climate variables). For percentage growth the ratio is 7:3, and—with minor rounding in favor of markets—the 85 percent joint contribution divides into 60 percent for markets and 25 percent (preliminary) for climate. This procedure credits most of a market-climate interaction effect to markets. Markets is deliberately favored because much the interaction effect seems to result from migration to the warmer states. The resulting buildup in consumer demand can reasonably be credited to markets instead of climate, even though both have a claim.

Estimates for the threshold influence involved minor deviations from the usual procedure. First, 1 percent of the original climate estimates was shifted to thresholds. This was done because experimental evidence pointed to about this much duplication of thresholds by climate: cold climates and subthreshold development coincide in Montana, Idaho, and Wyoming. Second, the threshold estimate for absolute growth was based partly on the estimate for percentage growth. Market variables, P and Y in particular, duplicate the threshold influence with absolute growth, making it hard to measure. But thresholds necessarily explains less with absolute growth than with percentage growth. Montana, Idaho, Wyoming, New Mexico, and Nevada are too underpopulated to have high potentials for absolute growth. But they don't need much absolute growth to attain respectable percentage growth rates. A small threshold-induced loss in absolute growth therefore amounts to a larger loss in percentage growth. Hence the threshold contribution must be somewhat less with absolute growth than with percentage growth.

Lack of a suitable resource variable necessitated indirect methods of evaluating the resource influence. Two approaches were used. The first used labor as a benchmark and judged the relative importance of resources by consulting other studies. There is general agreement that the resource influence has long been declining and is now minor. Only the McLaughlin-Robock study finds resources to be more important than labor—by a narrow margin. Fuchs judges labor to be roughly twice as important as resources (excluding climate). The Fantus study gives labor costs a 24 to 11 weighted score advantage over proximity to raw materials. On balance, the resource contribution averages about two-thirds that of labor.[7]

The second approach looks at unexplained residuals. Without using resource variables, we can get R's that leave unexplained variances of only 2 percent for absolute growth, 7 percent for per capita growth, and 3 percent for percentage growth. These residuals, of course, are not ceilings for the resource influence: resources may be duplicated by other influences represented in R. But resources might just as easily be counteracted by overlapping influences, in which case part of the residual belongs to influences whose contributions to R suffered through failure to hold resources constant. The procedure used gives resources the benefit of the doubt by crediting resources with the full amount of the unexplained variance *plus* small portions of the shares originally credited to climate and labor.

The portions transferred allow for possible duplication (a) of Gulf state petroleum resources by climate and (b) of agricultural resources by labor supply ($F^{1.5}$). The transfers are gauged to bring the residual method estimates up to or slightly above the benchmark estimate levels.

3 Simple Correlations

The study findings will be presented in four chapters. The first covers the simple correlations for all three measures of growth; the next three deal with partial and multiple correlations, a separate chapter being devoted to each growth variable. This chapter, which reports and analyzes the simple correlations, has three divisions. The first looks at unweighted variables; the second takes up weighted variables; and the third summarizes the findings.

Unweighted Variables

The correlations (r's) for all three growth variables—absolute, per capita, and percentage—have been arranged in tables in adjacent columns opposite the explanatory variables. This facilitates evaluation of the hypotheses being explored: it allows us to compare one dependent variable with another in relation to the same independent variable. The hypotheses, once more, deal with markets, agglomeration, thresholds, urban orientation, labor, resources, and climate. Because the urban orientation variables have market implications too, they will be consolidated with market variables in early tables and discussed only once.

Markets: Demand, Supply, and Isolation

The market variables introduced in chapter 2 included ones measuring (1) absolute demand and supply, (2) relative demand, (3) relative supply, (4) spatial isolation, and (5) developmental density. All categories except relative demand provide simple correlations pointing to a strong market influence. (Relative demand responds to partial correlations.)

Absolute Variables. The absolute variables are relevant mainly to absolute growth. Seven appear as dependent variables in table 3-1. The first three—P (population), Y (income), and CP (urban population)—describe the demand side of the supply-demand relationship; they measure the pull of consumer demand. Two others, E (manufacturing employment) and VA (value added by manufacture), measure industry, or the supply side; they ask whether industry seeks places where competitive production is low. The remaining two absolute vari-

51

Table 3-1
Simple Correlations: Absolute Variables

Independent Variables	Absolute Growth	Per Capita Growth	Percentage Growth
P	+ .42	− .04	− .22
Y	+ .42	− .05	− .21
CP	+ .40	− .06	− .20
E	+ .12	− .23	− .35
VA	+ .15	− .21	− .34
F	+ .28	+ .10	− .16
M	+ .42	+ .31	+ .46

Abbreviations: P = Population, Y = Income, CP = Urban Population, F = Farm Population, E = Manufacturing Employment, VA = Value Added, M = Square Miles

ables, F (farm population) and M (square miles), are not essentially market variables but are sufficiently intercorrelated with market variables to behave as market proxies until the market influence is held constant. No adjusted versions (logs, squares, etc.) of the variables are shown, because no adjustment attempted improved r.

When we look first at absolute growth, the expectation that total demand will be linked to total increase in manufacturing employment is realized in these r's: +.42 for P, +.42 for Y, and +.40 for CP. Since r must reach only ± .36 for significance at the 1 percent confidence level, these figures can be regarded as statistically significant. True, they are not very high: an r of +.42 gives an r^2 (coefficient of determination) of only .18, which means that population or income statistically explains only 18 percent of the variation in absolute growth. But this is misleading—for two reasons. First, the highest populations tend to be in the East, where the adverse influence of high levels of manufacturing retards growth. Thus we shall see in the next chapter that when manufacturing employment ($E^{1.5}$) is held constant, P and Y exhibit partial r's of +.82 and +.89. Second, we have not yet considered the interaction between demand and climate. Later in this chapter a +.92 r for $(T - 9)^{2.5} \times Y$—income weighted by temperature—will be presented.

The two industry variables, E and VA, do not show significant r's. Moreover, their r's of +.12 and +.15, being positive, seem to contradict the idea that industry seeks a vacuum. But again appearances are misleading. There are intercorrelations of +.92 and +.94 between E and VA, respectively, and Y. E and VA are therefore torn between a tendency to function as proxies for demand (i.e., to be significantly positive) and a tendency to speak for themselves (i.e., to be significantly negative). They compromise by displaying r's fairly close to zero. Only when P or Y is held constant do we get the true picture: holding Y constant results in partials of −.76 for both E and VA and one of −.87 for the adjusted variable $E^{1.5}$. The thing worth noting about the simple r's for E and

VA, therefore, is that they resist the tendency to become significantly positive as proxies for P, Y, and CP.

The +.28 r reached by F under absolute growth is barely significant at the 5 percent level, which is ± .28 for forty-eight cases. This r is really a combining of two positive tendencies: a mild tendency for F to behave as a proxy for P (their intercorrelation is +.47) and a further tendency for F to describe the relatively weak attraction of surplus labor. F's role as a labor variable will become clearer later on but is already suggested by the fact that F outscores E and VA, despite the fact that the latter two have far higher intercorrelations with P and Y.

The last absolute variable, M, is significant not only under absolute growth (+.42) but under per capita (+.31) and percentage (+.46) growth: no matter how growth is measured, the larger states are growing faster. M is clearly functioning as a proxy for markets and loses all significance when market variables are held constant. The biggest states are all in the West, where spatial isolation and wide gaps between supply and demand encourage rapid growth. The +.42 r seen under absolute growth reflects the fact that M is positively intercorrelated with P and Y yet (unlike P and Y) negatively intercorrelated with E: high demand becomes separated from the counterinfluence of high supply. The supply-demand gap is reinforced by isolation from the Manufacturing Belt: there is a +.71 intercorrelation between M and Lg. When we get to per capita and percentage growth, these same market influences are at work; but the supply-demand gap should now be viewed in terms of a -.64 intercorrelation between M and E/Y: large areas go with low ratios of supply to demand.

If we now focus on per capita and percentage growth, P, Y, and CP lose all significance—which is to be expected—and actually show negative r's. Because absolute demand no longer has positive significance, the +.92 intercorrelation between E and Y no longer obscures growth's inclination to favor states that lack industry. Now the industry variables, E and VA, can show their true colors: they become negative, approaching significance with per capita growth and reaching it (-.35 and -.34) with percentage growth. Although low, these r's are striking, because absolute variables are not the ideal way of measuring industry when relative variables are used to measure growth. It is not hard to anticipate the much higher negative r's we shall find for E/P, E/Y, E/M, and other relative measures of industry. We can also anticipate that when Y (demand) is held constant, E (supply) will achieve even higher negative r's with per capita and percentage growth. Incidentally, the negative r's shown for P, Y, and CP are explained by their intercorrelations with E and VA, which become the dominant variables in the last two columns.

Relative Demand. One expects relative growth to show higher r's with relative market variables than with absolute market variables. The first group of relative variables to be examined consists of Y/P (per capita income) and some rural-urban mix variables closely related to Y/P. Theoretically, a high Y/P should contribute to faster growth only to the extent that states are equally industrialized. That is, a high Y/P should be a stimulus insofar as it widens the supply-demand gap, in the sense of Y/E (or E/Y): E/P and Y/P in combination become a two-variable expression of Y/E. Of course, wide differences in E/P actually exist. High Y/P goes with high E/P in the northeastern United States, where heavy industrialization raises personal income; but high Y/P and low E/P go together in the West, where a high price-wage structure (reflecting transport costs on northeastern manufactured goods) raises Y/P. The Y/P variable can therefore be viewed as asking whether high Y/P contributes enough to consumer demand for Y/P's effect (if any) to be visible.

Table 3-2 shows the r's for Y/P and five rural-urban mix variables: CP/P (urban population percentage), F/P (farm population percentage), CP/F (the ratio of urban to farm population), F/CP (the reciprocal ratio), and the urban dummy, which is valued at one in the twenty states that are more than 57.7 percent urban (the minimum for Manufacturing Belt states) and at zero for all others. The rural-urban variables are so highly intercorrelated with Y/P and so inclined to follow or even lead Y/P in the realm of partial correlation that their usefulness as demand variables must be recognized. (CP/P and F/P have respective intercorrelations with Y/P of +.75 and -.75.) The reason for the connection is obvious: farm residents, particularly in the South, have lower incomes than urban residents—because cities offer a variety of higher paying occupations.

Y/P is insignificant and, indeed, close to zero in all three of its simple r's. All but one of the rural-urban mix variables are also insignificant. The one exception, CP/F, reaches -.39 in correlation with per capita growth: the urban states show significantly slower growth. Since urban states have higher per capita incomes, this might seem to contradict the market hypothesis. It is clear, though, that CP/F is in this instance acting as a proxy for the urbanized but overindustrialized northeastern states. (It has intercorrelations of +.61 with

Table 3-2
Simple Correlations: Relative Income and Rural-Urban Mix Variables

Independent Variables	Absolute Growth	Per Capita Growth	Percentage Growth
Y/P	+ .09	+ .02	- .06
CP/P	+ .18	- .08	- .09
F/P	- .08	+ .06	- .01
CP/F	- .03	- .39	- .23
F/CP	- .08	+ .01	- .02
CP/P > 57.7%	+ .19	+ .01	- .14

Abbreviations: Y = Income, P = Population, CP = Urban Population, F = Farm Population, CP/P > 57.7% = 20 most urbanized states (dummy)

E/P and +.58 with the MB dummy). If anything, CP/F supports the market hypothesis in its role of proxy for industry.[1]

Although Y/P fails the simple correlation tests, it has latent significance. Later in this chapter we shall observe how weighting Y/P by temperature exposes significantly positive r's. Weighting aside, Y/P also shows significant positive *partial* r's when either (*a*) industrialization and temperature or (*b*) industrialization and wages are jointly held constant. Controlling industrialization removes the connection between high Y/P and high levels of industrialization (unfavorable) in the Manufacturing Belt; controlling temperature cuts the link between *low* Y/P and a warm climate (favorable) in the South; controlling wages removes the tendency for Y/P to represent wages, which are high (unfavorable) where Y/P is high. We shall see Y/P going to +.58 under per capita growth when industrial density and temperature-weighted wages—E/M and (T - 9)/W—are held constant.

Relative Supply: Supply-Demand Ratios. The most important market variables, as far as the two relative growth variables are concerned, are those measuring relative supply—the supply-demand ratios. One expects growth to be fastest where the supply of locally (in-state) produced manufactured goods is low relative to the demand for them. The r's for ratios such as E/P, then, should be negative.

Table 3-3 summarizes the r's for the six supply-demand ratios introduced in chapter 2. The r's between these ratios and growth are nonlinear; the variables must be adjusted for curvilinear correlation. Hence, in the lower portion of the table, adjusted versions of the ratios are also shown. Because of space limitations, the table concentrates on ratios with supply as the numerator, for example, E/P instead of P/E. Except in the cases of CP/E (+.65 r with percentage growth) and CP/VA (+.62 r with percentage growth), the supply-over-demand version gave higher r's; and even CP/E and CP/VA were outperformed by log E/CP and log VA/CP.

The findings lend strong support to the market hypothesis. Absolute growth, of course, is not significantly correlated with the supply-demand ratios; absolute growth requires that we look at the partial r for, say, E with Y held constant (-.87) or for Y with E held constant (+.89). But per capita and percentage growth offer r's exceeding the 1 percent significance level. Per capita growth has r's of -.45 with both $(E/P)^3$ and $(VA/Y)^3$. Percentage growth does even better. Here the best r's are -.67 for log VA/CP, -.66 for log E/CP, -.62 for $\sqrt{VA/Y}$, and -.61 for $\sqrt{E/Y}$. Plainly, the least industrialized states—those where supply is lowest relative to demand—are growing faster.

An incidental finding is that Y and its twin, CP (+.997 intercorrelation with Y), serve better than P as measures of demand; ratios using Y and CP on the demand side generally yield higher r's. This is consistent with the finding that, with absolute growth, Y and CP show higher r's than P when the demand

Table 3–3
Simple Correlations: Supply-Demand Ratios

Independent Variables	Absolute Growth	Per Capita Growth	Percentage Growth
E/P	–.11	–.37	–.58
E/CP	–.12	–.28	–.60
E/Y	–.12	–.36	–.60
VA/P	–.07	–.33	–.56
VA/CP	–.10	–.28	–.63
VA/Y	–.09	–.36	–.62
Adjusted			
$(E/P)^3$	–.19	–.45	. . . .
$\sqrt{E/P}$	. . . .	. . . .	–.60
log E/CP	. . . .	. . . .	–.66
CP/E	. . . .	. . . .	+.65
$(E/Y)^3$	–.18	–.44	. . . .
$\sqrt{E/Y}$	. . . .	. . . .	–.61
$(VA/P)^3$	–.14	–.39	. . . .
$\sqrt{VA/P}$	. . . .	. . . .	–.58
log VA/CP	. . . .	. . . .	–.67
CP/VA	. . . .	. . . .	+.62
$(VA/Y)^3$	–.17	–.45	. . . .
$\sqrt{VA/Y}$	. . . .	. . . .	–.62

Note: Entries left blank indicate that the r is either (a) no better than the r for the unadjusted variable or (b) not statistically significant and not appreciably better.

Abbreviations: E = Manufacturing Employment, P = Population, CP = Urban Population, Y = Income, VA = Value Added

variables are weighted or when industry is held constant. However, P is almost as good a measure of demand, and the –.60 r between $\sqrt{E/P}$ and percentage growth is not far behind the –.66 between log E/CP and percentage growth. In some ways, moreover, P is a truer measure of demand; for CP gives secondary weight to rural-urban mix.

Spatial Isolation. The next facet of markets to be evaluated is spatial isolation, meaning isolation from the Manufacturing Belt. In some respects, spatial isolation is a proxy for relative industrialization: the level of industry declines as distance from the Manufacturing Belt increases (see table 1–1). Thus the western states are the most isolated and have the most favorable supply-demand ratios, that is, the least industry relative to population and income. But spatial isolation is also hypothesized to be a locational influence in its own right. As a state's distance from eastern, particularly northeastern, manufacturing centers increases, so does the cost of transporting goods from these distant centers to the state.

Table 3–4
Simple Correlations: Spatial Isolation Variables

Independent Variables	Absolute Growth	Per Capita Growth	Percentage Growth
Lg	+.26	+.37	+.54
West Dummy	+.18	+.32	+.54
Central-West Dummy	+.13	+.21	+.42
$(50 - \text{Lat}) \times (\text{Lg} - 65)$	+.46	+.53	+.76
$(60 - \text{Lat}) \times (\text{Lg} - 20)$	+.45	+.56	+.75
Adjusted			
$(50 - \text{Lat})^2 \times (\text{Lg} - 65)^2$	+.54	....	+.78
$(55 - \text{Lat})^2 \times (\text{Lg} - 50)^2$	+.51	....	+.79

Note: Entries left blank indicate that the r is lower than the r's for the unadjusted variables.

Abbreviations: Lg = Longitude, West dummy = 11 westernmost states, Central-West dummy = 22 states west of Mississippi River, Lat = Latitude

The distance "tariff" protects the hinterland states from outside competition and thereby (at least in theory) enhances their already favorable markets: lack of "inside" competition is coupled with protection against "outside" competition.

Table 3–4 presents the spatial isolation variables and their r's. The first three variables—Lg, the West dummy, and the Central-West dummy—represent east-west distance only; north-south distance is not yet taken into consideration. The West dummy describes the eleven states constituting the Census Bureau's West region (Mountain and Pacific states); Central-West refers to the twenty-two states west of the Mississippi River. The four latitude-longitude variables, including the two adjusted versions, combine east-west and north-south distance. In effect, a series of distance contour lines rippling out from the Northeast—increasing distance and decreasing industrialization—are described. Because latitude is also a proxy for temperature, however, the contour variables unavoidably incorporate a climate element into the formula.

The spatial isolation r's bolster the previous evidence that the market influence is significant. Lg, the strongest and most discriminating of the three east-west variables, shows r's of +.37 and +.54 with per capita and percentage growth respectively. Both r's are significant at the 1 percent confidence level; the +.54 r is strong enough to statistically explain almost 30 percent of the variation in percentage growth ($r^2 = .29$). The +.26 r between Lg and absolute growth is not significant. But it is nonetheless impressive when one considers that Lg is negatively intercorrelated with both P and Y. (With Y held constant, Lg moves to a +.36 partial r with absolute growth.)

The contour (latitude-longitude) variables make a very strong showing: they go well beyond the 1 percent confidence level (± .36) with all three measures of growth. The best r's are +.54 for absolute growth, +.56 for per capita growth, and +.79 for percentage growth. It is difficult to say how much of the improvement over the r's reached by Lg is due to the north-south aspect of spatial isolation and how much results from the climate element in latitude. But if we acknowledge that greater distances and mountain barriers make east-west isolation more important than north-south, and if we anticipate the striking results obtained by using temperature as a weight with market variables, it seems likely that climate deserves most of the credit. And of course we cannot at this point separate the effect of favorable supply-demand ratios from the effect of isolation per se either. In later experiments where temperature and industrialization are held constant, we shall obtain a clearer picture of the distance effect.

Underdevelopment (Density). Another hypothesis, which is really just another way of looking at markets, is that the least developed states are growing fastest. The suggestion that underdevelopment is essentially equivalent to a strong market assumes that underdevelopment is conceived of in terms of density—population and industry per square mile. In this case, low density goes hand-in-hand with low ratios of supply to demand and with spatial isolation. If, on the other hand, underdevelopment is defined as high farm population percentages and low per capita incomes—characteristics of the South—the demand side of the supply-demand relationship is so seriously weakened that strong markets are no longer described. The east-west spatial isolation facet of markets also vanishes, because the South is part of the East.

Table 3-5 shows the r's for six density variables plus A (average acres per farm), which is an indirect measure of density. As with the supply-demand ratios, the correlations are curvilinear; hence at the bottom of the table each variable is adjusted twice for curvilinearity. One of the two adjustments is optimal for per capita growth and the other optimal for percentage growth.

All but the two farm variables have significantly negative r's with per capita growth, and all without exception are significantly correlated with percentage growth. Of the six density variables, E/M shows the highest r's: $(E/M)^3$ goes to -.46 with per capita growth, and log E/M (along with log VA/M) reaches -.57 under percentage growth. That these variables are essentially measures of the supply-demand relationship is indicated not only by a $-.93$ intercorrelation between log E/M and $\sqrt{E/P}$ but by the near-identity of the r's for E/M and E/P. The -.46 for $(E/M)^3$ with per capita growth compares with the -.45 reached by $(E/P)^3$, and the -.57 for log E/M with percentage growth compares with the -.60 for $\sqrt{E/P}$.

Although E/M has the most significant r's, there is very little difference among the r's for the density variables. It might seem, therefore, that none is truly the leader and that all are virtually identical in economic substance. But here we must anticipate some partial r's, which demonstrate that E/M (really both E/M and VA/M) *is* dominant. Per capita growth provides the sharpest

Table 3–5
Simple Correlations: Developmental Density Variables

Independent Variables	Absolute Growth	Per Capita Growth	Percentage Growth
P/M	–.11	–.41	–.39
Y/M	–.10	–.37	–.37
E/M	–.15	–.45	–.37
VA/M	–.13	–.42	–.37
CP/M	–.10	–.41	–.36
F/M	–.00	–.02	–.39
A	–.10	+.17	+.66
Adjusted			
$(P/M)^2$	. . . .	–.43	. . . .
log P/M	. . . .	. . . .	–.53
$(Y/M)^2$	. . . .	–.38	. . . .
log Y/M	. . . .	. . . .	–.52
$(E/M)^3$	. . . .	–.46	. . . .
log E/M	. . . .	. . . .	–.57
$(VA/M)^2$	. . . .	–.40	. . . .
log VA/M	. . . .	. . . .	–.57
$(CP/M)^2$	. . . .	–.42	. . . .
log CP/M	. . . .	. . . .	–.48
$(F/M)^4$	. . . .	+.16	. . . .
log F/M	. . . .	. . . .	–.56
1/A	. . . .	–.24	. . . .
A^2	. . . .	. . . .	+.68

Note: Entries left blank indicate that the *r* is either (*a*) no better than the *r* for the unadjusted variable or (*b*) not statistically significant and not appreciably better.

Abbreviations: P = Population, M = Square Miles, Y = Income, E = Manufacturing Employment, VA = Value Added, CP = Urban Population, F = Farm Population, A = Average Acres per Farm

findings. If Y/M is held constant, both P/M and E/M stay significantly negative (–.40 and –.45), with E/M still the highest. Alternatively, if P/M is held constant, Y/M becomes significantly positive (+.35), revealing a latent tendency to describe per capita income (Y high relative to P); but E/M remains negative (–.27), still describing the effect of industry (fast growth where E is low relative to P). Even with both Y/M *and* P/M held constant, E/M remains significantly negative (–.32). Finally, if E/M is the variable held constant, both P/M and Y/M are transformed into demand variables, becoming positive (+.19 and +.37)–significantly positive in the case of Y/M. (In all these tests, F/M remains close to zero.) In other words, E/M is the only density variable whose negative significance is independent of that of the other density variables; E/M is in charge. One might add that the logic of having fast growth where there is low supply (E) rather than low demand (P or Y) is consistent with the evidence.

Farm Population Density. A temperature-weighted farm population density variable, $(T - 9)^2/\sqrt{F/M}$, will become quite important in subsequent analyses of percentage growth; hence an expanded discussion of F/M is warranted. Logic, intercorrelations, and partial correlations identify log F/M—the most significant version relative to percentage growth—as a market variable. It describes all three main facets of markets. First, and primarily, low F/M describes low supply: the least industrialized states, namely, the western states, are also the least densely farmed. Thus we find a +.76 intercorrelation between log E/M and log F/M. Second, low F/M describes high demand: high per capita income results from having relatively few farmers in the population mix. Not surprisingly, the intercorrelation between Y/P and F/M is -.34. And $\sqrt{E/Y}$, which combines the supply and demand factors, has a +.70 intercorrelation with log F/M. Third, low F/M describes spatial isolation: low rainfall and mountainous topography give the West the nation's lowest farm population densities. Lg and the West dummy therefore show respective intercorrelations of -.70 and -.81 with log F/M. Partial correlations in chapter 6 (table 6-2) confirm that log F/M combines the three market factors—supply, demand, and isolation—in one variable.

Although F/M predicts percentage growth very well, it can't handle per capita growth. The difficulty arises from the latent tendency of other versions of F/M—chiefly $(F/M)^3$ and $(F/M)^4$—to describe labor supply. With per capita growth exponential rather than log forms of the density variables best reveal the market influence: the dominant variable is $(E/M)^3$, not log E/M. And, in contrast to log F/M's +.76 intercorrelation with log E/M in the percentage growth context, $(F/M)^3$ has an insignificant—indeed negative—intercorrelation of -.11 with $(E/M)^3$ in the per capita growth context. The appropriate F/M variable—$(F/M)^3$— is no longer a market variable (by proxy); it is a labor supply variable, which is what tests described in subsequent chapters reveal $(F/M)^3$ to be.

The properties of logs and exponential forms of variables explain the substantive transformation of F/M. Logs (and roots) level off the highest values, thereby emphasizing the cases with the lowest values: log F/M emphasizes the western states, where the market attraction is strong. Exponents exaggerate differences among the highest values: $(F/M)^3$ accents the southern states, where low per capita income and limited isolation weaken the market attraction but surplus labor provides a different attraction. In short, F/M's inability to describe markets under per capita growth does not belie the assertion that log F/M is a very useful market variable when used with percentage growth.

Agglomeration: Ultra-High Density

The next two hypotheses, which concern agglomeration and thresholds, are not next in order of importance. But it is logical to consider them next because they are substantively related to the market hypothesis. For one thing, both agglomeration (industry attracts industry) and the threshold factor (adequate economic base) are measurable by the same density variables used in evaluating the density aspects of markets. Secondly, agglomeration and the threshold factor are partly market phenomena: both include the attraction of intermediate markets, and the threshold factor may also rest heavily on the need for adequate consumer markets. Finally, agglomeration is in another sense the opposite of a market attraction, because the hypothetical agglomeration attraction should be strongest where the market is weakest—in the Manufacturing Belt, where the supply of regionally produced manufactured goods is highest in relation to demand.

Table 3-6 presents the r's for thirteen agglomeration variables. These variables assess the tendency for industry to cluster. The first eight are based on the agglomeration concept getting the most emphasis in the Perloff study. This concept stresses clustering within the Manufacturing Belt (thirteen northeastern states—Massachusetts and Delaware to Illinois and Wisconsin). The NE dummy (includes northern New England), the MB dummy, and the six MB-weighted variables test the potency of established Manufacturing Belt industry as an attraction for new industry. Five additional dummy variables test the alternative Perloff concept, which theorizes that emerging agglomeration economies in the most industrialized and most urbanized states outside the Manufacturing Belt are becoming increasingly influential. These variables spotlight the Manufacturing Belt states (sometimes all but one or two) plus the most developed states elsewhere.

Table 3-6
Simple Correlations: Agglomeration Variables

Independent Variables	Absolute Growth	Per Capita Growth	Percentage Growth
NE	−.23	−.39	−.48
MB	−.18	−.32	−.41
MB × E	−.13	−.35	−.36
MB × VA	−.12	−.34	−.35
MB × E/M	−.17	−.45	−.35
MB × VA/M	−.15	−.43	−.35
MB × (E/M)^2	−.14	−.46	−.29
MB × E/P	−.19	−.39	−.42
E > 145,000 (dummy)	+.27	−.13	−.37
VA > $1 billion (dummy)	+.28	−.07	−.31
E/P > 7% (dummy)	−.16	−.28	−.49
E/P > 6% (dummy)	+.11	−.12	−.51
CP/P > 57.7% (dummy)	+.19	+.01	−.14

Abbreviations: NE = Northeast dummy (16 states), MB = Manufacturing Belt dummy (13 states), E = Manufacturing Employment, VA = Value Added, M = Square Miles, P = Population, CP = Urban Population

The agglomeration variables emphatically deny the agglomeration hypothesis and reaffirm the importance of markets. Even absolute growth shows negative r's opposite most of the agglomeration variables. This is noteworthy, because industrial agglomerations tend to coincide with population concentrations—high absolute levels of demand—which could easily result in positive r's. As it happens, four of the r's under absolute growth are positive; but they clearly describe the demand attraction: the VA dummy, which has the most positive r, goes from +.28 to -.02 if P is held constant. Under per capita and percentage growth, the r's are not only negative (except for one of +.01) but usually significantly so: slow growth prevails in the Manufacturing Belt states and in the more industrialized states generally. Under per capita growth, when we use the variable MB $\times$ (E/M)^2 to break out the Manufacturing Belt states and give heavy weight to those with the highest industrial density, r reaches -.46. Percentage growth shows r's of -.48 for the NE dummy, -.41 for the MB dummy, and -.49 and -.51 for the two E/P dummies.

Agglomeration could still have latent significance—markets, climate, and labor all impede growth in the Manufacturing Belt—but it obviously isn't a major influence. (By way of further reservation, the intermediate markets aspect of agglomeration undoubtedly influences growth—other research establishes this—but apparently depends mainly on *new* intermediate markets, which follow consumer markets and are largely reflected in the market variables.)

Thresholds: Ultra-Low Density

The threshold hypothesis, rather than suggesting that exceptionally high levels of industrialization (or developmental density) are beneficial to growth, supposes that exceptionally low levels of industrialization (or density) impede growth. As with agglomeration, the presence or absence of intermediate markets and external economies is important to the hypothetical phenomenon. But these attractions are now presumed to be widely available—obtainable in all but a few states. At the same time, new elements enter the picture. The principal new element is markets: perhaps the main reason that the least developed states have slower residual growth, if they do, is that their markets have not yet reached the point where most industries can realize necessary economies of scale. Another new element is urban amenities, which are scarce in the least developed states.

Table 3-7 shows the r's for the threshold variables. Briefly reviewing, the use of density reciprocals, such as 1/(P/M), as threshold variables is based on partial correlation experiments described in later chapters. The West-Rural dummy values the five least developed western states—Montana, Idaho, Wyoming, New Mexico, and Nevada—at one and the other forty-three states at zero. West-Metro values the six most developed western states—Colorado, Utah, Arizona,

Table 3-7
Simple Correlations: Threshold Variables

Independent Variables	Absolute Growth	Per Capita Growth	Percentage Growth
1/(P/M)	−.15	+.05	+.41
1/(Y/M)	−.17	+.05	+.46
1/(E/M)	−.16	+.00	+.41
1/(VA/M)	−.16	−.00	+.41
1/(CP/M)	−.17	+.00	+.36
1/(F/M)	−.09	+.10	+.42
West Dummy	+.18	+.32	+.54
West-Rural Dummy	−.15	−.06	+.22
West-Metro Dummy	+.36	+.47	+.48
West × 1/(P/M)	−.12	+.08	+.42
West × 1/(E/M)	−.13	+.05	+.44
West-Rural × 1/(P/M)	−.13	−.02	+.26
West-Rural × 1/(E/M)	−.13	−.02	+.30
West-Rural × 1/E	−.13	−.02	+.29
West-Rural × 1/VA	−.13	−.02	+.30
West × P/M	+.77	+.44	+.41[a]
West × CP/M	+.82	+.45[a]	+.39[a]
West × E/M	+.79	+.45	+.31[a]

[a]This r is based on the square root of the density variable on the left.

Abbreviations: P = Population, M = Square Miles, Y = Income, E = Manufacturing Employment, VA = Value Added, CP = Urban Population, F = Farm Population, West = 11 western states, West-Rural = 5 least developed western states, West-Metro = 6 most developed western states

Washington, Oregon, and California—at one and the other forty-two at zero. The dummy-weighted variables, such as West × 1/(P/M), give the "dummied in" states the values of the density variable and all other states a zero value.

The general rule for reciprocals (which does not always apply) is that the r's for a variable and its reciprocal are opposite in sign: as the variable gets bigger, its reciprocal gets smaller. The threshold hypothesis looks for low growth where density is low (positive r), which means low growth where the density *reciprocal* is high. This calls for negative r's if the hypothesis is supported. The West-Rural dummy should also be negative, indicating that growth is lowest where the dummy value is highest (one rather than zero). Likewise, the dummy-weighted reciprocals should be negative. But the West-Metro dummy, designating states that have crossed the threshold, should be positive or else insignificantly negative.

Are the expected r's obtained? Mostly no but partly yes. The positive r's under percentage growth seem to deny the threshold hypothesis. The trouble is that low density and West-Rural status describe not only thresholds but strong markets. Since percentage growth especially favors states where E is low (and density too), the threshold variables are at this stage—nothing held constant—

recording the market influence. The market influence is far stronger than the threshold influence, so all we can see are tendencies.

These tendencies are clearest under per capita growth. Here the density reciprocals hover around zero. Considering that the "rightside-up" density variables are significantly negative (table 3-5), the reciprocals would ordinarily be not only positive but fairly high. That they aren't is indirect—and very inconclusive—evidence of a threshold influence. Somewhat better evidence comes from the West-Rural dummy. It is negatively correlated with per capita growth, despite very favorable supply-demand ratios in the West-Rural states (as elsewhere in the West). The negative r (-.06), barely above zero, is not significant in a statistical sense but is significant in the sense that it isn't positive, and appreciably so.

Additional evidence of a tendency toward slow growth in the least developed states comes from a comparison of the West-Rural and West-Metro dummies. Under all three growth variables, the West-Metro states show fast growth: West-Metro has r's of +.36, +.47, and +.48. But the West-Rural states aren't doing as well: West-Rural has r's of -.15, -.06, and +.22. This contrast at least hints at the existence of a threshold influence.

Still more evidence comes from West $\times$ P/M, West $\times$ CP/M, and West $\times$ E/M. P/M, CP/M, and E/M are all negatively correlated with all three growth variables (table 3-5): low density goes with high growth. But now, when just the eleven western states are considered (the eastern states are valued at zero), the correlations become positive—significantly positive. For absolute and per capita growth, which give higher r's to the weighted variables than to the West dummy alone, this indicates that the most densely developed states within the underdeveloped (western) set are growing fastest. This is definitely suggestive of a threshold influence. For percentage growth, the positive r's must be credited entirely to the West dummy, which at +.54 is higher than the weighted variables. Since multiplying West by density lowers the correlation, we cannot say that the most developed western states have higher percentage growth. The apparent reason they don't is that percentage growth easily becomes very high where the manufacturing employment base (E) is abnormally low.

Labor: Wages, Unionization, and Labor Supply

The next hypothesis states that favorable labor conditions attract industry. "Favorable labor conditions" means (1) low wages, (2) a low degree of unionization, and (3) an abundant labor supply in the sense of surplus labor. All three conditions tend to go together and are associated with high farm population density. Agriculture, where technology has displaced numerous workers, is the principal source of surplus labor; surplus labor contributes to low wages; and both surplus labor and hostile attitudes in rural states hamper unionization.

Table 3-8
Simple Correlations: Labor Variables

Independent Variables	Absolute Growth	Per Capita Growth	Percentage Growth
W	+.07	+.04	+.09
E × W	+.13	−.23	−.34
U	+.05	−.13	−.18
E × U	+.10	−.24	−.34
F/M	−.00	−.02	−.39
F	+.28	+.10	−.16
Adjusted[a]			
$\sqrt{W}$	+.06	+.03	+.09
$\sqrt{U}$	+.03	−.17	−.18
$1/W^2$	−.02	+.03	−.06
$1/U^2$	+.08	+.25	+.11
$(F/M)^4$	+.09	+.16	−.11
$F^{1.5}$	+.28	....	....

[a]In this table, unlike the preceding ones, the adjustments shown are not those which maximize the simple r's. Instead, they are the adjustments that maximize partial r's in situations where the variables become significant. These partials are examined in later chapters. The r's shown in this table are, of course, the simple r's, whether a variable is adjusted or not.

Abbreviations: W = Wages (average hourly earnings in manufacturing), E = Manufacturing Employment, U = Unionization, F = Farm Population, M = Square Miles

These linkages give the most favorable labor conditions to the South, where the farm population percentage and farm population density are highest. However, low wages and (particularly) weak unions can also be found in scattered other places, such as northern New England, the Dakotas, and New Mexico.

Table 3-8 presents the labor variables. There are two unadjusted wage variables, W (average hourly wages in manufacturing) and E × W (total wage payments); two unadjusted unionization variables, U (relative unionization) and E × U (total unionization); and two unadjusted surplus labor variables, F/M (farm population density) and F (farm population). At the bottom of the table are some adjusted versions that generally yield the best r's in partial correlation experiments, covered in the next three chapters. W and U are high where wages are high and unions strong; hence we are looking for negative r's with these variables, that is, low growth where the variables are high. F and F/M are high where there is surplus labor, so these variables should be positively correlated.

The simple r's in table 3-8 give little support to the labor hypothesis. The r's for W are not only insignificant but positive. U shows some mildly negative r's—the right sign—under per capita and percentage growth, but it can be shown that these r's rest heavily on U's relationship to industrialization and climate:

the -.18 under percentage growth falls to -.02 if $\sqrt{E/P}$ is held constant and moves to +.09 if T is also held constant. The absolute variables, E $\times$ W and E $\times$ U give -.34 readings under percentage growth, and this seems to support the labor hypothesis. But these two variables turned out to have +.99 intercorrelations with E and are obviously proxies for E, which has a -.35 r with percentage growth. The -.39 for F/M under percentage growth seems to deny that surplus labor is a stimulus, but again the variable is really describing strong markets. Observe, however, that the adjusted variable $(F/M)^4$, which greatly emphasizes the surplus labor states, is much less negative. Finally, F goes to +.28 under absolute growth. In this situation, F is mainly a proxy for P and Y, yet it can still reach partial r's of +.17 with Y held constant and +.25 with both Y and P held constant.

In summary, the simple r's for the labor variables generally fail to support the labor hypothesis, although $(F/M)^4$ and F give tentative voice to a surplus labor stimulus. But the simple r's are misleading: the labor variables will display highly significant r's bearing the correct signs when we get to partial correlations. At the moment, though, other more important influences obscure the labor influence. The main problem is that high wages and strong unions (unfavorable) are linked with the West's strong markets (favorable). Another problem is that high wages and strong unions contribute to high per capita income, reinforcing the market linkage. When Lg and Y/P are held constant, the picture will change.

Climate: Temperature and Latitude

The last hypothesis concerns a badly neglected industrial location influence—climate. Cold climates should be linked with slow growth. The bases for this hypothesis include the effects of cold weather on construction and heating costs, on transportation, on outdoor operations and storage, on employee absenteeism, on the willingness of executives to live in certain states, and on migration.

Just two climate variables, T (temperature) and Lat (latitude) are used in this study. The simple r's for these variables are given in table 3–9. As explained before, 50 – Lat is used in place of Lat so that values will increase north to south. This allows the latitude variable to be used as a multiplier in latitude-longitude (contour) variables and gives T and 50 – Lat the same sign.

The findings give substantial support to the climate hypothesis. T^2, which performs slightly better than T, has r's of +.45 with absolute growth, +.47 with per capita growth, and +.45 with percentage growth. The comparable r's for 50 – Lat are +.32, +.41, and +.46. All of these r's except the +.32 reading for 50 – Lat are safely above the 1 percent significance level ($\pm.36$): the exception exceeds the 5 percent level ($\pm.28$). Except in the case of percentage growth, where T^2 and 50 – Lat have almost identical r's, T (or T^2) predicts better than 50 – Lat. This is logical, because temperature is what latitude is only a proxy for.

Table 3-9
Simple Correlations: Climate Variables

Independent Variables	Absolute Growth	Per Capita Growth	Percentage Growth
T	+.43	+.47	+.43
50 – Lat	+.32	+.41	+.46
Adjusted T^2	+.45	+.47	+.45

Abbreviations: T = Temperature (January mean, principal city), Lat = Latitude (center of state)

The results are remarkably consistent: the best r's are all within one point of +.46. This gives an r^2 of .21, which means that variation in climate can statistically explain about one-fifth of the variation in manufacturing growth, however measured. But one-fifth may be an understatement. For, as will be seen shortly, climate has an indirect effect as a catalyst for the market influence. This effect can be measured only by temperature-weighted market variables, which explain more than the sum of the independent effects of markets and climate. For example, T^2 and Y have an R^2 (coefficient of multiple determination) of .36 with absolute growth, but $(T - 9)^{2.5} \times Y$ goes to .84 (r^2) all by itself.

Aside from the extent of climate's relationship to growth, it is worth mentioning that the climate variables are the only variables other than market variables (or proxies therefor) that have simple r's significant at the 1 percent or even the 5 percent confidence level.

Intercorrelations

When examining r's between dependent and independent variables, it is helpful to know about intercorrelations among the independent variables. Inter-correlations, such as the +.92 r between E and Y, can reveal that an r between a dependent and an independent variable is influenced—or perhaps not influenced—by overlap between that independent variable and another. Under absolute growth, where E and VA begin as proxies for Y, it isn't hard to see why VA (+.15) goes higher than E (+.12): VA's +.94 intercorrelation with Y tops E's +.92 intercorrelation with Y.

Table 3-10 shows intercorrelations for a representative group of variables. The table is intended to allow the reader to answer for himself various questions that may arise and that are not adequately covered by the text. It also supports a few points deserving specific mention.

Table 3-10
Intercorrelations for Selected Variables

	P	Y	E	Y/P	E/P	E/Y	Lg	E/M	MB Dummy	West-Rural	1/(P/M)	W	U	T
Y	+.98													
E	+.91	+.92												
Y/P	+.29	+.42	+.40											
E/P	+.39	+.41	+.61	+.40										
E/Y	+.29	+.26	+.47	+.03	+.91									
Lg	-.21	-.16	-.35	+.11	-.68	-.77								
E/M	+.62[a]	+.64[a]	+.87[a]	+.41	+.93[a]	+.90[a]	-.76[a]							
MB Dummy	+.46	+.51	+.69	+.59	+.81	+.59	-.50	+.82[b]						
West-Rural	-.30	-.25	-.25	+.17	-.38	-.44	+.55	-.59[b]	-.21					
W	-.36	-.30	-.32	+.24	-.47	-.53	+.47	-.25	-.30	+.78	+.33			
U	+.22	+.31	+.28	+.74	+.07	-.24	+.31	+.03	+.31	+.24	+.01	+.67		
T	+.28	+.07	-.04	-.33	-.18	+.26	+.04	+.11	+.25	-.01	-.16	-.25	-.24	
CP	+.16	+.997	+.92	+.41	+.41	+.18	-.18	-.10	-.20	-.14	-.30	+.29	+.32	+.09
F	+.98	+.32	+.28	-.45	+.59	+.44	-.15	-.26	+.51	-.24	-.38	-.30	-.14	+.35
VA	+.47	+.94	+.996	+.43	-.58	-.64	-.31	+.55	-.10	-.35	-.31	+.32	+.36	-.05
M	+.92	+.10	-.15	+.05	-.57	-.31	+.71	-.46	+.69	-.24	+.39	+.29	+.08	+.16
F/P	+.12	-.43	-.45	-.75	+.58	+.33	+.15	-.55	-.44	+.52	-.02	-.53	+.02	+.02
CP/P > 57.7%	-.33	+.56	+.57	+.61	+.85[a]	+.82[a]	-.19	+.50	-.58	+.01	-.30	+.42	+.39	+.00
P/M	+.52	+.66[a]	+.84[a]	+.40	+.87[a]	+.79[a]	-.77[a]	+.98	+.72[b]	-.29	-.31	+.01	+.11	-.05
Y/M	+.65[a]	+.67[a]	+.83[a]	+.47	+.57[a]	+.70[a]	-.72[a]	+.98	+.79[b]	-.66[b]	-.28	+.07	+.13	-.08
F/M	+.62[a]	+.55[a]	+.73[a]	-.34	+.08	+.32	+.70[a]	+.76[a]	+.83[b]	-.57[b]	-.52	-.39	-.22	+.28
(F/M)[4]	+.64[a]	-.02	+.07	-.46	-.21	-.29	-.30	-.07	+.35[b]	-.81[b]	-.24	-.43	-.34	+.32
West-Metro	+.09	+.02	-.12	+.17	-.26		+.61	-.18	-.04	-.20	+.06	+.39	+.43	+.17
50 - Lat	-.03	-.01	-.11	-.45		-.09	-.08	-.18	-.25	-.13	-.10	-.39	-.53	+.88

[a]This r is based on the log of the variable heading the column and either the log or the square root of the variable on the left.

[b]This r is based on the log or square root of the variable on the left.

Three points concern the market variables. First, the three absolute demand variables—P, Y, and CP—are highly intercorrelated, and the +.997 intercorrelation between Y and CP makes them virtual twins in many applications. Second, Y/P's efforts to show the expected positive r's with growth are hampered by adverse intercorrelations with W (+.74), E/P (+.40), and T (−.33): the stimulus of high per capita income is neutralized by high wages, high supply, and cold climates. Third, the density variables have extremely high intercorrelations with the supply-demand ratios and with each other. The +.85 intercorrelation between log P/M and $\sqrt{E/P}$, as well as the +.98 intercorrelation between P/M and E/M, are further challenges to Fuchs' (chapter 1) idea that P/M measures available factory space.

The next point, concerning climate, is a vital one. The only variables with simple r's high enough to give T *its* high r's, assuming T were a proxy for something else, are the market variables. If T isn't really speaking for climate, it should show significant intercorrelations with some of the market variables. What T shows, however, are intercorrelations of +.07 with Y, −.18 with E/P, −.04 with E/Y, +.04 with Lg, and −.10 with E/M. There is, to be sure, the −.33 intercorrelation between T and Y/P, but the sign is wrong: high T (favorable) is tied to low Y/P (unfavorable).

Some reasons why two minor influences—labor and thresholds—fail to show significant simple r's are evident in table 3-10. W has intercorrelations of +.74 with Y/P, −.24 with E/Y, and +.47 with Lg: low wages are offset by attractive markets. The West-Rural dummy, which gives its high values to the subthreshold states, has intercorrelations of +.17 with Y/P, −.44 with E/Y, and +.46 with Lg: the ultraunderdeveloped states have strong markets—strong enough to offset the threshold handicap.

Weighted Variables

In addition to the variables already discussed, many others were tested. These additional variables were used to find out whether certain influences interact so as to enhance or detract from each other's effects. The interaction experiments used market and labor variables weighted by climate and by spatial isolation variables. The climate-weighted variables are based on the premise that the market stimulus (or else the labor stimulus) is inhibited by cold climates and reinforced by warm climates—particularly in places such as Florida and California, where climate-induced growth in consumer demand is not adequately reflected in the market variables. The distance-weighted variables inquire whether favorable supply-demand ratios and the like have a greater impact when combined with the protective "tariff" imposed on eastern manufactured goods by long shipping distances.

Absolute Market Variables Weighted by
Temperature

The first variables that will be shown weighted by temperature are the
absolute market variables—P, Y, CP, F, and E. One of these, F, is a market variable only by proxy but was nevertheless weighted to see what would happen.
The weighted variables and their r's are shown in table 3-11. For comparative
purposes, the unweighted variables are placed at the top of the table. The
"Minimum T Weight" variables weight the five market variables by T itself, rather
than by an altered version of T designed to give temperature more weight in the
formula. The next three categories eliminate F and E, whose weighting was
unfruitful, and apply successively heavier T weights to the demand variables
(P, Y, and CP). As explained in chapter 2, E is divided into rather than mulitplied
by T because E's essential relationship with growth is negative.

Table 3-11
Simple Correlations: Temperature-Weighted Absolute Variables

Independent Variables	Absolute Growth	Per Capita Growth	Percentage Growth
T^2	+.45	+.47	+.45
P	+.42	-.04	-.22
Y	+.42	-.05	-.21
CP	+.40	-.06	-.20
F	+.28	+.10	-.16
E	+.12	-.23	-.35
Minimum T Weight			
T × P	+.68	+.16	-.06
T × Y	+.69	+.14	-.06
T × CP	+.66	+.12	-.06
T × F	+.37	+.21	-.04
T/E	-.15	+.10	+.53
Medium T Weight			
(T − 9)P	+.73	+.22	-.01
(T − 9)Y	+.75	+.20	-.02
(T − 9)CP	+.73	+.18	-.01
Heavy T Weight			
$(T − 9)^2 P$	+.85	+.37	+.15
$(T − 9)^2 Y$	+.90	+.36	+.14
$(T − 9)^2 CP$	+.88	+.34	+.14
Optimal T Weight			
$(T − 9)^{2.5} × P$	+.87	+.40	+.20
$(T − 9)^{2.5} × Y$	+.92	+.39	+.19
$(T − 9)^{2.5} × CP$	+.90	+.38	+.19

The temperature weighting scheme was extremely impressive in its results. We shall focus on the findings for absolute growth, because that is where the unweighted and weighted absolute variables are significant. The minimum T weights, as in $T \times P$, bring sharp increases in the r's for the three demand variables; Y goes from +.42 by itself to +.69 for $T \times Y$. In contrast, $T \times F$ and T/E fail to improve upon the r's obtainable by T alone, which is why they were dropped from subsequent experiments. (Under percentage growth T/E does improve on T alone, but temperature-weighted *relative* market variables do much better.)

Successively heavier T weights bring successively higher r's. As explained before (chapter 2), subtracting a constant from a variable increases the ratio of maximum to minimum value and thereby increases the variable's weight in a formula. Increasing T's weight by this method raises the previous r's by about six points; $(T - 9)Y$ goes to +.75. Squaring $T - 9$ more drastically increases T's weight and brings a bigger jump in the r's; $(T - 9)^2 Y$ climbs all the way to +.90. The optimal weighting scheme is reached with $T - 9$ raised to the 2.5 power. This adjustment brings $(T - 9)^{2.5} \times Y$ to an r of +.92. The r^2 for +.92 is .85: temperature-weighted income can account for 85 percent of the variance in absolute growth. Since T^2 and Y, acting independently, have an R (multiple correlation) of only .602 and an R^2 of .36, we know that the weighted variable is not simply adding together two essentially independent influences. The fact that $(T - 9)^{2.5} \times Y$ can explain over twice as much of the variance as T^2 and Y jointly explain constitutes powerful evidence of an interaction effect. (However, as will be shown later, some of the interaction effect is really the interaction of high demand and low supply: Y is given heavier weight in places where it is high relative to E, because E is lower in the South.)

At this point it may be wise to digress on a matter of interpretation that can cause confusion. The steadily rising r's under per capita growth might seem to provide additional evidence of an interaction effect. But notice that the r's for the weighted demand variables stay below the +.47 r for T^2, which r in fact serves as a limit that can be approached but not exceeded. Whenever the r for a weighted variable is less than the r for one of its constituents, we can always raise the weighted variable's r by giving that constituent more and more weight. Carried to extremes, as in the earlier example of $E \times W$, this procedure reduces the weighted variable to the equivalent of the constituent. The only time we can get excited is when the weighted variable shows an r that is higher than that of any variable involved in the formula.

Relative Market Variables Weighted by Climate

The next four tables show relative market variables weighted by temperature and (in the first three tables only) by latitude. Table 3–12 shows per capita

Table 3-12
Simple Correlations: Per Capita Income Weighted by Climate

Independent Variables	Absolute Growth	Per Capita Growth	Percentage Growth
T^2	+.45	+.47	+.45
48 − Lat	+.32	+.41	+.46
Y/P	+.09	+.02	−.06
$Y^{0.8}/P$	−.23	+.07	+.20
Weighted			
(T − 9) × Y/P	+.58	+.53	+.44
(48 − Lat) × Y/P	+.45	+.49	+.51
Adjusted			
$(T − 9)^{1.5} × (Y^{0.8}/P)$	+.38	+.59	+.65

income, Y/P; table 3-13 shows two supply-demand ratios, E/P and E/Y; table 3-14 covers longitude, Lg; and table 3-15 looks at three density variables—P/M, E/M, and F/M. At the top of each table the unweighted climate and market variables are displayed for comparison with the weighted versions; this enables us to see at a glance whether any particular weighted variable does better than its constituent variables. The next section of each table weights the basic version of the market variable(s) by T − 9 and also, in the first three tables, by 48 − Lat or 50 − Lat. One or two additional sections of each table show refined weighting schemes and adjustments for curvilinearity. These refinements and adjustments were derived by trial-and-error and are the versions that give the maximum *r* vis-à-vis one or more of the growth variables.

Per Capita Income. Despite its unpromising performance as an unweighted variable, Y/P has latent significance. This can be anticipated from the preceding analysis of the weighted absolute variables, where all versions of T × Y excel over the equivalent versions of T × P. Since T × Y = T × P × Y/P, the findings suggest that Y/P is a factor. Moreover, it isn't hard to see that Y/P is to per capita growth as Y is to absolute growth. Therefore, if absolute growth shows a strong relationship to T × Y, it is reasonable to expect that per capita growth will be related to T × Y/P. Thus it is that our basic temperature-weighted per capita income variable, (T − 9) × Y/P, shows an *r* of +.53 with per capita growth in table 3-12. Since +.53 is more than the +.47 achieved by the best temperature variable, T^2, we have evidence of at least a slight interaction effect. Supporting evidence comes from the latitude-weighted variable, (48 − Lat) × Y/P, which outshines 48 − Lat by +.49 to +.41.

The better variable, (T −9) × Y/P, was reweighted and otherwise adjusted to maximize the *r*. The result was $(T − 9)^{1.5} × (Y^{0.8}/P)$. This variable goes to +.59 under per capita growth, which is the highest *r* obtainable for per capita growth in relation to any independent variable. In fact, this variable becomes the keystone variable in all of the best multiple correlation combinations for per capita growth, regardless of how many variables are combined. It is also crucial in the strongest control combinations in the partial correlation experiments. Confirmation that Y/P and T interact—that T is a catalyst for Y/P—appears in the percentage growth column of table 3-12. Here $(T - 9)^{1.5} \times (Y^{0.8}/P)$ goes even higher, reaching +.65.

As further indication that interdependence is involved, the weighted variable has an r higher than the R for its two constituent variables combined. With per capita growth, T^2 and Y/P combined give an R of .545, and T^2 and $Y^{0.8}/P$ combined give an R of .544—compared to the r of +.59 for $(T - 9)^{1.5} \times (Y^{0.8}/P)$. With percentage growth, T^2 and Y/P combined reach .465, and T^2 and $Y^{0.8}/P$ go to .615—compared to the r of +.65 for $(T - 9)^{1.5} \times (Y^{0.8}/P)$.

Supply-Demand Ratios. A weighted absolute variable based on $T \times Y$ (or $T \times P \times Y/P$) is the top performer with absolute growth; a weighted per capita income variable based on $T \times Y/P$ does best with per capita growth. But when it comes to percentage growth, a weighted supply-demand ratio based on $T \times Y/E$ works best. Since $T \times Y/E = T \times P/E \times Y/P$ (the Ps cancel), this gives us still more evidence (a) that consumer demand is a vital factor in manufacturing growth and (b) that not only population but the per capita income of the population must be considered in measuring consumer demand.

The new evidence just referred to is summarized in table 3-13. Only the

Table 3-13
Simple Correlations: Supply-Demand Ratios Weighted by Climate

Independent Variables	Absolute Growth	Per Capita Growth	Percentage Growth
T^2	+.45	+.47	+.45
48 – Lat	+.32	+.41	+.46
E/P	–.11	–.37	–.58
E/Y	–.12	–.36	–.60
Weighted			
$(T - 9) \times P/E$	+.12	+.37	+.81
$(T - 9) \times Y/E$	+.18	+.40	+.85
$(48 - Lat) \times P/E$	+.06	+.28	+.73
$(48 - Lat) \times Y/E$	+.10	+.31	+.78
Reweighted			
$(T - 9)^{1.5} \times Y/E$	+.25	+.46	+.86
$(T - 9)^{1.5}\sqrt{Y/E}$	+.39	+.53	+.76
Optimal Weights			
$(T - 9)^{2.5} \times [(Y/M^{0.65}/(E/M)]$	+.13	+.40	+.89

two most basic supply-demand ratios, E/P and E/Y, are presented, but VA can be substituted for E in either ratio with only a slight diminution of the r's. Although E/P and E/Y appear in the table as P/E and Y/E, this is just a more convenient form of notation: $T \times P/E = T/(E/P)$. The two ratios are weighted by both temperature and latitude; temperature gives the better results. Under percentage growth, $(T - 9) \times P/E$ goes to +.81 and $(T - 9) \times Y/E$ to +.85. With 48 – Lat as the weight, the Y/E version is again better than the P/E version.

As the best of the preliminary weighted ratios, $(T - 9) \times Y/E$ was selected for refinement. With percentage growth, r was advanced to +.86 by slightly increasing the weight assigned to temperature, making the variable $(T - 9)^{1.5} \times Y/E$. The same reweighting of temperature combined with a down-weighting of Y/E gave the best version for per capita growth, $(T - 9)^{1.5} \times \sqrt{Y/E}$. It reaches +.53. Back in the percentage growth column, an even better r was obtained by switching from Y/E to (Y/M)/(E/M)—which is identical to Y/E—and then slightly adjusting the numerator to create $(Y/M)^{0.65}/(E/M)$. The optimal weighted ratio became $(T - 9)^{2.5} \times [(Y/M)^{0.65}/(E/M)]$. Its r is +.89; r^2 is .79. In other words, a single temperature-weighted supply-demand ratio can explain about four-fifths of the variation in percentage growth. In comparison, the best R obtainable for variations of the two basic variables, acting independently, is the R of .742 for T^2 combined with $\sqrt{E/Y}$. Here R^2 is .55, well below the above r^2 of .79. We have convincing evidence not only that markets and climate are the dominant influences in manufacturing growth but that they interact. Where demand is high relative to the regionally produced supply of manufactured goods, industry grows rapidly—provided that (or especially if) the climate is favorable.

Longitude. A third type of relative market variable to be weighted by climate is longitude. It is a proxy variable that is intended primarily as a substitute for transport costs on eastern manufactured goods marketed in the West,

Table 3-14
Simple Correlations: Longitude Weighted by Climate

Independent Variables	Absolute Growth	Per Capita Growth	Percentage Growth
T^2	+.45	+.47	+.45
50 – Lat	+.32	+.41	+.46
Lg	+.26	+.37	+.54
Weighted			
$(T - 9) \times (Lg - 50)$	+.54	+.58	+.68
$(50 - Lat) \times (Lg - 50)$	+.46	+.54	+.74
Reweighted			
$(T - 9) \times (Lg - 65)$	+.52	+.55	+.68
$(50 - Lat) \times (Lg - 65)$	+.46	+.53	+.76
$(50 - Lat)^2 \times (Lg - 65)^2$	+.54	....	+.78

but it also represents the favorable supply-demand ratios and low developmental density found in the West. Earlier in this chapter (table 3-4) longitude was weighted by latitude to obtain so-called contour variables. These describe concentric distance contour lines rippling out from the northeastern Manufacturing Belt; latitude (as well as longitude) is used to measure distance. To be sure, latitude describes climate as well as distance, but the earlier analysis centered on distance. Now our attention shifts to climate. Toward this end we shall exploit a nuance of distinction between latitude (distance) and temperature (climate). The new variables based on T × Lg are quite similar in substance to the contour variables, but our perspective is different.

Table 3-14 introduces the new temperature-weighted longitude variables. It also presents for comparison corresponding latitude-weighted variables, including two from table 3-4. Under absolute and per capita growth, $(T - 9) \times (Lg - 50)$ achieves respective r's of +.54 and +.58. These are enough ahead of the r's for T^2 to suggest interaction but no better (marginally better under per capita growth) than the r's for the best contour variables. Under percentage growth both $(T - 9) \times (Lg - 50)$ and $(T - 9) \times (Lg - 65)$ go to +.68. This is appreciably better than the +.54 r for the highest constituent variable, Lg; interaction is again suggested. However, the best contour variable is ten points higher at +.78. The findings, then, support the interaction hypothesis but do not encourage the substitution of temperature-weighted longitude for latitude-longitude variables in subsequent analyses.

Density Variables. With the density (per square mile) variables we are almost back to supply-demand ratios: we have seen that, although density is most nearly a measure of the spatial concentration of industry (E/M is the dominant variable), it also describes supply-demand ratios. (One recalls the +.93 intercorrelation between log E/M and $\sqrt{E/P}$.) This gives us grounds for optimism about the likelihood that density, like the supply-demand ratios, will respond to weighting by temperature. This optimism is upheld by the r's in table 3-15, where P/M, E/M, and F/M are shown weighted by temperature. Because density is negatively correlated with growth, it must be used as a divisor.

Once again the r's skyrocket in the percentage growth column. Under each of the weighting schemes shown, the three density variables remain tightly clustered. However, the best versions obtainable by adjusting the denominator only ("Heavy T Weight") and by separately adjusting both numerator and denominator ("Optimal T Weight") put E/M ahead—just as it is before being weighted. The best of the weighted density variables is $(T - 9)^2/\sqrt{E/M}$. Its r of +.88 is just one point below the +.89 reached by $(T - 9)^{2.5} \times [(Y/M)^{0.65}/(E/M)]$. Unsurprisingly, the two variables have a +.98 intercorrelation.

Almost as good as the E/M variable is $(T - 9)^2/\sqrt{F/M}$, which reaches +.87. This variable is of special interest, because it rather than $(T - 9)^{2.5} \times [(Y/M)^{0.65}/(E/M)]$ becomes the principal variable in some—not all—of the best

Table 3-15

Simple Correlations: Temperature-Weighted Density Variables

Independent Variables	Absolute Growth	Per Capita Growth	Percentage Growth
T^2	+.45	+.47	+.45
P/M	−.11	−.41	−.39
E/M	−.15	−.45	−.37
F/M	−.00	−.02	−.39
log P/M	....	....	−.53
log E/M	....	....	−.57
log F/M	....	....	−.56
Moderate T Weight			
(T − 9)/(P/M)	−.09	+.17	+.59
(T − 9)/(E/M)	−.11	+.12	+.58
(T − 9)/(F/M)	−.04	+.18	+.55
Heavy T Weight			
$(T − 9)/(P/M)^{0.4}$	+.15	+.46	+.81
$(T − 9)/(E/M)^{0.25}$	+.19	+.47	+.83
$(T − 9)/(F/M)^{0.25}$	+.35	+.52	+.80
Optimal T Weight			
$(T − 9)^2/\sqrt{P/M}$	+.23	+.49	+.84
$(T − 9)^2/\sqrt{E/M}$	+.11	+.41	+.88
$(T − 9)^2/\sqrt{F/M}$	+.32	+.51	+.87

multiple correlation combinations for percentage growth. Intercorrelations and partial correlations with one or the other of the two variables held constant reveal two substantive differences between $(T − 9)^2/\sqrt{F/M}$ and $(T − 9)^{2.5}$ $\times [(Y/M)^{0.65}/(E/M)]$. The former gives better representation to the longitude facet of markets (F/M becomes extremely low in the arid, mountainous West), whereas the latter is more representative of the industrialization and supply-demand facets of markets. These differences give $(T − 9)^2/\sqrt{F/M}$ sufficient independence to permit its use in further testing the hypothesis that markets and climate are interdependent. If they are, the weighted variable's r (+.87) should exceed the R measuring the combined independent effects of its constituent variables. The best R for the constituent variables comes from a combination of T^2 and log F/M; the R is .776. Thus the interdependency hypothesis is again affirmed.

Labor Variables Weighted by Temperature

Two labor variables, W (wages) and U (unionization), were weighted by temperature. Because weighted wages became significant in partial correlation

Table 3-16
Simple Correlations: Temperature-Weighted Labor Variables

Independent Variables	Absolute Growth	Per Capita Growth	Percentage Growth
T^2	+.45	+.47	+.45
W	+.07	+.04	+.09
U	+.05	-.13	-.18
Minimum T Weight			
T/W	+.30	+.37	+.30
T/U	+.22	+.40	+.30
Medium T Weight			
$(T - 9)/W$	+.32	+.40	+.33
$(T - 9)^2/W^2$	+.29	+.37	+.32

tests where T was held constant, refined versions were developed for wages but not for unionization. The two refined versions of greatest interest (they are shown in later partial and multiple correlation experiments) are $(T - 9)/W$ and $(T - 9)^2/W^2$.

The r's for the weighted labor variables appear in table 3-16. All are less than the r's for T and T^2; the weighted variables at this point are essentially proxies for T and T^2. When certain variables are held constant so that the unweighted wage variables become significant, $(T - 9)/W$ and $(T - 9)^2/W^2$ will be seen moving ahead of their constituent variables. Under these conditions, temperature-weighted wages is not only significant but generally more so than any of the wage variables. Both $(T - 9)/W$ and $(T - 9)^2/W^2$ are well represented in the best multiple correlation combinations for all three growth variables— absolute growth, per capita growth, and percentage growth. The interaction effect is not yet visible, however, because variables such as Lg and Y/P must be partialed out in order to make W significant.

Market Variables Weighted by Distance

The distance-weighting experiments yielded improved r's with absolute growth but, subject to minor exceptions, not with relative growth. Three absolute market variables—P, CP, and Y—were weighted by several longitude variables, by the West and West-Metro dummies, and by contour (latitude-longitude) variables. In these experiments CP duplicated Y, so only P and Y findings will be discussed. Table 3-17 shows the r's of greatest interest. Under the optimal Lg weight, we move from r's of +.42 for unweighted P and Y to ones of +.85 for $(Lg - 65)P$ and +.84 for $(Lg - 65)Y$. By treating the eastern and central states as having zero population and income, the West dummy raises r still higher: West $\times$ Y goes to +.87. The apparent interaction between demand

Table 3–17
Simple Correlations: Distance-Weighted Variables

Independent Variables	Absolute Growth	Per Capita Growth	Percentage Growth
Lg	+.26	+.37	+.54
(50 – Lat) × (Lg – 65)	+.46	+.53	+.76
West Dummy (11 states)	+.18	+.32	+.54
West-Metro Dummy (6 states)	+.36	+.47	+.48
P	+.42	–.04	–.22
Y	+.42	–.05	–.21
CP/E	–.01	+.17	+.65
$\sqrt{E/Y}$	–.08	–.31	–.61
log F/M	+.03	–.14	–.56
Lg-Weighted			
(Lg – 65)P	+.85	+.30	+.06
(Lg – 65)Y	+.84	+.28	+.06
(Lg – 65) × CP/E	+.04	+.22	+.67
(Lg – 65) × Y/E	–.04	+.11	+.52
(Lg – 65)/$\sqrt{F/M}$	–.00	+.21	+.56
Dummy-Weighted			
West × Y	+.87	+.42	+.23
West-Metro × Y	+.88	+.43	+.22
Contour Weight			
(50 – Lat) (Lg – 65)Y	+.91	+.35	+.14
(50 – Lat) (Lg – 65) × CP/E	+.14	+.31	+.79
(50 – Lat) (Lg – 65)/$\sqrt{F/M}$	+.08	+.29	+.69

and distance is concentrated in the six most developed western states, for by substituting West-Metro as the distance weight we can go even higher; West-Metro × Y reaches +.88. This is just a little shy of the +.92 reached by $(T - 9)^{2.5}$ × Y; both variables lean heavily on California and Arizona. Finally, by using a contour weight—which adds a note of climate—we can go to +.91 with (50 – Lat) (Lg – 65)Y. These findings lend credence to the idea that demand and spatial isolation interact.

Several relative market variables—Y/P, some supply-demand ratios, and some developmental density variables—were weighted by longitude and other distance variables. The results were disappointing. Weighted Y/P variables gave consistently lower r's than obtainable with the distance variable (whichever one was used) alone. Other relative market variables did better, but only one had a higher r when weighted than either it or the weight had by itself. Table 3–17 shows the three relative market variables that responded best to weighting: CP/E, E/Y, and F/M. Note that the +.67 for (Lg – 65) × CP/E barely exceeds the +.65 for CP/E alone, and the +.79 for (50 – Lat) (Lg – 65) × CP/E barely exceeds the +.76 for the contour variable alone. Perhaps, to judge by the different results achieved with absolute growth, interaction between distance and supply-demand factors exists but is already reflected adequately in the supply-demand variables. However, the relative growth findings certainly do not support the distance interaction hypothesis.

Comparative Ratings

The returns have only begun to come in, but important trends are already developing. It is evident from the simple r's that markets and climate are the dominant influences, with markets in front. Labor and thresholds show signs of latent significance but do not begin to approach markets and climate in importance. Other influences as yet have nothing to show.

First place is tentatively awarded to markets—partly on the basis of comparative performances by the best market and climate variables and partly on the basis of the inability of a single market variable to describe adequately the market influence. Actually, the best variables under absolute growth show climate with a slight edge: P and Y reach +.42, but T^2 reads +.45. However, P and Y describe only the demand side of markets, and knowledge of the significantly negative r's achieved by E/P and E/Y under per capita and percentage growth allows us to surmise that E and Y can jointly explain more than T^2. When we move on to per capita growth, the best unweighted market and climate variables are $(E/M)^3$ and T^2. Their respective r's are -.46 and +.47, which seems to put climate barely ahead. Again, however, it is reasonable (and correct) to suppose that several market variables describing several facets of markets can jointly explain more than T^2 can. Turning to percentage growth, we needn't anticipate what additional market variables can explain: the supply-demand ratios give us r's such as -.67 for log VA/CP and -.61 for $\sqrt{E/Y}$, but climate's best r's are +.46 for 50 - Lat and +.45 for T^2.

4

Absolute Growth: Partial and Multiple Correlations

The next analyses seek to identify latent influences and to assess the relative importance of all competing influences. Partial and multiple correlations are used to find influences that at first don't register, or else have deceptively low r's, because they overlap other influences (often stronger) with the opposite effect on growth. We are primarily concerned with finding out whether labor, thresholds, and other hypothetical influences without significant simple r's have latent significance. But we are also interested in verifying that climate is not a proxy for markets (or vice versa), in further testing the market-climate interaction hypothesis, and in estimating what proportion of the variation in growth is explained by each influence. The partial and multiple correlation findings relating to absolute growth are presented in this chapter; the findings for per capita and percentage growth are in the two following chapters.

Partial Correlations

The absolute growth findings provide overwhelming support for the hypothesis that markets and climate—particularly markets—attract industry and that the two influences interact. When several market factors are held constant, the labor attraction can also be seen. In addition, there is new—but still tentative —evidence of a threshold influence. Indirect evidence suggests that the resource influence is minor. And there is evidence of a very weak urban attraction— something left over after per capita income has been accounted for. These findings are summarized in three tables. One shows minimal controls (one or two variables held constant), another shows moderate controls (two or three variables held constant), and the last shows strong controls (four or five variables held constant).

Minimal Controls

Table 4-1 presents the minimal control situation. Six columns show the partial r's resulting when four single variables and two two-variable combinations are held constant (controlled, partialed out). Since other influences are not yet significant, the controls emphasize the two dominant influences—markets and climate. Heading the six control columns are the best climate variable (T^2),

Table 4-1
Partial Correlations of Selected Variables with 1947–63 Absolute Growth: Minimal Controls (One or Two Variables Held Constant)

Selected Independent Variables	Simple r with Growth	Variables Held Constant ("Partialed Out")					
		T^2	Y	$E^{1.5}$	W Lg	T^2 Y	$(T-9)Y$
(MULTIPLE R)		(.450)	(.421)	(.052)	(.273)	(.602)	(.753)
Demand							
P	+.42	+.41	+.05	+.82	+.56	-.23	-.77
Y	+.42	+.45	....	+.89	+.57	....	-.76
(T – 9)P	+.73	+.66	+.75	+.87	+.79	+.69	+.02
(T – 9)Y	+.75	+.71	+.88	+.94	+.83	+.86	....
(T – 9)²Y	+.90	+.87	+.91	+.94	+.92	+.89	+.83
Supply							
E	+.12	+.17	-.76	+.34	+.30	-.73	-.84
E¹·⁵	+.05	+.12	-.87	....	+.20	-.84	-.86
Spatial							
Lg	+.26	+.26	+.36	+.28	....	+.38	+.41
(50 – Lat) (Lg – 65)²	+.49	+.39	+.55	+.51	+.48	+.47	+.49
Other							
T²	+.45	....	+.47	+.46	+.46	....	+.30
F	+.28	+.16	+.17	+.28	+.33	+.02	+.05
West-Rural Dummy	-.15	-.08	-.05	-.14	-.31	+.03	+.04
West-Metro Dummy	+.36	+.33	+.39	+.37	+.28	+.36	+.36
West-Metro × CP	+.88	+.89	+.86	+.88	+.89	+.87	+.77
MB Dummy	-.18	-.07	-.51	-.28	-.03	-.42	-.60

Abbreviations: T = Temperature, Y = Income, E = Manufacturing Employment, Lg = Longitude, Lat = Latitude, F = Farm Population, West-Rural = 5 least developed Western states, West-Metro = 6 most developed Western states, CP = Urban Population, MB = Manufacturing Belt dummy (13 states) the best demand variable (Y), the best supply variable ($E^{1.5}$), a combination of spatial isolation and wages (Lg and W), a combination of the best climate and the best overall market variable (T^2 and Y), and a temperature-weighted market variable—$(T - 9)Y$. Note that this table differs from earlier ones in that the column headings do *not* designate one of the two variables being correlated; these are *not* correlations between the variables in the rows and those heading the columns; *the column headings this time designate variables held constant.* Parenthetical figures immediately below these headings (opposite "MULTIPLE R" in the stub column) show the multiple correlations between the control variables and absolute growth. (Where only one variable is controlled, "R" is really a simple r.) The nonparenthetical r's listed in each column are the partial r's for the variables in the stub column correlated *with absolute growth.* Preceding the six partial r columns is another showing the simple r for each variable on the left.

Demand. With ten market variables to examine, it is convenient to break them down into demand, supply, and spatial variables. The partials for the demand variables indicate that (1) P and Y are more closely related to absolute growth than their simple r's suggest, (2) Y is better than P as a measure of consumer demand, (3) Y's influence is so strong that, when its adverse inter-correlation with $E^{1.5}$ is controlled, its r jumps to +.89, and (4) temperature-weighted versions of P and Y are not only more powerful but are virtually unaffected when T^2, Y, or both are held constant—convincing evidence of market-climate interaction.

Because T^2 has hardly any intercorrelation with P or Y, we don't expect the r's for P and Y to be much affected by holding T^2 constant. And they aren't: P drops a point to +.41, while Y edges up to +.45. Y's slight increase results because the adverse effect of low income in the South is partly offset by the South's warm climate. The fact that the demand variables hold up well with climate held constant is important, for it establishes that Y and P are not proxies for the only other influence strong enough to pull them along (assuming demand and climate were highly intercorrelated). T^2 has the highest r (+.45) of any unweighted variable and is the only such variable higher than P and Y (both +.42). If it isn't pulling up P and Y, what else could?

Even better evidence of the demand influence comes from the third control column, where $E^{1.5}$ (the best version of E) is held constant. The negative simple r's observed in the last chapter for E, E/M, and E/P in relation to per capita and percentage growth already indicate that growth favors the least industrialized states. But these states, the lowest in supply, are also lowest in demand (P and Y). Unfavorable demand conditions thus get tangled up with favorable supply conditions in the case of absolute growth, and this obscures both influences. Thus when $E^{1.5}$ is partialed out, P leaps to +.82 and Y to +.89.

The significance of demand is obscured not only by the coincidence of low demand (unfavorable) with low supply (favorable) but by the further connection of low demand with spatial isolation (favorable) and with low wages (favorable). That is, total income (Y) is relatively low in the sparsely populated but isolated western states and in the South, where wages are low. When these conflicts are removed by control of Lg and W (fourth column), Y goes from +.42 to +.57, with P going to +.56.

These very significant positive r's might seem to be contradicted by the significantly negative r's of −.77 for P and −.76 for Y in the last column. But these merely illustrate the fact that partial r's often involve proxy relationships (as do many simple r's), *particularly when a variable closely related to the one being observed has been held constant.* In the last column, controlling (T − 9)Y effectively controls Y—and P also. With demand now relatively constant, Y becomes a proxy for E, with which it has a +.92 intercorrelation. Notice that something comparable happens when $E^{1.5}$ is held constant: E becomes a better proxy for Y than originally and climbs to +.34, echoing Y's climb to +.89.

The three temperature-weighted demand variables—(T − 9)P, (T − 9)Y, and $(T − 9)^2 Y$—offer still more evidence that demand attracts industry. No matter what is held constant (other than temperature-weighted demand variables), these variables display high to extremely high r's. When $E^{1.5}$ is controlled, sending Y to +.89, both (T − 9)Y and $(T − 9)^2 Y$ go to +.94. Since the r^2 for an r of +.94 is .88, either weighted variable can account for 88 percent of the residual variation in growth (i.e., growth not explainable by variations in industry). Even with both T^2 and Y controlled (column five) the weighted variables remain strong, with $(T − 9)^2 Y$ holding at +.89. This is just about as strong evidence of an interaction effect as one could ask for: climate and markets interact in a manner that makes their joint effect greater than the sum of their independent effects. I suspect that this is partly because *increases* in demand are more crucial than the level of demand at the start of a growth period. Increases are based on P (relatively uniform birth rates) but are greater relative to initial population where a warm climate spurs in-migration (as in Florida, Arizona, and California).

Supply.   Until demand—some version of P or Y—is held constant, the supply of manufactured goods serves as a proxy for population and income; E and VA move up and down in their r's with P and Y. (Compare Y and E in the "Simple r" column and in the first, fourth, and third control columns—in that order—noting how E moves up every time Y moves up.) But whenever P or Y, weighted or unweighted, is partialed out, the supply variables sharply reverse themselves. $E^{1.5}$ goes from its simple r of +.05 to a partial of −.77 when P is controlled (not shown) and to one of −.87 when Y is controlled (column two). This is equivalent to Y's jump to +.89 when $E^{1.5}$ is controlled. If T^2 and Y are simultaneously held constant, $E^{1.5}$ reads −.84 (column five). And with

$(T - 9)Y$ controlled, $E^{1.5}$ reads $-.86$ (column six). In other words, absolute growth is faster where supply is low *relative to* demand.

Here it is appropriate to digress on causality. Although high correlations do not prove causality, causality is clearly implied in the extremely high and negative partials for $E^{1.5}$. In the first place, there is a sound theoretical basis for inferring that industry will move in where competition is weak. Alternative interpretations border on the absurd. Who will argue that the fast-growing states have less manufacturing employment because they have grown faster? Or, if low employment is suspected of functioning as a proxy for something else when it shows a $-.87$ partial, a proxy for what? Certainly not climate: T^2 reads $+.47$ in that column. Wages? The wage partial (not shown) is $-.07$, still immature; temperature-weighted wages, $(T - 9)/W$, is $+.37$. Finally, the market interpretation is supported by the evidence and conclusions of other studies and by other evidence from this study.

Spatial Isolation. Because absolute growth is dominated by eastern attractions—population and income especially—spatial isolation is less influential here than with per capita and percentage growth. But when Y, which is the strongest eastern attraction, is partialed out, Lg moves up to $+.36$ (column two), the 1 percent confidence level. Control of both T^2 and Y or else of $(T - 9)Y$ brings slightly better partials for Lg, $+.41$ in the latter instance (last column). If another eastern attraction, wages, is also controlled by holding both $(T - 9)Y$ and W constant, Lg climbs to $+.55$ (not shown). Admittedly, Lg is mostly a spokesman for E—low E is a western attraction—in these situations. But Lg would still be significant if E and the remaining eastern attractions (population and surplus labor) were controlled also. Evidence for this assertion takes us beyond simple controls but perhaps should be given anyway: if industry, population, and surplus labor are thrown into the control mix by holding constant five variables— $(T - 9)Y$, W, $E^{1.5}$, $(T - 9)P$, and $(F/M)^4$ —Lg remains significant at $+.36$. The isolated states show higher residual growth.

The contour variable, $(50 - Lat)(Lg - 65)$, is even more significant. This is partly because latitude introduces climate as well as north-south isolation into the formula. Thus controlling T^2 changes the simple r of $+.49$ to a partial of $+.39$. Similarly, the partial of $+.55$ reached with Y held constant becomes one of $+.47$ when T^2 is controlled along with Y. Yet all six of the partials shown in table 4-1, including the three where climate is represented in the control variables, exceed the 1 percent confidence level. Moreover, when both $(T - 9)Y$ and W are controlled, the contour variable moves to $+.56$ (not shown). This is fairly good evidence that spatial isolation is an influence in its own right.

Climate. The findings in table 4-1 agument the evidence from the previous chapter that climate influences growth. We have already observed how the temperature-weighted demand variables maintain extremely high partials based on a variety of controls; the +.94 r for $(T - 9)^2 Y$ with $E^{1.5}$ held constant is hard to argue with. Equally convincing are the high partials maintained by T^2. A warm climate (favorable) could really not be a proxy for demand—the most populous, highest income states are in the Northeast—and the +.47 partial for T^2 when Y is held constant confirms this. A warm climate conceivably could be a proxy for lack of industry or low wages—here the South comes to mind—but T^2 holds at +.46 when either $E^{1.5}$ or Lg and W combined are controlled.

By way of reservation, there is a situation where the r's for climate variables are influenced by markets. Although T^2 reads +.47 when Y is held constant, this partial is affected by the -.87 partial for $E^{1.5}$. Thus when both Y and $E^{1.5}$ are controlled (not shown), T^2 drops to +.27. Even here, $(T - 9)^2 Y$ stands at +.71; yet there is no denying that holding Y constant allows climate to describe not only itself but cases where E is low relative to Y. This development has no counterpart with per capita and percentage growth: control of E/Y gives T a +.48 partial with per capita growth and T^2 a +.50 partial with percentage growth.

Other Influences.   The only other influences showing even tentative signs of significance in the table 4-1 control situations are labor and the threshold influence. Regarding labor, total farm population, F, is being used as an indirect measure of surplus labor. In table 4-1, it is always positive and sometimes significant at the 5 percent level. The significant partials (+.28 and +.33) are partly spurious, resulting mainly from a +.47 intercorrelation between F and P and secondarily from a +.35 intercorrelation between F and T. Therefore, F drops to -.03 when P and T^2 are jointly controlled (not shown). Nevertheless, the observed positive tendencies in F foreshadow legitimate r's coming up soon.

Wage and unionization variables offer no significant r's in the face of simple controls and are not shown. The control variables used in the table cause W and U to oscillate between a partial of +.23 (wrong sign) for W with T^2 held constant—here W is a proxy for Y—and one of -.18 for U with $(T - 9)Y$ held constant, where U is mostly a proxy for E. Moderate controls will reveal significantly negative partials for both influences, but at the moment W and U are too weak to speak for themselves.

The threshold influence is dimly visible in—but not really substantiated by—the partial r's for the West-Rural and West-Metro dummies. (The West-Rural states are the western states without major metropolitan areas: Montana, Idaho, Wyoming, New Mexico, and Nevada. The West-Metro states are the other six: Colorado, Utah, Arizona, Washington, Oregon, and California.) Whereas West-Rural is mostly negative, sometimes barely positive, in its r's, West-Metro is always significantly positive. The more developed western states show faster growth.

Even more suggestive of a threshold influence is West-Metro $\times$ CP, which weights the West-Metro states according to urban population. (It is valued at $1 \times CP = CP$ in the West-Metro states and at $0 \times CP = 0$ elsewhere.) West-Metro $\times$ CP has extremely high partials, ranging from +.77 to +.89. CP, however, measures consumer demand as well as development. These partials must be regarded as primarily indicating the attraction of markets. The heavy weight given California also allows West-Metro $\times$ CP to incorporate some of the market-climate interaction effect. Still, West-Metro and West-Metro $\times$ CP maintain their high partials in the three columns where Y is held constant. This is mostly because West-Metro becomes partly a proxy for E, which becomes highly significant: West-Metro is high where E is low—in the West. West-Metro $\times$ CP describes the ideal relationship of high demand (CP) to low supply (West-Metro), with a liberal dose of isolation thrown in for good measure. Yet it is revealing that West-Rural, which is even more favorably related to E when Y is controlled, does not show the same strength.

One other hypothetical influence, agglomeration, shows no evidence of significance but deserves mention for the opposite reason: it shows strong evidence of insignificance. The MB dummy (valued at one for the thirteen Manufacturing Belt states) is consistently negative. If we hold Y constant, so that MB no longer represents both industry *and* demand, the industry-attracts-industry hypothesis is sharply rebutted by a $-.51$ partial. Are severe winters at fault? When T^2 is partialed out in addition to Y, MB registers $-.42$. The Manufacturing Belt is not a magnet for new industry.

Moderate Controls

From minimal controls we proceed to moderate ones. These hold two or three variables constant at once. Table 4-2 presents five moderate control combinations. The combinations employ market and climate variables exclusively. This is done primarily to uncover the latent influence of labor and to further examine thresholds: viewing the secondary influences requires getting the primary ones out of the way. The controls also facilitate further inspection of the market influence.

Demand.   Four variables are listed under "Demand" in the stub column of table 4-2. The first two, Y and Y/P, provide the best evidence yet that income is a better measure of consumer demand than is population—and that demand is a major influence. When P alone is held constant (not shown), the residual pull of Y is momentarily neutralized by the negative pull of $E^{1.5}$, which is highly intercorrelated with Y and has a partial r of $-.77$. But when both P and $E^{1.5}$ are partialed out, as shown in the first control column, Y climbs back to +.62. Since $Y = P \times Y/P$, the finding can be interpreted as affirming the importance of Y/P also. The +.38 partial for Y/P verifies this. In the third column the experi-

Table 4-2
Partial Correlations of Selected Variables with 1947–63 Absolute Growth: Moderate Controls (Two or Three Variables Held Constant)

Selected Independent Variables	Simple r with Growth	Variables Held Constant ("Partialed Out")				
		P $E^{1.5}$	P Y $E^{1.5}$	$(T-9)^2 P$ $E^{1.5}$	$(T-9)^2 P$ $(T-9)^2 Y$ $E^{1.5}$	$(T-9)^2 P$ $(T-9)^2 Y$ Lg
(MULTIPLE R)		(.819)	(.894)	(.875)	(.948)	(.914)
Demand						
Y	+.42	+.62	....	+.63	+.38	-.51
Y/P	+.09	+.38	-.12	+.39	-.21	-.35
$(T-9)^2 P$	+.85	+.57	+.64	....	....	....
$(T-9)^2 Y$	+.90	+.80	+.73	+.75	....	....
Industry						
$E^{1.5}$	+.05	....	....	....	....	-.62
$MB \times E$	-.13	-.34	-.37	-.30	-.39	-.67
Lg	+.26	+.30	+.09	+.32	+.08	....
Labor						
$F^{1.5}$	+.28	-.48	+.04	-.16	+.64	+.29
$(F/M)^4$	+.09	-.08	+.48	-.03	+.58	+.45
$1/W^2$	-.02	-.12	+.31	-.24	+.31	+.51
$1/U^2$	+.08	+.01	+.36	-.10	+.36	+.41
Threshold						
West-Rural Dummy	-.15	+.20	+.10	+.04	-.13	-.17
West-Metro Dummy	+.36	+.43	+.25	+.38	+.12	+.12
West-Metro $\times$ CP	+.88	+.87	+.77	+.76	+.32	+.57

Abbreviations: P = Population, E = Manufacturing Employment, Y = Income, T = Temperature, Lg = Longitude, MB = Manufacturing Belt Dummy (13 states), F = Farm Population, M = Square Miles, U = Unionization, W = Wages, West-Rural = 5 least developed western states, West-Metro = 6 most developed western states, CP = Urban (City) Population ment is repeated with $(T - 9)^2 P$ substituted for P: $(T - 9)^2 P$ and $E^{1.5}$ are held constant. This time Y goes to $+.63$ and Y/P to $+.39$. The control combination of $(T - 9)P$ and $E^{1.5}$ is now shown but yields partials of $+.60$ for Y and $+.43$ for Y/P. Very clearly, when states are equal in population and industry, growth favors those where income is proportionately higher than population, that is, where the consumer's purchasing power is highest.

At this point, another warning about proxies and spurious correlation is needed. The negative partials for Y and Y/P in the last column do not contradict the conclusion of the above analysis. In this column weighted versions of Y and P are held constant, which effectively deprives Y of any independent significance. Y responds by becoming a proxy for E, with which it has a $+.92$ intercorrelation. When $E^{1.5}$ goes to $-.62$, Y goes to $-.51$. Y/P, in turn, becomes partly a proxy for Y and partly a proxy for $1/W^2$, with which it has a $-.73$ intercorrelation. When the wage reciprocal becomes significantly positive (equivalent to negative for the nonreciprocal variable, W), Y/P imitates by becoming negative. Note that the proxy variables have lower partials than the variables they represent.

Table 4-2 also provides additional evidence that markets and climate interact. In the first column, with P and $E^{1.5}$ controlled, Y reaches $+.62$ but $(T - 9)^2 Y$ goes to $+.80$. Here the comparative r^2's for Y and $(T - 9)^2 Y$ are .38 and .64, indicating that weighted income has two-thirds again as much explanatory power as unweighted income. The next control column is even more convincing, because now Y is controlled in addition to P and $E^{1.5}$. Even so, $(T - 9)^2 Y$ reaches $+.73$. In the third column, weighting the second-best demand variable, P, is not good enough; Y demands to be weighted, with $(T - 9)^2 Y$ showing a partial of $+.75$.

Industry.   The remaining market variables—two supply variables and a spatial variable—are combined under "Industry." The principal supply variable is $E^{1.5}$. If P and Y are simultaneously held constant (not shown), $E^{1.5}$ has a partial of $-.87$. If $(T - 9)P$ and $(T - 9)Y$ are jointly controlled, $E^{1.5}$ goes to $-.88$. And if $(T - 9)^2 P$ and $(T - 9)^2 Y$ are the demand controls, $E^{1.5}$ has a $-.67$ partial r. These partials offer reasonably conclusive evidence that growth favors states where supply is low relative to demand. But there is still uncertainty about the extent to which low supply describes the added stimulus of spatial isolation. The last column of table 4-2, where Lg is among the control variables, tells us that $E^{1.5}$ is speaking mainly for itself: holding $(T - 9)^2 P$, $(T - 9)^2 Y$, and Lg constant leaves $E^{1.5}$ with a partial of $-.62$. The alternative control combination of $(T - 9)P$, $(T - 9)Y$, and Lg gives more weight to P and Y and less to T, with the result that $E^{1.5}$ goes to $-.85$ (not shown).

These findings are verified by a different supply variable, MB $\times$ E, which is also an agglomeration variable. MB $\times$ E values the Manufacturing Belt states at E ($= 1 \times E$) and the remaining states at zero ($= 0 \times E$): every state that is less industrialized than the Manufacturing Belt states gets the optimal (lowest) supply value. In the first four columns, even though $E^{1.5}$ is controlled, MB $\times$ E shows significantly negative partials: the relative oversupply situation found in the Manufacturing Belt is inimical to growth. In the last column, where $E^{1.5}$ is *not* held constant, MB $\times$ E climbs to $-.67$. The alternative control combination of $(T - 9)P$, $(T - 9)Y$, and Lg brings MB $\times$ E to $-.87$ (not shown).

The last market variable shown, Lg, provides limited additional evidence that spatial isolation encourages manufacturing growth. In each of the first four control columns, $E^{1.5}$ and P (sometimes weighted by T) are controlled. This in effect controls E/P, with which Lg has a $-.68$ intercorrelation; hence Lg is indirectly controlled to a degree. Even so, Lg remains positive and, in two instances, significant at the 5 percent confidence level. In columns two and four, where Lg is quite weak, labor variables have become significant and are pulling growth eastward: the westward pull of spatial isolation is neutralized. But if we take the column four control set—$(T - 9)^2 P$, $(T - 9)^2 Y$, and $E^{1.5}$—and add $(F/M)^4$ and $1/W^2$ so as to dampen the labor supply and wage attractions, Lg regains its strength: it pops back to $+.35$ (not shown). The threshold influence is still interfering with growth in the least developed western states, however; so further improvement comes when the West-Rural dummy is added to the control set (six variables now held constant). This pushes Lg on to $+.41$, above the 1 percent level.

Labor Supply.   The moderate controls shown in table 4–2 give us our first good evidence of labor's influence in industrial location. The first labor influence to be examined is labor supply, represented by the two farm population variables, $F^{1.5}$ and $(F/M)^4$. The exponential adjustments applied to F and F/M, particularly the exponent 4 used with F/M, give exaggerated weight to states with extremely high values. This has the effect of saying that variations in labor supply are important mainly among states where the supply of surplus labor is quite high.

The labor analysis must begin with another warning about spurious correlation. One is naturally suspicious about the negative partials for $F^{1.5}$ and $(F/M)^4$ appearing in the first and third control columns. Here we must recall that farm population percentage (F/P) has a $-.75$ intercorrelation with per capita income (Y/P): other factors being equal, income is lower in agricultural states. Thus in the first control column, where P is held constant, high F is equivalent to high F/P, which in turn corresponds to low Y/P and low Y: F is a reverse proxy for Y (low F = high Y). And the $-.48$ partial for $F^{1.5}$ reflects the $+.62$ partial for Y. Similarly, in the third column, the $-.16$ partial for $F^{1.5}$ reflects the $+.63$ partial for Y. Consequently, when Y and $(T - 9)^2 Y$ are respectively added to these two control combinations, creating the new combinations shown in columns two and four, $F^{1.5}$ again becomes positive; it can no longer represent Y.

The labor supply partials on which to focus are therefore the ones in the second, fourth, and fifth control columns, where Y is controlled and F does not represent Y. In column two, $(F/M)^4$ makes a dramatic leap from obscurity to significance, reaching +.48. But the controls over P and Y are not the best: the demand variables must be weighted by climate to achieve full effect. Column four substitutes temperature-weighted versions—$(T - 9)^2P$, $(T - 9)^2Y$, and $E^{1.5}$ are controlled—and $(F/M)^4$ moves up ten points to +.58. But now the absolute variable, $F^{1.5}$, is even more significant: it reads +.64. The alternative combination (not shown) of $(T - 9)P$, $(T - 9)Y$, and $E^{1.5}$ puts $(F/M)^4$ ahead of $F^{1.5}$ by a margin of +.62 to +.59. In the last column, Lg replaces $E^{1.5}$ and less adequately controls a tendency for low F to represent low E. The labor supply partials therefore decline but are still significant—+.45 for $(F/M)^4$ and +.29 for $F^{1.5}$.

The labor supply influence, previously overshadowed by the more powerful market influence, has emerged. Labor's influence is not visible at the outset, because dense farm populations are associated with (1) low per capita income, or weak demand, and (2) the higher levels of manufacturing found in the East (even in the South) vis-à-vis the West. But when Y and P (hence Y/P) are controlled, and E also, these adverse intercorrelations are no longer a problem.

How can we be sure, though, that labor supply is the influence being measured? The answer must be given largely in theoretical terms. Other studies have concluded that surplus labor attracts industry, notably in the South; so the surplus labor interpretation is at least plausible. And, as argued earlier, the farm origin of most surplus labor (technological displacement in agriculture) makes farm variables promising as measures of surplus labor. The partials for $(F/M)^4$ and $F^{1.5}$ are much too high and occur too consistently to be regarded as spurious; even per capita and percentage growth show significant partials with $(F/M)^4$. Moreover, these high partials often occur in situations where all other variables, intercorrelated or not, have lower partials, which makes proxy relationships highly unlikely. Surplus labor is of course related to low wages; but often as not the surplus labor variables have higher partials, and in other instances a wage variable has been held constant. At the same time, the wage and farm variables *do* tend to become significant in the same control situations, supporting the theory that they are related as labor variables. Finally, it is extremely implausible that causality runs from manufacturing growth to farm population growth: farm population is declining.

Wages and Unionization. Like labor supply, wages and unionization are too unimportant in the overall scheme of influences to show significant simple *r*'s. Moreover, as pointed out before, these influences are hidden by the connection of high wages with (1) high per capita income, (2) spatial isolation, and (3) low industrialization. High wages help produce high income, total and per capita. High consumer demand thus attracts market-oriented firms even while labor-oriented ones are being rebuffed. At the same time, high wages occur

not only in the Manufacturing Belt but in the West. There the high cost of
shipping eastern manufactured goods to western markets leads to somewhat
higher prices and wages. (This is a watered-down version of the high price-wage
structure in Alaska.) The tendency toward high wages in the West shows up
in a +.47 intercorrelation between Lg and W. And it results in overlap between
high wages (unfavorable) and both spatial isolation and lack of industry (both
favorable). Unionization is affected the same way insofar as it is linked with
wages. Strong unions on the West Coast also create a direct conflict between
unionization and spatial isolation. But unions are generally weak in the West
compared to the Northeast, so that low industrialization tends to reinforce
rather than counteract the attraction of weak unions.

Remarkable things happen when per capita income (P and Y together) and
either industrialization (E and P together) or spatial isolation (Lg) are held
constant. Table 4-2 illustrates this, using $1/W^2$ to represent wages and $1/U^2$ for
unionization. *Remember, positive r's for these reciprocals are equivalent to*
negative r's for W and U. Simultaneous control of both per capita income and
industrialization is provided in columns two and four. The resulting partials are
the same in both columns (i.e., regardless of whether or not P and Y are
weighted by T): $1/W^2$ goes to +.31 and $1/U^2$ to +.36. (As an indication of the
importance of adjusting for curvilinear correlation, the unadjusted variables
W and U have respective partials of $-.18$ and $-.20$ under the column two
controls, and $-.19$ and $-.04$ under the column four controls—considerably
lower than reached by the reciprocals.)

Lg is a more effective control than $E^{1.5}$. Thus when $(T-9)^2 P, (T-9)^2 Y$,
and Lg are jointly partialed out, $1/W^2$ climbs to +.51 and $1/U^2$ to +.41 (last
column). This last finding typifies the usual relationship between wages and
unionization: wages scores higher.

The findings, then, support the conclusion of other studies that industry is
attracted by low wages and weak unions. However, there is reason to doubt that
unionization is much more than a double proxy representing wages and labor
supply. Although unions could have a limited amount of independent significance, we shall see abundant evidence that wages and labor supply are the
controlling factors. In columns two and four, for example, $1/W^2$ will move
ahead of $1/U^2$ if $(F/M)^4$—labor supply—is added to the control combinations.
(In these two instances, wages and unionization both become insignificant—
evidence that both tend to duplicate labor supply.) If $(F/M)^4$ is added to the
control set heading column five—the most effective control set—the outcome is
striking: $1/W^2$ declines modestly from +.51 to +.45, but $1/U^2$ plunges from
+.41 to +.27.

Thresholds. Table 4-2 provides additional but still inconclusive evidence
of a threshold factor holding back the least developed states. All five control
combinations give the West-Metro dummy a substantially more positive partial
than the West-Rural dummy. These five comparisons together with the simple *r*

comparison (West-Metro, +.36; West-Rural, -.15) and the six partial r comparisons from table 4-1 give West-Metro a twelve-for-twelve record in contests with West-Rural; table 4-3 will bring this to seventeen-for-seventeen. In these comparisons we can never be certain that higher levels of consumer demand are not the real explanation; absolute growth simply is not well adapted to testing for a threshold influence. However, demand is rather thoroughly controlled in the last two columns, which suggests that thresholds are the answer.

Another pair of partial r's not shown in the table also seem to refute the market interpretation of West-Metro. When $(T - 9)P$ and $(T - 9)Y$ are controlled but E is not, unweighted P and Y become proxies for E, which is highly negative: $E^{1.5}$ goes to -.88, P to -.78, and Y to -.80. Now West-Metro's relatively high values (vis-à-vis West-Rural) for E, P, and Y should if anything put West-Metro behind West-Rural. But West-Metro still holds a +.38 to +.05 advantage.

Still more evidence of a threshold influence comes from the weighted variable, West-Metro $\times$ CP. This variable allows for degrees of threshold advantage; it assumes that the farther across the threshold a state is, the faster it grows—provided it is still basically underdeveloped. West-Metro $\times$ CP gives consistently high partials, very significant in all but the fourth column. These partials do not rest on any peculiarity of CP, for almost identical readings can be obtained by substituting P or Y; even West-Metro $\times$ E gives partials almost as high. Since some of these partials occur in situations where not one but two demand variables are held constant, it is unlikely that CP is strictly a measure of demand.

Other Influences.   Findings bearing on two other influences also appear in table 4-2. The first is climate. Most of what needs to be said about it has already been said in connection with the temperature-weighted demand variables. It is worth pointing out, though, that in the last two columns temperature-weighted variables must be controlled to develop the high labor partials shown. This implies that climate is an influence.

The agglomeration variable, MB $\times$ E, has been viewed from the market but not the agglomeration standpoint. When used to test for agglomeration, this variable tries to say that industry attracts industry but only when Manufacturing Belt levels of industrialization are reached; states outside the Manufacturing Belt are treated as having no industry at all ($0 \times E = 0$). But the attempt to say that new industry clusters around old industry fails: MB $\times$ E shows negative partials in every column. By itself, the MB dummy (not shown) is also consistently negative. It reads -.47 in the last column, where MB $\times$ E reads -.67.

Strong Controls

Table 4-3 proceeds to strong controls. The control combinations shown all entail holding constant at least four variables, thereby statistically explaining

Table 4-3
Partial Correlations of Selected Variables with 1947–63 Absolute Growth: Strong Controls (Four or Five Variables Held Constant)

Selected Independent Variables	Simple r with Growth	Variables Held Constant ("Partialed Out")				
		Lg $F^{1.5}$ $(T-9)Y$ $(T-9)P$	Lg $E^{1.5}$ $(T-9)Y$ $(T-9)P$	$F^{1.5}$ $E^{1.5}$ $(T-9)Y$ $(T-9)P$	$(T-9)^2/w^2$ $E^{1.5}$ $(T-9)Y$ $(T-9)P$	$(F/M)^4$ $(T-9)^2/w^2$ $E^{1.5}$ $(T-9)Y$ $(T-9)P$
(MULTIPLE R)		(.804)	(.950)	(.968)	(.952)	(.971)
Markets						
$(T-9)^2 Y$	+.90	+.91	+.08	+.41	-.02	+.04
$E^{1.5}$	+.05	-.90	...	...	...	...
MB × E	-.13	-.91	-.37	-.31	-.38	-.39
East × P/M	-.17	-.26	-.37	-.24	-.37	-.51
Labor						
$F^{1.5}$	+.28	...	+.59	...	+.73	+.59
$(F/M)^4$	+.09	+.25	+.65	+.48	+.62	...
$\sqrt{W}$	+.06	-.46	-.34	-.31	-.18	-.08
$\sqrt{U}$	+.03	-.38	-.17	-.22	-.09	+.04
$1/W^2$	-.02	+.46	+.45	+.40	+.30	+.16
$1/U^2$	+.08	+.34	+.41	+.39	+.35	+.11
$(T-9)^2/W^2$	+.29	+.48	+.23	+.56	...	...
Threshold						
West-Rural Dummy	-.15	-.16	-.11	+.01	-.07	-.03
West-Metro Dummy	+.36	+.21	+.09	+.23	+.09	+.15
West-Metro × CP	+.88	+.83	+.42	+.44	+.41	+.26

Abbreviations: T = Temperature, P = Population, Y = Income, F = Farm Population, Lg = Longitude, E = Manufacturing Employment, W = Wages, MB = Manufacturing Belt dummy (13 states), East = dummy for 37 eastern and central states (all but the 11 western states), M = Square Miles, U = Unionization, West-Rural = 5 least developed western states, West-Metro = 6 most developed western states, CP = Urban (City) Population anywhere from 65 to 94 percent (R^2) of the variation in absolute growth. While giving us further glimpses of the market and climate influences, the controls emphasize the secondary influences—labor and the threshold factor. All control combinations are based on holding (T - 9)P and (T - 9)Y constant, and all but one include $E^{1.5}$ as a third control variable. Parallel experiments, not recorded in the table, substituted $(T - 9)^2 P$ and $(T - 9)^2 Y$ with very little difference in the results.

Markets. The first four variables in the stub column of table 4–3 present the latest evidence of the market influence. Because the demand variables controlled—(T - 9)P and (T - 9)Y—give less weight to T than they might, $(T - 9)^2 Y$ is still able to show a partial r of +.91 in the first column. This is a little deceiving, because T used as a weight with Y or P begins to duplicate E whenever T is raised to a power. Note that $E^{1.5}$ reads -.90 in the same column, suggesting a proxy relationship. As further evidence of duplication, $E^{1.5}$ drops from -.87 with Y controlled, to -.86 with (T - 9)Y controlled, to -.61 with $(T - 9)^2 Y$ controlled, and to -.42 with $(T - 9)^{2.5} \times Y$ controlled— because Y is given increasing weight in states where it happens to be high *relative to* E. On the other hand, if $E^{1.5}$ is added as a fifth control variable in column one, $(T - 9)^2 Y$ still has a partial of +.41 (not shown). The evidence again suggests that demand is an important influence and that it interacts with climate.

Two industry variables, $E^{1.5}$ and MB $\times$ E, represent the supply side of markets. In the first column, the only one in which $E^{1.5}$ is not itself a control variable, $E^{1.5}$ finally reaches -.90—despite some overlap with Lg, held constant. This modest improvement over earlier partials results from the inclusion of $F^{1.5}$, representing labor supply, in the control combination. With the eastward pull of labor supply on growth at least partly checked, the westward pull of underindustrialization can register better. In fact, a different control combination using *two* labor supply variables—(T - 9)P, (T - 9)Y, $F^{1.5}$, and $(F/M)^4$—sends $E^{1.5}$ on up to -.94 (not shown). Who can argue with that? Meanwhile, MB $\times$ E goes to -.91 in the first column. This tells us that new industry is avoiding the industrially oversupplied states of the Manufacturing Belt—particularly the ones with the most industry. In the last four columns, even with $E^{1.5}$ partialed out, MB $\times$ E continues to show significantly negative partials.

The last market variable, East $\times$ P/M, is of interest as the variable that enters fifth in the best ten-variable multiple correlation combination (table 4–5). East is a dummy valued at one for the thirty-seven easternmost states and at zero for the eleven western states. Multiplying population density, P/M, by East gives all western states the same value—0 $\times$ P/M = 0—instead of giving the smallest values to the five least developed states. Thus East $\times$ P/M can be thought of as P/M adjusted to compensate for thresholds: it compensates by giving the West-Metro states values just as low (good) as the West-Rural values. P/M, in turn, is a proxy for markets. Low density, we have seen, describes the underdevelopment found in states with wide gaps between supply and demand. Although relative variables like P/M generally perform poorly with absolute growth, this one is capable of describing residual aspects of the market influence—once the most crucial absolute variables are controlled. The consistently negative and often significant r's for East $\times$ P/M depict faster residual growth in the least developed states. In the last column, the $-.51$ partial is significant well beyond the 1 percent level.

Labor Supply. Table 4-3 repeats the two labor supply variables shown in the previous table, $F^{1.5}$ and $(F/M)^4$. Only in three of the columns is $F^{1.5}$ excluded from the control combination. But in these columns its partials of $+.59$ (twice) and $+.73$ easily exceed the 1 percent significance level. The $+.73$ partial, moreover, rises well above those for all other variables, the closest of which is $(F/M)^4$. These observations validate the previous conclusion that the high partials for $F^{1.5}$ are not spurious and not based on proxy relationships with nonlabor variables. Interestingly, the $+.73$ partial occurs in a situation where a wage variable, $(T-9)^2/W^2$, is held constant: $F^{1.5}$ is not a proxy for wages either. In short, the states with the most surplus labor—those with the highest farm populations—show the fastest residual growth after markets and climate have explained most of what they can explain.

As long as $E^{1.5}$ is controlled so that the westward pull of markets does not neutralize the eastward pull of labor supply, $(F/M)^4$ also does well. Its $+.65$ partial in the second column exceeds the $+.59$ achieved by $F^{1.5}$; its $+.62$ partial in column four is second-best but still very high. And in column three, even with its cousin $F^{1.5}$ controlled, $(F/M)^4$ reaches $+.48$. Moreover, these very significant partials occur in the face of negative r's for East $\times$ P/M, which is to say despite the residual pull of western markets. Hence if East $\times$ P/M is added as a fifth member to the column four control set, $(F/M)^4$ climbs from $+.62$ to $+.69$ (not shown).

To check the interpretation of $F^{1.5}$ and $(F/M)^4$ as labor supply variables, an analysis of residuals was made. An analysis of residuals compares residual (unexplained) growth before and after a variable being examined is added to a group of variables held constant. The original group is used to predict growth by means of a multiple regression equation. Predicted growth is then subtracted from actual for each state to get the error, which is the residual. The new variable is then added to the equation, and the computations are repeated. A before-and-after comparison identifies the states experiencing the biggest error reductions. In the case at hand, the original group of control variables included $(T-9)P$, $(T-9)Y$, $E^{1.5}$, East $\times$ P/M, Y/M, and West-Metro $\times$ CP. With these six variables held constant, the labor supply partials were $+.60$ for $F^{1.5}$ and $+.65$ for $(F/M)^4$.

The tests saw $F^{1.5}$ and $(F/M)^4$ taking turns being variable number seven in a regression equation predicting growth. In both instances North Carolina had easily the largest reduction in residual (unexplained) growth, and this resulted from an increase in predicted growth. North Carolina is identified in the Perloff study as the state with the largest 1939–54 upward shift in textile mill employment;[1] the textile mills were attracted to North Carolina and other parts of the South by abundant low cost labor.[2] Again for both farm variables, the third largest reduction in residual growth was in Pennsylvania, where a previously excessive growth estimate was cut back. Pennsylvania is a textile loss state; its textile losses were exceeded only by those of Massachusetts.[3] Massachusetts had the eighth largest reduction with $F^{1.5}$ and the seventh largest reduction with $(F/M)^4$; predicted growth was lowered in both cases. South Carolina, the state with the second largest textile gains, had the sixth largest reduction in unexplained growth under $(F/M)^4$, and this resulted from an increase in predicted growth.

Beyond the textile pattern, the most important improvements under $F^{1.5}$ came from increases in predicted growth for Minnesota, Wisconsin, and Tennessee and decreases in predicted growth for Louisiana and Alabama. The leading improvements not already noted for $(F/M)^4$ came from an increase in Tennessee's predicted growth and decreases in the predictions for Louisiana and Alabama. Everything except the slow growth in Alabama and Louisiana is reasonably consistent with a labor supply explanation. There seems to be a shift from the Manufacturing Belt to *nearby* states with surplus labor. Wisconsin and Minnesota are not low-wage states, of course, and southern Wisconsin is in the Manufacturing Belt. But these two states do have surplus labor emanating from agriculture (and from iron ore mining in Minnesota). Outward expansion of manufacturing at the western end of the Manufacturing Belt has absorbed some of this labor.[4]

Two alternatives to the labor supply interpretation have a degree of plausibility, particularly when it comes to $F^{1.5}$. The first is that the agricultural resource attraction as it relates to food products manufacturing is being picked up. The Perloff study identifies Wisconsin and North Carolina as having had the second and sixth largest upward shifts in food and kindred products employment and further identifies Pennsylvania, Massachusetts, and Louisiana as having had the third, fourth, and sixth largest downward shifts.[5] These five states are among the top eight in the analysis of residuals for $F^{1.5}$, and four of them (all but Wisconsin) are among the top seven under $(F/M)^4$. A weaker alternative is that farm-oriented industries—feed, fertilizer, farm equipment, and the like—are attracted to the farm market in states with many farmers; this is a market interpretation. But the states in question are mostly southern states where subsistence farming accounts for most of the dense farm population: the farm market interpretation is not convincing.

On balance, these interpretations are not attractive alternatives to the labor supply interpretation for $(F/M)^4$, which very closely resembles the other labor variables in its behavior. But for $F^{1.5}$, the response of Wisconsin and Minnesota creates a fair possibility that both the labor and the food resource or farm market attractions are being recorded.

Wages. The previous table and supporting text made the point that the wage influence breaks through to significance when per capita income (P and Y combined) and spatial isolation (or else industry) are jointly held constant. The table also showed that the most effective control combination gave wages $(1/W^2)$ a higher partial than unionization $(1/U^2)$. Table 4-3 amplifies these findings. Using more extensive controls, it demonstrates more conclusively than before that wages is an independent influence. It also brings to light a new interaction influence—interaction between wages and climate.

The first three columns, where no wage variable is controlled, are the ones to look at. Column one builds on the last column of table 4-2 (slightly modified as to the weight given T) by adding $F^{1.5}$ as a fourth control variable. The resulting wage partials are $-.46$ for $\sqrt{W}$ and $+.46$ for $1/W^2$. This finding reaffirms the significance of wages. And, since $F^{1.5}$ has been controlled, we know that wages is more than a proxy for labor supply (assuming that $F^{1.5}$ has been correctly interpreted). Furthermore, since $\sqrt{W}$ is eight points ahead of $\sqrt{U}$ ($-.46$ vs. $-.38$), wages does not seem to be a proxy for unionization.

Columns two and three show slightly lower partials for the wage variables. Column two substitutes $E^{1.5}$ for $F^{1.5}$. All that happens is that $1/W^2$ changes from $+.46$ to $+.45$. This shows that wage levels are not just an alternative measure of industry. (Wages *is* a fairly good proxy for industry in the East, where the lesser degree of manufacturing in the South vis-à-vis the Manufacturing Belt corresponds to lower wages. But in the West manufacturing is even lower, whereas wages are back to Manufacturing Belt levels.) Column three drops Lg as a control and reinstates $F^{1.5}$. This causes $1/W^2$ to drop to $+.40$. However, the decline is clearly the result of failure to control Lg, not the result of controlling $F^{1.5}$: if Lg is added back as a fifth control variable, $1/W^2$ returns to $+.46$ (not shown). In all of these situations, $1/W^2$ stays ahead of $1/U^2$ (which reads $+.40$ when all five variables are controlled). All indications are that wages is an independently significant influence.

Column three also provides a new insight: wages responds to weighting by temperature. Although $1/W^2$ reads only $+.40$ in this column, $(T-9)^2/W^2$ reaches $+.56$. (It remains at $+.56$ if Lg is added as a fifth control variable.) Even in the first column, $(T-9)^2/W^2$ is marginally better than $1/W^2$. Although temperature-weighted wage variables are not always better, they do work best in the strongest multiple correlation combinations. In fact, regardless of whether we are dealing with absolute, per capita, or percentage growth, the highest R's come from combinations that include weighted wage variables—usually $(T-9)^2/W^2$. Also, the highest partials reachable by weighted wage variables are higher than the highest reachable by unweighted wage variables. In practical terms, these findings indicate that the lowest wage states outside of the South (Maine, New Hampshire, Vermont, Rhode Island, and the Dakotas) have lower residual growth when nonwage influences are held constant. A cold climate seems to interfere with the wage stimulus.

Repeating, the weighted wage variable that most often gives the highest partial is $(T - 9)^2/W^2$, or $(T - 9)^2 \times 1/W^2$. In table 4-3 we can observe this variable with no more than four other variables held constant. The best it can do with four variables held constant is a very respectable +.56. But with more extensive controls, it climbs higher. If entered last in the best ten-variable multiple correlation combination (table 4-5)—that is, if nine variables are held constant—$(T - 9)^2/W^2$ goes to +.69. This control combination, incidentally, sends $1/W^2$ to +.57 and $\sqrt{W}$ to -.52.

Unionization. The table 4-3 findings also reveal significant partials for the unionization variables, $\sqrt{U}$ and $1/U^2$, but leave doubt as to whether these variables speak for themselves. In the first three columns, before $(T - 9)^2/W^2$ is controlled, we find partials of -.38 ($\sqrt{U}$), +.41 ($1/U^2$), and +.39 ($1/U^2$). All three partials are significant at the 1 percent confidence level. At the same time, though, all three are less than the best wage partials; one suspects a proxy relationship. True, $1/U^2$ stays at +.35 in the fourth column, where a wage variable is held constant. But a further proxy relationship to $(F/M)^4$ seems responsible. Consequently, when $(F/M)^4$ is added to the control set in the last column, $1/U^2$ drops to +.11.

The proxy relationship between unionization and labor supply—between $1/U^2$ and $(F/M)^4$—requires elaboration. Some evidence of dependency was brought out in the discussion of table 4-2: we saw $1/U^2$ going from +.41 to +.27 when $(F/M)^4$ was added to the most effective (for labor) control combination. Let us now see what happens when $(F/M)^4$ becomes a fifth control variable in columns one, two, and three of table 4-3. Here are the before-and-after partials for wages and unionization:

	Column 1		Column 2		Column 3	
	Before	*After*	*Before*	*After*	*Before*	*After*
$1/W^2$ (or $\sqrt{W}$)	(-.46)	(-.45)	+.45	+.39	+.40	+.31
$1/U^2$ (or $\sqrt{U}$)	(-.38)	(-.34)	+.41	+.19	+.39	+.23

It is apparent, first of all, that both wages and unionization get some support from labor supply: both decline in their partials when $(F/M)^4$ is controlled. But the wage variables show relatively small declines, whereas the unionization variables show larger ones. In the column one situation, unionization is still alive in the "after" situation—primarily because $E^{1.5}$ is not controlled and $\sqrt{U}$ has some ability to function as a surrogate for $E^{1.5}$. But the second and third tests leave $1/U^2$ moribund. If $1/W^2$ is now added as a sixth control variable in the three control sets, the demise of unionization is just about completed: $1/U^2$ develops respective partials of +.08, +.02, and +.12.

As a further and particularly rigorous test of the hypothesis that weak unions stimulate growth, all variables but the two labor variables from the best ten-variable multiple correlation combination (table 4-5) were held constant. Then $(F/M)^4$ was added as a ninth control to see what happened to the wage and unionization variables. Finally, $1/W^2$ and $1/U^2$ were alternated as the tenth control variable. The results:

	Step 8	Step 9: $(F/M)^4$	Step 10: $1/W^2$	Alt. 10: $1/U^2$
$(F/M)^4$	+.53	....	....	....
$1/W^2$	+.58	+.57	....	+.56
$1/U^2$	+.40	+.21	-.15	....
$(T - 9)^2/W^2$	+.60	+.69	+.50	+.68

Even before any other labor variable is controlled, $1/U^2$ trails its nearest competitor, $(F/M)^4$, by +.53 to +.40. And when $(F/M)^4$ joins the control combination, $1/U^2$ becomes insignificant at +.21. Now it is a proxy—not a very good one—for wages alone. Therefore, when $1/W^2$ becomes the tenth variable held constant, $1/U^2$ falls beyond zero to -.15 (the wrong sign). On the other hand, if $1/U^2$ is used as the tenth control variable, $1/W^2$ and $(T - 9)^2/W^2$ are virtually unaffected. Conclusion: unionization is a proxy for labor supply and wages.

Thresholds. Table 4-3 concludes by repeating the three threshold variables from table 4-2. It must again be pointed out that absolute growth is not well adapted for testing the threshold hypothesis, since ultra-low levels of development are badly tangled up with ultra-low levels of consumer demand, not to mention manufacturing employment and farm population. Tests with per capita and percentage growth, where the threshold influence registers very clearly, demonstrate that this influence cannot be seen until market influences have been controlled. But with absolute growth the principal market variables are P, Y, and E. All are at or near their minimum values in the five subthreshold states—Montana, Idaho, Wyoming, New Mexico, and Nevada; so, for that matter, is F. By the time the absolute variables have been controlled, most of the threshold variation has been indirectly controlled as well.

Nevertheless, residual traces of a threshold influence can be found. The West-Rural and West-Metro dummies do not show significant r's, but they do differ considerably from each other. West-Metro is always positive (good residual growth) and usually well above zero; West-Rural is negative (poor residual growth) except in one column, where its partial is +.01. By subtracting the West-Rural partial from the West-Metro partial in each column, we get differences of +.37, +.20, +.24, +.16, and +.18. Statistical significance cannot be attached to these differences, but they do suggest that the West-Rural states are troubled.

The suggestion is much stronger in the third threshold variable, West-Metro X CP. This variable is still ambiguous, for it could mean nothing more than that the six West-Metro states have more consumers and income with which to attract industry. Holding $(T - 9)P$ and $(T - 9)Y$ constant does not rule out a residual demand pull resulting from the interaction of demand and spatial isolation in the western states. Still, considering that Lg is controlled in two of the columns, partials such as +.83 and +.42 are definitely suggestive of a threshold influence. Equally suggestive is the fact that West-Metro X CP equals or exceeds West X CP, and of course West-Rural X CP, in all control situations. If the last two variables were shown in the table, the comparison would be as follows:

	Col. 1	Col. 2	Col. 3	Col. 4	Col. 5
West-Metro X CP	+.83	+.42	+.44	+.41	+.26
West X CP	+.83	+.42	+.44	+.40	+.25
West-Rural X CP	-.13	-.10	+.01	-.07	-.03

Any interaction between spatial isolation and demand should benefit the West-Rural states as well—unless there is a threshold barrier. But even when we allow for variation in demand in the least developed states, either by treating them separately or by grouping them with West-Metro under the West dummy (eleven states), they show no sign of a residual demand influence; only the West-Metro states react.

Agglomeration. Table 4-3 looks at one other hypothesis—agglomeration. MB X E, viewed earlier as a supply (market) variable, searches for positive r's; these would indicate faster residual growth in the Manufacturing Belt. But the r's are all negative: -.91, -.37, -.31, -.38, and -.39. The last four occur despite the partialing out of $E^{1.5}$. Oversupply in the Manufacturing Belt is thus fairly well controlled, so that any latent agglomeration attraction should be visible. Other MB-weighted variables, such as MB X VA, run a bit lower but tell the same story. MB itself (valued at one in the thirteen states, zero elsewhere) has partials of -.53, -.21, -.20, -.22, and -.34 under the five control combinations shown in the table. In short, strong controls reveal that residual growth in the Manufacturing Belt is significantly lower, not significantly higher. Control of markets, climate, and labor—all hostile to the region—makes no difference.

Multiple Correlations

Another way to gain insights about what influences are important is to examine multiple correlations, or Rs. These measure the relationship between the dependent variable (growth) and several independent variables in combination. R has no sign, for it may rest on a combination of positively and negatively correlated variables. The best Rs for any fixed number of independent variables are often produced by combinations which omit some variables with high—even the highest—simple r's. Such combinations substitute less important variables having less tendency to duplicate (or be duplicated by) other variables included. By noting which variables produce the highest Rs, we can learn more about what does or doesn't have independent significance, that is, about which factors must be included in a comprehensive explanation of growth.

Multiple Correlation Tables

Tables 4-4 and 4-5 summarize the best Rs achieved in experiments with absolute growth. The tables show how the Rs are constructed in stepwise fashion, one variable added at a time, until a certain number of steps (variables added) is reached. (Entering the same variables in different orders has no effect on R.) The first column shows the step at which the variable in the second column was added. Column three gives the simple r (step one) or partial r (later steps) for each variable when it enters, that is, immediately before it joins the group held constant. The partial r's, of course, are those which result when the preceding variables are held constant. Thus in the first combination in table 4-4, $(T - 9)Y$ enters first with a simple r of $+.75$. With $(T - 9)Y$ held constant, $E^{1.5}$, which enters second, has a partial of $-.86$.

The columns headed by R and R^2 show the coefficient of multiple correlation and its square for however many variables have entered as of the specified step. Nonstatisticians may find a review of what R^2 means helpful at this point. The r's, simple or partial, can be squared to get r^2, the coefficient of determination. Read as a percentage, it tells how much of the variation (the unexplained variation in the case of partial r^2's) in the dependent variable is statistically explained by the variable whose r^2 is being examined. Rs work exactly the same way: they are squared to get R^2, the coefficient of multiple determination. The R^2 of .920 at step 3 under "Best for Step 2" means that the three variables being combined statistically account for 92 percent of the variation in absolute growth among the forty-eight contiguous states.

The order of entry for the variables in these and subsequent multiple correlation tables is semiarbitrary. The variable with the highest simple r in the group has not necessarily been entered first; the variable with the highest partial r at step 2 has not necessarily been entered second. Rather, I have tried to show the variables in sequences that illustrate certain points, facilitate certain comparisons, or allow partials of unusual interest to mature. However, beyond step 3 most of the variables have been entered in their natural order, with the variable having the highest partial as of any given step entering at that step.

The last column, headed "$F (= T^2)$ to Remove" is mainly for statisticians. F and T (italicized) as used here are statistical measures, not to be confused with farm population and temperature, for which F and T are used as abbreviations elsewhere in the tables. Statistical F and statistical T are measures of significance. They are used with tables of F and T in looking up percentage levels of significance. In the significance tables, F and T are read in conjunction with "degrees of freedom," which is equal to the number of cases (forty-eight in these experiments) minus one, minus the number of variables held constant. For forty degrees of freedom (seven variables held constant) an F of 5.42 designates the .025 level of significance, 7.34 is the .01 level, and 12.61 is the .001 level. Forty-four or thirty-eight degrees of freedom are not appreciably different from forty when it comes to significance. In the "Comparative" combination in table 5.4, the F of 9.93 for the variable Y indicates that Y is significant at better than the .01 confidence level: its contribution to R and R^2 could be as large purely by chance only once in 100+ experiments.

"To Remove" in the F column heading means that the F values shown relate to the drop in R that would occur if the variable described were removed from the combination. Obviously this drop is the same as the increase in R that would result if the variable were the last to enter, that is, if all of the other variables in the combination preceded it. In other words, the F column treats each variable as though it were the last to enter, even if it actually entered first or second. If just one variable were removed from a combination, removing the one with the biggest F would cause the biggest drop in R (and R^2), and removing the one with the smallest F would bring the smallest drop. However, *the Fs are not in linear proportion to the change in R; F* goes up proportionately faster than R or R^2; if one F is ten times another, the first variable's contribution to R^2 might be only four or seven times the second's.

Another caveat: aside from their nonlinear proportionality, the F scores can be very misleading when two or more variables in a combination have considerable overlap (are highly intercorrelated). In this case dropping one has relatively little effect on R because the other is still around to represent whatever the variables represent. If there are two market variables of the same type in a combination, the drop in R that would result from removing one is less (F is smaller) than it would be if the variable removed had carried the full load for the market factor in question. To illustrate, when the first combination in table 4-5 was being constructed, MB X E had an F of 109.19 (not shown) after step 5. But when its twin, MB X VA, entered at step 6, the F value for MB X E plummeted to 15.93 (and then crept back up a little as the last three variables were added). One should therefore be extra cautious about using F values to judge the relative importance of variables when it appears that two or more of the variables are closely related. The Fs are shown primarily to establish the significance of the variables in the combinations, not to provide definitive answers about the relative importance of different influences.

Two to Four Variables

The best Rs obtainable for combinations of two, three, or four variables are shown in table 4-4. A "Comparative" combination showing a modified version of the best two-variable combination is also presented. The two-variable combinations are both extended to step 3 to give a better view of the competing influences and to permit additional comparisons. In all of the combinations, markets and climate immediately spring into prominence—exactly as the preceding simple and partial r's would lead us to expect. The extra variable in the best two-variable combination also gives tentative recognition to the threshold influence. The labor influence, in turn, is represented in both the third and fourth sets.

Best for Step 2.   Looking first at the set labeled "Best for Step 2," we find that two market variables—$(T - 9)Y$ and $E^{1.5}$, or demand and supply—can by themselves explain almost 90 percent of the variation in absolute growth; their R^2 is .887. This extremely impressive R^2 is not a product of markets alone, of course; it also involves a substantial contribution by climate via the market-climate interaction influence. The "Comparative" combination immediately below indicates that R^2 at step 2 would be about .09 lower if Y were not weighted by T - 9. But this tends to understate climate's contribution, because $E^{1.5}$ and T involve considerable duplication once demand is held constant.

In two other ways the "Comparative" set elaborates on the point that markets and climate interact. First, by way of review of evidence presented earlier, $(T - 9)Y$ has a simple r of +.75, compared to the r of +.92 for $(T - 9)^{2.5}$ $\times$ Y. Second, when Y and $E^{1.5}$ are jointly held constant, $(T - 9)^2 Y$ can still show a partial r of +.71. This is despite the fact that the entry of $E^{1.5}$ at step 2 duplicates T^2 to the extent that the latter's partial falls from +.47 to +.27. In other words, the +.71 partial for $(T - 9)^2 Y$ is not just an imitation of T^2, and it cannot be an imitation of Y (held constant); it is the product of interaction between T and Y.

When the best two-variable set is extended to three steps, the variable entering third is West-Metro $\times$ CP. This variable combines market and threshold elements. Markets is in charge at first: CP describes demand, while West-Metro describes both spatial isolation and lack of industry. But by the time $(T - 9)Y$ and $E^{1.5}$ have been controlled, the threshold element gains stature. It is impos-

Table 4–4

Multiple Correlations for 1947–63 Absolute Growth: Best and Comparative Combinations for Two to Four Variables

Step	Variable Entered	r or Partial r at Entry Step	R	R^2	$F (= T^2)$ to Remove
Best for Step 2					
1	$(T-9)Y$	+.75	.753	.567	76.20
2	$E^{1.5}$	−.86	.942	.887	50.41
3	West-Metro × CP	+.53	.959	.920	17.19
Comparative					
1	Y	+.42	.421	.177	9.93
2	$E^{1.5}$	−.87	.894	.799	20.48
3	$(T-9)^2 Y$	+.71	.950	.903	45.73
Best for Steps 3–4					
1	$(T-9)P$	+.73	.734	.539	194.84
2	$(T-9)^{1.5} \times Y$	+.77	.902	.814	350.36
3	$F^{1.5}$	+.80	.965	.931	84.63
4	$(T-9)/W$	+.53	.975	.951	16.68
Next Best Step 4					
1	$(T-9)P$	+.73	.734	.539	38.80
2	$(T-9)Y$	+.25	.753	.567	132.83
3	NE × E	−.90	.957	.916	298.97
4	$(F/M)^3$	+.60	.973	.947	24.29

Abbreviations: T = Temperature, Y = Income, E = Manufacturing Employment, West-Metro= Metropolitan West dummy (1 = Colorado, Utah, Arizona, Washington, Oregon, California; 0 = other 42 states), CP = Urban (City) Population, F = Farm Population, W = Wages, NE = Northeast dummy (1 = 13 Manufacturing Belt states plus northern New England; 0 = other 32 states), M = Square Miles

sible to say how much of the .033 contribution to R^2 is due to markets and how much due to thresholds. One important market variable, $(T-9)P$, has not been controlled. If entered first, it would cut West-Metro × CP's contribution to .018, which should be fairly close to the threshold amount. Another consideration suggesting that thresholds might deserve most of the credit is that CP by itself has a partial of −.03 at step 3—compared to +.53 for West-Metro × CP. Some western states have become a subset where CP—demand, development, or both—remains influential. The subset excludes the West-Rural states; for West × CP (which includes them) has a lower partial, +.52, and West-Rural × CP reads +.01.

If "Best for Step 2" were extended still another step to four steps, the next variable to enter would be F^2. Its step 4 partial of +.48 is barely higher than the +.47 partials reached by another labor supply variable, $(F/M)^4$. One of the labor supply variables has become significant at step 4 in the "Comparative" combination also: $(F/M)^4$ reads +.39. But in this instance the next variable to enter would be West-Metro $\times$ CP, with a partial r of +.51.

Best for Steps 3-4.   The highest Rs that can be reached using either three or four variables come from a combination that starts out with two temperature-weighted demand variables, $(T - 9)P$ and $(T - 9)^{1.5} \times Y$. With the P variable held constant at step 1, a residual demand attraction remains in states where Y is high relative to P, that is, where per capita income is high. The per capita income aspect of demand is described by the +.77 partial for $(T - 9)^{1.5} \times Y$. In this and other combinations using weighted versions of both P and Y, the P variable adopts a negative regression coefficient as soon as the Y variable and an industry variable enter; and if the P variable follows the others it enters with a negative partial. This could easily be misinterpreted by anyone overlooking the fact that Y is held constant. What it really means is that, when Y is held constant, growth is fastest where P is low *relative to* Y. P is low relative to Y where Y is high relative to P. Hence a negative partial for, say, $(T - 9)P$ when $(T - 9)Y$ is partialed out is equivalent to a positive partial for $(T - 9)Y$ when $(T - 9)P$ is held constant; these are alternative ways of describing per capita income. Either way, both variables must be interpreted as demand variables.

At step 3 the variable with the highest partial—the one shown entering the combination—is $F^{1.5}$. (Its nearest rival, other than close relatives, is an industry variable, NE $\times$ E, whose partial is -.72; $E^{1.5}$ reads -.67.) The fact that this labor supply variable is part of the best three-variable set is a good indication that labor is among the more important factors affecting manufacturing growth. The three variables combined have an R of .965 and an R^2 of .931; they account for 93 percent of the variation in absolute growth.

Step 4 introduces a second labor variable, $(T - 9)/W$. Its entry partial of +.53 is just a little ahead of the competing r's of -.49 for NE $\times$ E and +.48 for T. With $(T - 9)/W$ entered, the best four-variable combination includes two market variables—these carry most of the weight—and two labor variables. A third influence, climate, is represented as a weight in three of the four variables. The four variables are good for an R of .975 and an R^2 of .951. All but 5 percent of the variation in absolute growth is explained.

"Best for Steps 3-4" has no threshold variable. But if the combination is extended another step, West-Metro $\times$ $(CP/P)^3$ enters. Its partial is +.34, just a little above a +.32 partial reached by West-Metro alone. Combined with the first four variables, West-Metro $\times$ $(CP/P)^3$ increases R to .978 and R^2 to .956.

Next Best Step 4.   The fourth and last combination in table 4-4 is a different set of four variables that produce nearly as high an R at step 4 as the best combination. Steps 1 and 2 employ almost the same variables, but the temperature weight in the income variable has been reduced. This helps in two ways to "set up" an industry variable at step 3: it more adequately controls Y (gives it more weight), so that the original proxy relationship between E and Y is more effectively eliminated; and it minimizes the effect of the overlap between E and T that develops when demand is held constant.

The revised demand controls bring numerous industry variables to high significance levels. There are partials of $-.84$ for VA, $-.85$ for E, $-.88$ for $E^{1.5}$, $-.90$ for MB $\times$ E, and $-.90$ for NE $\times$ E. The variable incorporating the sixteen-state Northeast dummy (NE) is a shade better than the Manufacturing Belt version: NE $\times$ E enters at step 3. (Its nearest rival, other than close relatives, is West-Metro $\times$ CP, with an r of $+.84$. West-Metro $\times$ CP overlaps NE $\times$ E to the extent that both describe the lack of industry in some of the western states vis-à-vis the Northeast, but West-Metro $\times$ CP also has demand and threshold characteristics.) The entry of NE $\times$ E gives us a set of three market variables, two of them weighted by climate, that can explain about 92 percent of the variance.

NE $\times$ E sets up the labor supply variables. These could do no better at step 3 than a $+.08$ partial for $F^{1.5}$ and a $+.14$ partial for $(F/M)^4$. The problem evidently was that the eastward pull of labor supply was neutralized by the stronger westward pull of low supplies of manufactured goods. This conflict can also be viewed as overlap between overindustrialization (unfavorable) and high levels of surplus labor (favorable) in the East, including the Northeast. Thus with NE $\times$ E held constant, we get partials of $+.50$ for $F^{1.5}$ and $+.60$ for $(F/M)^3$, now a point better than $(F/M)^4$. (West-Metro $\times$ CP has fallen to $+.35$.) The resulting combination of three market variables plus a labor supply variable explains barely less than 95 percent of the variation in growth.

When this combination is extended, the fifth variable is the VA dummy (VA exceeds \$1 billion). Its entry partial is $+.36$. The dummy will be interpreted when it appears again under "Best for Steps 5-9."

Five to Ten Variables

Table 4-5 presents the two best combinations for five to ten variables. Through step 4 the two sets differ only in detail: both employ two temperature-weighted demand variables, an industry (supply) variable, and a labor supply variable. The principal differences are that the first set (*a*) gives more weight to climate, (*b*) places more emphasis on industrial oversupply in the Manufacturing Belt, and (*c*) uses $F^{1.5}$ instead of $(F/M)^4$ as the labor variable entering at step 4. Note, however, that both sets ultimately utilize both $F^{1.5}$ and $(F/M)^4$.

Best for Steps 5-9. Now let us concentrate on the first set of variables, the one beginning with $(T-9)^2 P$. The step 5 variable in this set is $(T-9)^2/W^2$,

Table 4-5
Multiple Correlations for 1947-63 Absolute Growth: Best Combinations for Five to Ten Variables

Step	Variable Entered	r or Partial r at Entry Step	R	R^2	$F(= T^2)$ to Remove
Best for Steps 5-9					
1	$(T-9)^2 P$	+.85	.854	.729	28.47
2	MB × E	−.42	.881	.776	30.30
3	$(T-9)^2 Y$	+.77	.954	.910	68.85
4	$F^{1.5}$	+.63	.972	.945	8.08
5	$(T-9)^2/W^2$	+.52	.980	.960	6.90
6	MB × VA	+.45	.984	.968	21.01
7	VA Dummy: VA > \$1 billion	+.30	.985	.970	9.72
8	$(F/M)^4$	+.35	.987	.974	5.97
9	West-Metro × $(CP/P)^4$	+.39	.989	.978	6.80
Best for Step 10					
1	$(T-9)P$	+.73	.733	.537	38.71
2	$E^{1.5}$	−.68	.868	.753	391.81
3	$(T-9)Y$	+.78	.950	.903	111.67
4	$(F/M)^4$	+.62	.970	.941	24.96
5	East × P/M	−.47	.977	.955	8.41
6	$F^{1.5}$	+.32	.979	.958	14.33
7	$(T-9)^2/W^2$	+.50	.984	.968	32.75
8	T	−.23	.985	.970	11.79
9	Y/M	+.31	.987	.974	6.52
10	$(F/P)^4$	−.49	.990	.980	11.50

Abbreviations: T = Temperature, P = Population, MB = Manufacturing Belt dummy (1 = Massachusetts, Rhode Island, Connecticut, New York, New Jersey, Pennsylvania, Delaware, Maryland, Ohio, Michigan, Indiana, Illinois, Wisconsin; 0 = other 35 states), E = Manufacturing Employment, Y = Income, F = Farm Population, W = Wages, VA = Manufacturing Value Added, M = Square Miles, West-Metro = Metropolitan West dummy (1 = Colorado, Utah, Arizona, Washington, Oregon, California; 0 = other 42 states), CP = Urban Population, East = dummy (1 = 37 easternmost states; 0 = 11 western states), T = Temperature

a wage variable that will become increasingly familiar as we move on to per capita and percentage growth. Its entry partial is a healthy +.52. We now have a five-variable combination with an R of .980 and an R^2 of .960. This combination includes three market and two labor variables. Three of the five variables are weighted by climate. Here is very strong evidence that three influences—markets, climate, and labor—control the absolute growth scene.

The step 6 variable, MB × VA, is valued at VA (value added) in the Manufacturing Belt states and at zero elsewhere. This variable is a counter-variable to MB X E. A counter-variable is one that starts out as a near-duplicate of another and suddenly reverses sign, becoming significant in the opposite direction, when the other variable is held constant. The sign reversal (negative to positive in this case) shows that the variable has undergone a change in character. What MB X VA originally stood for was the supply of manufactured goods, adjusted to give all states outside the Manufacturing Belt the minimum value. But MB X E has controlled that influence. What we are now looking at is situations within the Manufacturing Belt where VA is high or low *relative to* E, held constant.

MB X VA could represent (1) the ratio of capital to labor, with a low VA/E ratio—VA with E held constant—identifying textile states, (2) agglomeration, probably centering on the auto industry in Michigan and Ohio, or (3) residual demand, with VA being a proxy for Y. To investigate these possibilities another analysis of residuals was undertaken. This time the first five variables plus $(F/M)^4$ were partialed out—here MB X VA goes to +.49—to get "before" residuals; then MB X VA was added in as a seventh variable in the regression equation to get "after" residuals.

The findings are ambiguous but lean toward the textile theory. The two biggest error reductions were in Pennsylvania (-464) and Massachusetts (-281) and resulted from lower growth predictions. These states were the two biggest textile losers. Rhode Island, ranking third in textile losses, showed the third biggest error reduction (-77) for states where predicted growth was lowered. The textile theory therefore looks good. Agglomeration, in contrast, does poorly: Michigan and Ohio showed lower growth predictions and increased residuals (+8 and +50)—the opposite of what agglomeration calls for. The third possibility, residual demand, would probably lead to large reductions in predictive error at the western end of the Manufacturing Belt—in Illinois and Wisconsin, where demand is highest relative to supply. But Illinois' error increased (+263) due to lower predicted growth, and Wisconsin's was virtually unchanged.

The VA dummy, designed to represent agglomeration, enters at step 7. It shows a partial of only +.30, barely significant, but this becomes +.45 if the variable is held back until step 9. The dummy identifies eighteen states, all states where VA exceeds $1 billion. Included from outside the Manufacturing Belt are Virginia, North Carolina, Georgia, Minnesota, Missouri, Texas, and California. To see whether the VA dummy gets its strength inside or outside of the Manufacturing Belt, residuals were again analyzed. The first six variables plus $(F/M)^4$ were held constant—this sends the dummy to +.37—for the "before" residuals. The "after" figures showed substantial error reductions only in Connecticut (-146), Georgia (-128), Iowa (-117), and Minnesota (-110). The three industrialized states—Connecticut, Georgia, and Minnesota—improved through increases in predicted growth; Iowa, previously overestimated, involved a decrease.

Industry's preference for Minnesota (Twin Cities) over Iowa tentatively supports an agglomeration interpretation. But, given the fact that three of the four states are outside the Manufacturing Belt, this is not primarily agglomeration in the traditional sense. Rather, the attraction appears as a pull exerted by some of the more developed states outside the Manufacturing Belt. Moreover, the VA dummy could almost as easily be given a demand interpretation: all eighteen "dummied in" states have income levels above \$3.5 billion. Metropolitan area markets could be involved.

The eighth variable, $(F/M)^4$, has been adequately discussed elsewhere; we can proceed directly to the ninth, West-Metro $\times$ $(CP/P)^4$. The West-Metro dummy is the basic ingredient in the weighted variable; the dummy alone stands at +.34 at step 9, compared to +.39 for West-Metro $\times$ $(CP/P)^4$. Since the preceding variables provide extensive control over market influences, it is reasonably safe to give this variable a threshold interpretation. It shows faster residual growth in the six most developed of the eleven least developed states. The $(CP/P)^4$ appendage on the weighted variable emphasizes thresholds by giving additional weight to the most developed—most urbanized—states within the West-Metro group. West-Metro $\times$ $(CP/P)^4$ achieves its biggest cuts in residual growth in the previously underestimated states of Colorado, Washington, and Utah.

The "Best for Steps 5–9" combination runs out of significant variables after step 9. At this point R has climbed to .989 and R^2 to .978; about 98 percent of the variation in absolute growth has been explained.

Best for Step 10. The analysis of "Best for Step 10" begins at step 5, where this and the preceding combination part company. At step 5 East $\times$ P/M enters with a partial of –.47. There is no significant difference between this variable and P/M itself; both reach –.47, with East $\times$ P/M scoring .002 higher. The weighted version may be slightly more realistic in refusing to give a bigger advantage to the West-Rural states vis-à-vis the West-Metro. But for all practical purposes East $\times$ P/M = P/M, as their +.998 intercorrelation shows. As to interpretation, it is reasonably clear that P/M operates here as it operates with per capita and percentage growth—as a market variable. It says that, once the principal absolute variables are controlled, the least developed states show the fastest growth.

Steps 6 and 7 bring in two more labor variables, $F^{1.5}$ and $(T - 9)^2/W^2$. $F^{1.5}$ doesn't look very significant at +.32, but this is because $(F/M)^4$ has stolen some of its thunder. Entered last it climbs back to +.53; entered ninth, ahead of $(F/M)^4$, it attains a partial r of +.71. For its part, $(T - 9)^2/W^2$ will go to +.69 if held back until step 10. These highly significant partials and the fact that the first seven variables include three labor variables provide a solid basis for the conclusion that labor is a significant influence.

The seventh variable, T, looks insignificant because it has been entered out of turn to allow the partial for a variable of greater interest, $(F/P)^4$, to ripen;

$(F/P)^4$ is really ahead at this point with a partial $-.29$. Entered last, T goes to $-.49$, which is why it shows about the same F (significance) value as $(F/P)^4$ in the last column. If we forgot that three temperature-weighted variables have already been controlled, we could easily misinterpret this negative partial: it would seem to refute the idea that industry likes warm climates. But it is only because climate is already largely under control that T can show a negative partial: T *never* becomes negative except in some instances where one or more climate-weighted variables have been partialed out.

What, then, does T represent? It still represents temperature (climate). What we see is a correction for curvilinearity in the relationship between temperature and growth. It often happens that two versions of the same variable will enter a combination with opposite signs in situations where no proxy relationship to another variable is conceivable and where the one with the "wrong" sign, though significant, is much less significant than the one with the right sign—$(T - 9)Y$ in this case. These seemingly spurious r's are not really spurious; they are an indirect way of adjusting for curvilinear correlation. Two variables do the work of one; a large addition is tempered by a small subtraction based on a modified pattern.

Numerous experiments with absolute, per capita, and percentage growth show that when T is grouped with one of the more powerful temperature-weighted market variables it becomes negative. This happens because T – 9, when used as a weight, penalizes the coldest states too severely: the -9 places an extremely heavy growth penalty on the two coldest states, Minnesota and North Dakota, when used in variables such as $(T - 9)Y$. Thus, when T enters the regression equation (accompanied by a large constant), the two biggest reductions in residual growth result from higher predictions for Minnesota and North Dakota.

At step 9, the $+.31$ partial for Y/M is also deceptive—in two respects. First, as to magnitude, it understates the variable's significance: Y/M moves on up to $+.39$ if entered last. Second, regarding sign, Y/M is positive only because P/M has been partialed out. This transforms Y/M into a counter-variable measuring per capita income: the positive partial describes faster residual growth where Y is high relative to P. Of course, $(T - 9)Y$ and $(T - 9)P$, taken together, already provide a large measure of control over the Y/P relationship. But, by giving more weight to P and Y in the warmer states, the temperature-weighted demand variables are apparently a little imprecise in controlling Y/P in the northern states. Thus the biggest reductions in unexplained growth achieved by Y/M are in five northern states: reduced residuals result from higher growth estimates for Connecticut, New Jersey, and Washington and lower growth estimates for West Virginia and Massachusetts.

Step 10 introduces an exponential version of farm population percentage, $(F/P)^4$. This and other very similar rural-urban mix variables, such as $1/(CP/P)$ and F/CP, regularly become significant at about step 8 or 9 in the best combinations for all three measures of growth. These variables—$(F/P)^4$, $1/(CP/P)$, and F/CP—all have the effect of magnifying the highest farm population percentages and leveling off the highest urban percentages. It is likely, therefore, that the influence detected is something that deters growth in the most rural states, as opposed to something that stimulates growth in extremely urbanized states. The possibilities include (1) lack of suitable urban locations, metropolitan areas in particular, for industry to locate in, (2) lack of agglomeration economies and urban amenities, and (3) low levels of consumer demand associated with rural poverty and not adequately reflected in the income variables.

Another analysis of residuals provides clues. By far the biggest improvement in the regression estimates of growth occurs in Mississippi. Mississippi has not only the highest farm population percentage but the highest black population percentage and the lowest median family income in the nation. This suggests that $(F/P)^4$ picks up a qualitative aspect of consumer demand. It may be that southern rural poverty—predominantly but not exclusively black poverty—gives its victims so little income that the proportion spent on manufactured goods is unusually low. In this case, the population and income variables would miss certain nuances of demand.

But poverty may not be the whole story. The biggest reductions in unexplained growth after Mississippi (–370) are in North Dakota (–168), Minnesota (–144), Georgia (–96), and South Dakota (–77). Mississippi, North Dakota, and South Dakota improve via decreases in the previous growth estimates; Minnesota and Georgia improve via increases (growth previously underestimated). This begins to look like a matter of urban orientation. Indeed, Minnesota (Twin Cities) and Georgia (Atlanta) we recall as states that responded strongly to the VA dummy used in the previous combination. Whereas before we saw what was in effect a diversion of industry to Minnesota from the neighboring state of Iowa, we now see diversion from the neighboring states of North and South Dakota. Rural poverty could still be a factor in the Dakotas— median income is lower than in surrounding states—but something broader is suggested: states with major metropolitan areas seem to have a special attraction.

After ten steps, the "Best for Step 10" combination is still not ready to quit: West-Metro $\times$ CP is in the wings with a partial of +.40. But R is up to .990 and R^2 has reached .980; it seems rather pointless to go on. Let us simply say, then, that the ten variables listed in the table can explain 98 percent of the variation in absolute growth.

Comparative Ratings

The rank order of importance of the several factors influencing absolute growth and the percentage contributions of these factors to variations in growth can be judged by (1) the simple r's for different variables, (2) partial

r's, viewed in conjunction with the extent of control required for latent partials to mature, (3) the variables that participate in the best Rs, (4) the statistical F (significance) values for these variables, and (5) their individual contributions to R^2 under varying entry orders.

These criteria put markets and climate far ahead as the dominant locational influences—with markets a strong first. Only market and climate variables have significant simple r's, except where proxy representation of markets (as with M) is evident. Only market and climate variables can achieve partial r's significant at the 1 percent level when just one or two variables are held constant. The best two-variable R comes from two market variables, one of them weighted by climate. The two variables—$(T - 9)Y$ and $E^{1.5}$—have an R^2 of .887, and this involves little if any duplication of other influences. In the best ten-variable set we find five market variables, two of them weighted by climate, plus temperature and a temperature-weighted wage variable. The two or three highest F values under all of the best Rs belong to markets and climate. The estimating procedure described in chapter 2 has markets explaining 55 to 75 percent of the variation in absolute growth. Climate accounts for 14 to 28 percent.

Labor ranks third. The labor variables are not very significant until at least two and preferably three market or market-climate variables are controlled. They become significant, however, when we break the link between unfavorable labor conditions and favorable conditions of demand and spatial isolation. Three labor variables—$F^{1.5}$, $(F/M)^4$, and $(T - 9)^2/W^2$—are among the first seven in the best ten-variable combination. Labor explains 3 to 9 percent of the variation in absolute growth.

Despite the lack of correlation evidence, we can judge that resources belongs in fourth place. The benchmark method of estimating (chapter 2) gives resources two-thirds as much as the labor estimate—about 4 percent. The residual method credits resources with the 2 percent unexplained variance from the best ten-variable R plus small transfers from some preliminary climate and labor estimates—again 4 percent. The range is 1 to 8 percent.

The threshold influence is weak relative to absolute growth, ranking fifth. It registers in higher partials for the West-Metro dummy vis-à-vis West-Rural. It also shows up in the contributions of West-Metro $\times$ CP and West-Metro $\times$ $(CP/P)^4$ to some of the best Rs. The threshold influence can explain 1 to 5 percent of the variation in absolute growth.

The urban attraction is the only other influence with significant r's. Not observable until at least four variables are held constant, it is picked up by the VA dummy and $(F/P)^4$. Analyses of residuals show both variables detecting something that leads industry to eschew rural states and seek urban states *outside the Manufacturing Belt*. Also, both variables point to strong residual growth in Georgia (Atlanta) and Minnesota (Twin Cities), among other places. The variables thus appear to be similar in substance. This substance explains 0+ to 4 percent of the variance.

Let us try to bring everything into perspective by focusing on the somewhat fuzzy central tendencies. This obviously involves false precision, but the qualifications and reservations have had their day: it is time to do what must be done to afford clear comparisons. As nearly as one can judge, markets accounts for 65 percent, climate for 21 percent, labor for 6 percent, resources for 4 percent, thresholds for 3 percent, and urban attraction for 1 percent of the variation in absolute growth. There is no evidence that new industry gravitates to the Manufacturing Belt, although agglomeration attractions elsewhere are probably part of the urban attraction.

5 Per Capita Growth: Partial and Multiple Correlations

The second dependent variable is 1947–63 per capita growth in manufacturing employment: absolute growth divided by 1950 population. The partial and multiple correlations for per capita growth support conclusions very similar to those reached with absolute growth. At the same time, the new findings are sharper and more conclusive in matters of detail. Markets, climate, and labor still rank one, two, three; and thresholds, resources, and the urban attraction still bring up the rear. Also, there is fresh evidence of the market-climate and wage-climate interaction effects. But now the per capita income and spatial aspects of markets are better defined. The threshold influence becomes quite prominent and moves ahead of resources to the fourth-ranked position. The urban attraction also claims a larger share of growth than before and thereby confirms its identity as an influence, whatever its exact substance might be.

Partial Correlations

As in the preceding chapter the partial correlation findings will be summarized under three headings: minimal controls (one or two variables held constant), moderate controls (two or three variables held constant), and strong controls (three to six variables held constant). Minimal controls cannot uncover the secondary influences, except for giving us a patchy view of labor and thresholds. But they do bring out all sides of the market influence and confirm that neither markets nor climate is a proxy for the other. Moderate controls allow us to see the labor influence clearly and the threshold influence a little better than before. Strong controls generate some formidable partial r's for a variety of labor and threshold variables and, in addition, bring the urban attraction into view.

Minimal Controls

Table 5-1 summarizes the partial correlations resulting from six approaches to minimal controls. The controls include the best climate variable (T), the best demand variable (Y/P), one of the better industry variables (P/M), the best industry and overall market variable (E/M), a combination of the best climate and the best market variable (T and E/M), and the best temperature-weighted market variable—$(T - 9)^{1.5} \times (Y^{0.8}/P)$.

Table 5–1
Partial Correlations of Selected Variables with 1947–63 Per Capita Growth: Minimal Controls (One or Two Variables Held Constant)

Selected Independent Variables	Simple r with Growth	Variables Held Constant ("Partialed Out")					
		T	Y/P	P/M	E/M	T E/M	T(Y^0.8/P)
(MULTIPLE R)		(.465)	(.022)	(.411)	(.449)	(.617)	(.589)
Demand							
CP/P	-.08	-.09	-.14	+.29	+.32	+.32	-.20
Y/P	+.02	+.21	....	+.22	+.25	+.48	+.02
Y/M	-.37	-.38	-.43	+.35	+.37	+.37	-.43
$(T-9)^{1.5} \times (Y^{0.8}/P)$	+.59	+.42	+.59	+.63	+.62	+.49	....
Industry							
$(E/P)^3$	-.45	-.40	-.51	-.22	-.14	-.01	-.41
$(E/Y)^3$	-.44	-.43	-.44	-.26	-.21	-.19	-.39
$(E/M)^3$	-.46	-.49	-.50[a]	-.27[a]	....	....	-.56
$(P/M)^2$	-.43	-.45	-.46	....	+.19[a]	+.06[a]	-.50
Spatial							
Lg	+.37	+.40	+.37	+.18	+.18	+.21	+.31
$(50 - Lat)(Lg - 65)^3$	+.49	+.43	+.49	+.40	+.41	+.34	+.29
Other							
T	+.47	....	+.50	+.49	+.47	....	-.11
West-Rural Dummy	-.06	+.00	-.07	-.17	-.16	-.10	-.11
West-Metro Dummy	+.47	+.45	+.47	+.43	+.44	+.43	+.38
West-Metro × $(CP/P)^3$	+.51	+.47	+.51	+.49	+.49	+.47	+.43
MB Dummy	-.32	-.26	-.41	-.03	-.00	+.10	-.28

[a]This partial r is for E/M or P/M rather than $(E/M)^3$ or $(P/M)^2$.

Abbreviations: T = Temperature, Y = Income, P = Population, M = Square Miles, E = Manufacturing Employment, $T(Y^{0.8}/P) = (T - 9) \times (Y^{0.8}/P)$, $(T - 9)^{1.5} \times (Y^{0.8}/P)$, CP = Urban (City) Population, Lg = Longitude, Lat = Latitude, West-Rural = 5 least developed western states, West-Metro = 6 most developed western states, MB = Manufacturing Belt dummy (13 states)

Demand.   Under the demand heading, CP/P and Y/P are closely related, having a +.75 intercorrelation. Since urban consumers have generally higher incomes, it is not unexpected that the two variables tend to become significant in the same situations. In their simple r's, both are close to zero. Part of the problem is that low levels of urbanization and low per capita incomes (both unfavorable) overlap warm climate (favorable) in the South. A further problem is that, in the Manufacturing Belt, high urbanization and income (favorable) coincide with a high degree of industrialization (unfavorable). When the first conflict is removed by controlling T (first control column), Y/P moves up to +.21—not yet significant but getting there. Alternatively, when either P/M or E/M is controlled to remove the industrialization conflict, Y/P again approaches significance and CP/P actually achieves significant partials of +.29 and +.32. Appropriately, the higher partial (+.32) accompanies the stronger of the two industrial control variables (E/M).

With two conflicts to deal with, a single control variable does not do an adequate job. But when both T and E/M are partialed out at the same time, Y/P moves well beyond the 1 percent confidence level to +.48. CP/P remains at +.32, midway between the 1 and 5 percent confidence levels. Once the adverse intercorrelations are neutralized, we see what we previously saw in different perspective with absolute growth: faster growth in states with the highest levels of consumer demand. It might be added that there is still another adverse relationship to be cleared away—wages, which are high (unfavorable) where CP/P and Y/P are high.

Another warning about spurious correlation: the negative partial r for CP/P in the last column is deceiving. Here temperature-weighted per capita income is held constant. This undermines the ability of CP/P to represent demand. It becomes a proxy for something new: the high levels of industrialization (and to some extent the high wages) found in the Manufacturing Belt. The -.20 partial for CP/P echoes the one of -.56 for (E/M)[3].

The third "demand" variable is not really a demand variable until industry is held constant. Y/M (income per square mile) initially describes the same thing as E/M and P/M, namely, the degree of developmental density and the associated degree of industrialization. Thus in every column where neither P/M nor E/M is controlled, Y/M shows significantly negative partials—but never as negative as those for P/M and E/M. When P/M is held constant, however, Y/M describes the relationship between Y and P, or Y/P. P/M has largely controlled relative industrialization, allowing the effect of high per capita income to be seen. The +.35 partial for Y/M says that growth is faster where income is high *relative to* population and industry. In the fourth control column, E/M gives slightly better control over industry, and Y/M moves up to +.37: growth is faster where demand (Y) is high *relative to* supply (E). Y/M's partial can be pushed to +.49 by holding constant both P/M and the labor supply variable, (F/M)[3]. (The surplus labor attraction, associated with low income, dims the stimulus of high income.)

The fourth demand variable, $(T - 9)^{1.5} \times (Y^{0.8}/P)$, brings us the latest evidence of interaction between markets and climate. This variable, easily recognized as an adjusted version of $(T - 9) \times Y/P$, will be recalled from chapter 3 as the variable with the highest simple r (+.59) vis-à-vis per capita growth. The similarity of this finding to the finding that $(T - 9)^{2.5} \times Y$ is the highest variable vis-à-vis absolute growth requires no elaboration. Even before we get to partial r's, interaction is visible in the fact that weighted Y/P has a higher simple r (+.59) than its best constituent, T (+.47). The evidence is expanded in the first control column, where T is held constant. Here $(T - 9)^{1.5} \times (Y^{0.8}/P)$ drops only to +.42, well above the +.21 partial for unweighted Y/P. The alternative control, Y/P, leaves the weighted variable with a partial of +.59. In all of the remaining columns, $(T - 9)^{1.5} \times (Y^{0.8}/P)$ maintains high partials. It mimics Y/P by going above its original level (to +.63 and +.62) when P/M and E/M are held constant. Interpreting, industry grows faster where per capita income is high, provided that the climate is not unfavorable.

Industry. As we move to the supply side of markets, the term "industry" fits better than "supply": unlike E and $E^{1.5}$, the principal supply variables examined under absolute growth, the variables under the industry heading in table 5-1 describe not only the relative level of manufacturing but the supply-demand relationship. All four industry variables—$(E/P)^3$, $(E/Y)^3$, $(E/M)^3$, and $(P/M)^2$—are lowest where relatively wide gaps exist between supply and demand. Population density (P/M), for example, gets progressively lower as we go from Northeast to South to West, just as manufacturing employment per capita (E/P) does.

For a preview of the behavior of the new industry variables, we can recall that with absolute growth E went to -.76 and $E^{1.5}$ to -.87 when Y was held constant: growth was far greater where supply was low relative to demand. Although E has been replaced by relative variables in table 5-1, it is worth mentioning what it can do in a similar test with per capita growth. With Y held constant, E goes to -.49. These findings prepare us for significantly negative partials from the new industry variables.

The four industry variables—$(E/P)^3$, $(E/Y)^3$, $(E/M)^3$, and $(P/M)^2$—are closely related. Their intercorrelations, adjusted for curvilinear correlation, are extremely high: log E/M shows r's of +.98 with log P/M, +.93 with log E/P, and +.91 with log E/Y. (This is what Fuchs failed to recognize in his study, criticized in chapter 1, when he rejected the market hypothesis and interpreted P/M as a measure of land available for factories.) We therefore find that when P/M or E/M is held constant, the others show sharp drops in their partials. But our immediate concern is with the first, second, and last control columns in table 5-1. In column one, holding T constant has almost no effect: the supply-demand ratios go down slightly and the density variables up slightly. This tells us that climate and industry, which produce the highest simple r's, are independent of each other—are not proxies. Columns two and six hold Y/P, unweighted or weighted, constant. Since $(E/Y)^3$ reflects Y/P, it doesn't respond; but the other industry variables generally do. E/M climbs to -.50 with Y/P controlled, and $(E/M)^3$ gets to -.56 when $(T - 9)^{1.5} \times (Y^{0.8}/P)$ is held constant. In other words, when states are equal in terms of relative demand, those that are relatively lowest in supply have the highest growth rates.

Another point of some interest has to do with the relationships between E/M, P/M, and Y/M, all of which will appear in the best multiple correlation combinations. They start out describing essentially the same thing—developmental density. But, we have seen, when either E/M or P/M is controlled, Y/M becomes a demand variable describing either Y/E or Y/P. P/M also becomes a demand variable when E/M is held constant, in which case P/M becomes positive (+.19), describing faster growth where demand (P) is high relative to supply (E). E/M, in turn, firmly establishes itself as the purest industrialization variable among the three by retaining an almost-significant negative partial of -.27 when P/M is controlled: residual growth remains higher where E is low relative to P. A more complete description of the relationships between E/M, P/M, and Y/M is as follows:

| | Variables Held Constant | | | | | |
	E/M	P/M	Y/M	P/M E/M	Y/M E/M	Y/M P/M
E/M	....	-.27	-.45	....	....	-.32
P/M	+.19	....	-.40	....	-.23	....
Y/M	+.37	+.35	....	+.39	....	....

Note that E/M is always negative, no matter which of its companions is partialed out: growth is faster where E is low relative to P or Y, especially Y. P/M is generally negative but becomes positive when describing the relationship between E and P. When Y/M is used to control demand, though, the relationship between Y and P takes hold: growth is faster where Y/P is high, that is, where P is low relative to Y.

Spatial Isolation.   With the spatial variables we are still looking at relative industrialization: the western states (which have the highest longitudes) are the least industrialized and have the widest gaps between supply and demand. But we are also looking at something else, namely, the increasing transport costs eastern manufacturers must pay to compete in western markets. The transport aspect of spatial isolation registered poorly with absolute growth. This poor showing resulted because population and income are dominant where absolute growth is concerned: they pull growth away from the West and toward the East, particularly the Northeast. Per capita growth neutralizes the counter-attraction of population by, in effect, holding population constant. Therefore, we can anticipate that spatial isolation will provide better evidence of significance with per capita growth than it did with absolute growth.

Looking first at the simplest spatial variable, Lg, we find it significantly positive at the outset (+.37) and consistently positive in all control situations. With T partialed out, Lg is just a little stronger than originally; it climbs to +.40. Lg remains at +.37 when Y/P is controlled instead. Controlling the industry variables does make a difference, for Lg loses the proxy boost it was getting from industry. Nevertheless, Lg remains positive and well above zero when either P/M or E/M is held constant. It would be significantly positive were it not for the eastward pull of low wages. Thus, when we get to table 5-2, we shall see Lg climbing back to +.29 (significant) when $(T - 9)/W$ is partialed out in addition to E/M. It might be added that Lg developes a partial r of +.45 when $(T - 9)/W$ alone is controlled and one of +.42 when $1/W^2$ is controlled (not shown).

The developmental contour variable, $(50 - Lat)(Lg - 65)^3$, describes distance contour lines rippling out from the Northeast and representing (a) progressively lower levels of industrialization and (b) progressively higher transport costs. Since this variable gets some of its strength from climate, represented by $50 - Lat$, its r dips from +.49 to +.43 when T is controlled. It is also, in part, a proxy for industry; hence it falls to +.41 when E/M is controlled. Yet when T and E/M are controlled simultaneously, depriving the spatial variable of both proxy supports, it remains significant with a partial of +.34. As with Lg, this partial is handicapped by the adverse intercorrelation between Lg and wages. If the control combination is changed to $(T - 9)/W$ and E/M, the contour variable snaps back to +.43. Controlling $(T - 9)/W$ alone fixes the partial at +.50; controlling $1/W^2$ makes it +.53. This variety of positive r's supports the hypothesis that isolation from the Manufacturing Belt fosters growth.

Climate. The already-abundant evidence that climate is significant becomes even more abundant when we examine the climate findings in table 5-1. As a preliminary point, we have seen that the weighted per capita income variable— $(T - 9)^{1.5} \times (Y^{0.8}/P)$—offers further evidence of the market-climate interaction effect. This of course implies that climate is an influence. But our main concern at the moment is to find out whether the climate influence is an illusion created by a proxy relationship to markets. Why markets? Because markets is the only influence strong enough (if assisted by something else) to pull T up to its simple r of +.47.

Table 5-1 now provides new evidence that neither markets nor climate depends on the other for significance. T moves from its simple r of +.47 to +.50 when Y/P is controlled and to +.49 when P/M is controlled; it stays at +.47 when E/M is controlled. Holding $(E/P)^3$ constant lowers T just a little, to +.42

(not shown)—because Y/P becomes almost significant (+.27), and the climate stimulus is slightly offset by low income in the South. This last development underscores the need to control both demand and supply to adequately isolate climate from markets. Double control makes quite a difference: T goes to +.53 with $(E/P)^3$ *and* Y/P controlled, to +.60 with E/M and Y/P controlled, to +.62 with P/M and Y/P controlled, and to +.65 with P/M and Y/M controlled. We cannot doubt that climate walks unaided by markets.

At the risk of overkill, it might be wise to say just a few words about the link between climate and wages—lest there remain a lingering suspicion that climate somehow gets much of its strength from low wages in the South. With W held constant, T has a partial of +.49, two points above its simple *r*. If W and E/M are simultaneously held constant, T's partial edges up to +.50. The fact is that the wage influence is still latent and could not possibly explain T's significant partials.

Other Influences.   The minimal controls used in table 5-1 yield nothing more significant for the labor variables than partials of −.12 for $\sqrt{U}$ (when P/M or E/M is held constant). However, if space had permitted, two simple controls that do create significant labor partials could have been shown.

	Simple r with Growth	Lg	$(50 - Lat)(Lg - 65)^3$
		Variables Held Constant	
$1/W^2$	+.03	+.21	+.24
$1/U^2$	+.25	+.34	+.36
$(F/M)^3$	+.14	+.31	+.37

Labor, which is an attraction only in the South, exerts an eastward pull on industry; but markets pull to the West. The market influence is far stronger; it hides the labor influence. But either of the two spatial variables can neutralize the East-West clash. Unionization and labor supply—$1/U^2$ and $(F/M)^3$—both become significant at the 1 percent level. The wage influence is still obscured by two forces: (1) per capita income, which is high (favorable) where wages are high (unfavorable) and (2) industrialization, which is low in the West (favorable), where wages are high.

The threshold influence also begins to solidify under simple controls. The contrast between the simple *r*'s of +.47 for the West-Metro dummy and −.06 for the West-Rural dummy are supported by comparably disparate *r*'s in every column; the six more developed western states show significantly faster growth than the five least developed states. The contrast is even greater when the West-

Metro states are weighted by degree of urbanization; West-Metro $\times$ $(CP/P)^3$ shows this. West-Metro's readings, though, are helped by the spatial facet of markets. Climate (California, Arizona) also helps West-Metro. Alternative controls give these results:

		Variables Held Constant	
		T	
	Lg	Lg	$(50 - Lat)(Lg - 65)^3$
West-Rural	$-.28$	$-.23$	$-.30$
West-Metro	$+.33$	$+.28$	$+.23$
West-Metro $\times$ $(CP/P)^3$	$+.39$	$+.33$	$+.26$

What we are starting to see is significantly faster residual growth in the West-Metro states accompanied by significantly slower growth in the West-Rural states. Cut loose from the stimulus of spatial isolation (which includes part of the supply-demand stimulus), the West-Rural states are in trouble. The residual growth is concentrated in the more developed western states and, moreover, tends to favor the most urbanized of these.

The agglomeration hypothesis is tested by the MB (Manufacturing Belt) dummy, valued at one in thirteen northeastern and Great Lakes states. MB fails to develop the positive r's needed to support the idea that established industry attracts new industry to the Manufacturing Belt. In fact, the r's for MB are almost always negative. About the only time MB becomes positive is when Y/P is not controlled and develops much higher positive r's; MB becomes a proxy for Y/P, high in the Manufacturing Belt. Note in control columns one, three, four, and five how MB's partials follow Y/P's, becoming less negative every time Y/P becomes more positive. The $+.10$ for MB in column five is a faint echo of the $+.48$ for Y/P. Also note that when Y/P is controlled, MB sinks to $-.41$—which reflects MB's intercorrelations of $-.82$ with $(E/M)^3$ and $-.83$ with $(E/P)^3$. It seems that the Manufacturing Belt, as an oversupplied market, repels rather than attracts new firms.

Moderate Controls

Moderate controls holding two or three variables constant at once provide additional evidence that markets and climate are significant. Such controls also bring labor into prominence and add to the growing evidence of a threshold factor. Table 5–2 displays the most effective moderate control combinations tried. Wages, per capita income, industrialization, and longitude are well represented among the controls: these forces interfere with each other, obscuring our view of them.

Demand.   Consumer demand, when described in terms of urbanization (CP/P) or per capita income (Y/P), is hard to detect as an influence. As said before, three conflicts interfere: the high income states of the Manufacturing Belt suffer from (1) a relative excess of industry, (2) harsh winters, and (3) high wages—and the high income states of the West also have high wages. We saw in table 5-1 that Y/P therefore moves from a simple r of +.02 to partials of +.25 with E/M controlled, +.21 with T controlled, and +.48 with E/M and T jointly controlled. What happens when a wage variable gets into the act?

In the first column of table 5-2 an industry variable and a temperature-weighted wage variable—E/M and (T - 9)/W—are held constant. Controlling just these two variables sends Y/P on up to +.58; CP/P climbs to +.41. If temperature is left out and the control set is changed to E/M and $1/W^2$ (not shown), the partials become +.39 for Y/P (compared to +.25 when just E/M is controlled) and +.41 for CP/P. If temperature is now reintroduced as a third control—E/M, $1/W^2$, and T held constant—Y/P goes to +.54 and CP/P to +.28 (not shown). These partials, incidentally, are not contradicted by the -.40 r for CP/P in the second column: there Y/P is held constant and CP/P becomes a proxy for the industry variables.

These findings, taken in conjunction with earlier findings and with the logical theoretical connection between demand and growth, justify a firm conclusion: *ceteris paribus*, high per capita income and urbanization encourage manufacturing growth. Urbanization is the weaker of the two stimuli and works largely through its effect on per capita income. But evidence of a residual urbanization stimulus remaining after Y/P is controlled—we will get to this shortly—suggests something extra. Very likely the more urbanized states are secondarily attractive as regional market centroids; they carry the demand centers of gravity; the consumers are more concentrated and accessible, usually because of the existence of major metropolitan areas. Proximity to intermediate (industrial) markets found in urban states could also be a factor. So could rapid population growth in urban areas, external economies, and urban amenities.

All five control columns provide evidence that markets and climate interact. In each column the weighted per capita income variable, $(T - 9)^{1.5} \times (Y^{0.8}/P)$, has partials exceeding the 1 percent significance level (±.37 when two variables are held constant). These partials reach +.67 and +.64 in the third and fifth columns, despite control of income variables. Although the +.67 partial leans heavily on a +.65 partial for T, $(T - 9)^{1.5} \times (Y^{0.8}/P)$ can still reach +.25 if T is also partialed out. And the only reason it is this low is that labor supply and the threshold factor are becoming significant: high per capita income tends to describe shortages of unskilled labor and (because incomes are high in the West, where thresholds operate) subthreshold status. This problem is overcome by adding $(F/M)^3$ and $1/(E/M)$ to the control set. With five variables thus controlled, $(T - 9)^{1.5} \times (Y^{0.8}/P)$ climbs back to +.56—despite direct control of T and indirect control of Y/P.

Table 5-2
Partial Correlations of Selected Variables with 1947–63 Per Capita Growth: Moderate Controls (Two or Three Variables Held Constant)

Selected Independent Variables	Simple r with Growth	Variables Held Constant ("Partialed Out")				
		E/M $(T-9)/w$	Y/P $(T-9)/w$	Y/M P/M	Y/P Lg	$(E/M)^3$ Y/P Lg
(MULTIPLE R)		(.568)	(.478)	(.523)	(.369)	(.521)
Demand						
CP/P	−.08	+.41	−.40	+.15	−.00	+.17
Y/P	+.02	+.58	. . . .	−.04	. . . .	. . . .
$(T-9)^{1.5} \times (Y^{0.8}/P)$	+.59	+.54	+.40	+.67	+.56	+.64
Industry						
$(E/P)^3$	−.45	−.04	−.58	−.29	−.37	−.19
E/M	−.45	. . . .	−.65	−.32	−.38	−.04
Lg	+.37	+.29	+.46	+.08	. . . .	. . . .
Labor						
$1/W^2$	+.03	−.31	−.13	+.23	+.30	+.40
$1/U^2$	+.25	+.02	+.16	+.32	+.37	+.37
$(F/M)^3$	+.14	−.06	+.01	+.39	+.34	+.31
Other						
T	+.47	+.34	+.17	+.65	+.51	+.58
West-Rural Dummy	−.06	−.09	−.02	−.26	−.28	−.29
West-Metro Dummy	+.47	+.49	+.49	+.40	+.34	+.42
West-Metro $\times (CP/P)^3$	+.51	+.53	+.50	+.46	+.40	+.47
MB Dummy	−.32	+.34	−.62	−.15	−.31	+.03

Abbreviations: T = Temperature, W = Wages, E = Manufacturing Employment, M = Square Miles, Y = Income, P = Population, Lg = Longitude, CP = Urban (City) Population, U = Unionization, F = Farm Population, West-Rural = 5 least developed states, West-Metro = 6 most developed western states, MB = Manufacturing Belt dummy (13 states).

Industry. The industry variables are by now so well established that it hardly seems necessary to develop further evidence. But we have not yet heard the full story. Just as three other influences interfere with the demand influence, so do three other influences interfere with the industry influence. First, demand interferes: there is a limited but definite tendency for supply and demand to go up and down together, and this weakens the ability of the industry variables to describe the *relationship* of supply to demand. Second, wage levels interfere: in the West, generally high wage levels (unfavorable) are connected with low levels of industrialization (favorable). Third, climate interferes to a very limited extent: although the West is more or less uniformly lacking in industry, climate contrasts between the northern and southern parts of the West create some disproportionality between industry levels and growth.

By holding demand, wages, and climate constant, we can get a truer idea of the relationship between growth and industrialization. We have already seen that, when Y/P (demand) is held constant, E/M moves from its simple r of $-.45$ to a partial of $-.50$ (table 5-1). If Y/P and $1/W^2$ are both held constant, E/M continues to $-.56$ (not shown). Alternatively, if Y/P and T are jointly controlled, E/M goes to $-.60$ (not shown). Now, returning to table 5-2, let us see what happens when all three interfering influences are controlled at once. The second column of the table has Y/P and $(T - 9)/W$ partialed out. This drives E/M on up to $-.65$. Whereas E/M originally could explain 20 percent (r^2) of the variation in per capita growth, it can now explain 33 percent [partial $r^2 \times (1 - R^2)$]. The other industry variables also climb: $(E/P)^3$ goes to $-.58$ and Lg to $+.46$. In addition, there are partials for variables not shown in the table of $-.63$ for P/M and $-.66$ for $MB \times E/M$. In other words, regardless of whether markets is viewed from the demand or the supply standpoint, growth is faster where the demand for manufactured goods exceeds the "home grown" supply.

The second column r of $+.46$ for Lg is much lower than the other industry r's. Could it be that spatial isolation is nothing more than a proxy for lack of industry? If E/M is controlled in addition to Y/P and $(T - 9)/W$, Lg falls to $+.10$; an independent spatial influence *seems* doubtful. But this is because the threshold influence now interferes with the spatial influence: the three control variables give the West-Rural dummy a partial of $-.26$. West-Metro, though, now has a partial of $+.41$, which becomes $+.47$ if T is added as a fourth control. And when West-Rural is partialed out fifth to control thresholds, $(50 - Lat) (Lg - 65)^3$ goes to $+.43$ and West-Metro to $+.44$. It appears that spatial isolation is a stimulus but primarily in the better developed western states.

In the first and the last three columns, one or more industry variables are partialed out. This of course explains why the remaining industry variables decline in their partials. But it is worth noting that in the fourth column, where Y/P and Lg are held constant, E/M and $(E/P)^3$ remain significant at the 1 percent confidence level. This confirms what never really was in doubt: the industry variables have a built-in spatial isolation factor but describe more than the spatial facet of markets.

Wages and Unionization.   In table 5-2 the labor variables approach maturity. Partials significant at the 1 percent level appear for all three types of labor variables—wage, union, and labor supply. Wages and unionization will be discussed first because, in contrast to the situation with absolute growth, they generally show higher partials than labor supply.

In the section on minimal controls, we saw that unionization but not wages becomes significant when a spatial variable is controlled. Wages does not become significant because it is adversely related not only to spatial isolation— wages and longitude are both high in the West—but to per capita income and industrialization as well. High wages (unfavorable) overlap high income (favorable) and, in the West, lack of industry (favorable). To see the wage influence, therefore, we must control not only a spatial variable but an income and an industrial variable.

First, though, let us note what control of income and industry can accomplish without simultaneous control of longitude. One recalls that, with absolute growth, partials of +.31 for $1/W^2$ and +.36 for $1/U^2$ arose when P, Y, and $E^{1.5}$ were controlled. A comparable combination for per capita growth is Y/P and E/M (relative variables). When Y/P and E/M are held constant, the labor partials (not shown) are almost the same as before: $1/W^2$ reads +.30 and $1/U^2$ reads +.35. Remember, because these variables are reciprocals their positive r's are equivalent to negative ones for W and U.

Returning to control combinations based on Lg, we can observe what happens when Lg is assisted by Y/P and an E/M variable. The two-variable combination, Lg and Y/P, heads the fourth column in table 5-2. Here $1/W^2$ remains at +.30 but $1/U^2$ creeps ahead to +.37. This suggests that wages is a weaker influence than—perhaps just a proxy for—unionization. But in column five, where $(E/M)^3$ joins the control set, $1/W^2$ moves ahead of $1/U^2$, +.40 to +.37. High wages no longer describe the West's lack of industry.

Although not far across the 1 percent significance line, both variables become more significant when additional variables are controlled. For example, if a second demand variable, CP/P, is added to the control set, $1/W^2$ climbs to +.46 and $1/U^2$ to +.43. Another increase occurs if West-Rural $\times$ 1/(P/M) is also controlled. (West-Rural $\times$ 1/(P/M) is a threshold variable giving its highest values to the least densely populated states.) Now—with Lg, Y/P, $(E/M)^3$, CP/P, and West-Rural $\times$ 1/(P/M) controlled—the labor partials are +.50 for $1/W^2$ and +.45 for $1/U^2$.

The preceding chapter developed evidence that unionization has little if any independent significance but instead is a double proxy for labor supply and wages. Experiments with per capita growth support the same conclusion. The wage partials are generally higher than those for unionization once the key variables are controlled. Also, adding $(F/M)^3$ to a control set hurts $1/U^2$ more than $1/W^2$, which may not be hurt at all. If $(F/M)^3$ is added to the last control set in table 6-2, for example, the best wage and unionization partials become

−.40 for $\sqrt{W}$ and −.35 for $\sqrt{U}$: unionization has slipped two points, but wages is as high as before. In this instance, the damage to unionization is minor, because $(F/M)^3$'s partial of +.31 wasn't high enough to lend much support in the first place. But in other situations to be examined shortly, partialing out the labor supply variable is very damaging to unionization.

Labor Supply.   It bears repeating that surplus labor emanates from farms. The southern states are generally highest in farm population density, but farm workers are rapidly being displaced by technology. These displaced workers migrate to cities to find jobs. This is the basis for assuming that labor supply, in the sense of abundant surplus labor, can be measured by farm population variables. Two such variables became significant with absolute growth. These were F and F/M—actually variations of them, such as $F^{1.5}$, $(F/M)^3$, and $(F/M)^4$. In table 4-3 we saw $F^{1.5}$ going to +.73 and $(F/M)^4$ to +.65 when four variables were held constant.

One does not expect the absolute variable, F, to do very well in correlation with a relative (per capita) measure of growth. And it does not. The F/M variables, on the other hand, are good performers; $(F/M)^3$ generally does best. In table 5-2, $(F/M)^3$ becomes significant in the same situations where $1/W^2$ and $1/U^2$ become significant. The positive partials of +.39, +.34, and +.31 in the last three columns signal high residual growth in states with dense farm populations, that is, in the South. The best partial (+.39) results when P/M and Y/M are jointly held constant. P/M substitutes for E/M—it controls industrialization— and allows $(F/M)^3$ to be divorced from the westward pull of strong markets; Y/M controls per capita income (but only when P/M is first held constant) and serves to release $(F/M)^3$ from its adverse intercorrelation (−.45) with Y/P.

The $(F/M)^3$ partials might appear to depend partly on a proxy relationship to wages, yet there is a surprising degree of independence. If we take the +.31 partial for $(F/M)^3$ in the last column of table 5-2 and boost it up to +.35 by holding CP/P and West-Rural × 1/(P/M) constant, it falls only to +.33 when $1/W^2$ (+.50) is partialed out sixth. (In contrast, the same procedure lifts $1/U^2$ to +.45, then drops it to +.26.)

Other Influences.   The influences remaining to be discussed are climate, the threshold factor, and agglomeration. For climate, the first two columns in the table don't mean very much, because (T − 9)/W has been partialed out. But the last three columns are quite revealing. These are the first control situations in which both a supply variable and a demand variable have been held constant. This tightening of control over the market influence raises T to new heights in its partials. In the middle column, where both P/M and Y/M are held constant, T goes from the +.49 partial it held when P/M alone was controlled to +.65. This evidently happens because T was handicapped by the overlap between warm climate and low per capita income in the southern states. A partial r of +.65

yields a partial r^2 of .42. Applied to the 73 percent variation in growth not explained by the control variables $(1.00 - .52^2 = .73)$, this can explain 31 percent of the total variation in per capita growth.

Now that the labor variables have become significant, the partials for T might seem to depend a lot on the coincidence of favorable labor and climate conditions in the South. But this is not the case. T's highest partial, found in the middle column, merely slips from +.65 to +.62 when labor's best variable of the moment—$(F/M)^3$—is held constant. And if $1/W^2$ is also held constant, the partial stays at +.62. T's second-highest partial simply moves from +.58 to +.57 when the last-column labor champion, $1/W^2$, is held constant. (However, this does not belie a certain amount of duplication, since when a labor variable is partialed out r^2 applies to a reduced amount of unexplained variance and will therefore explain less than before.)

The three threshold variables—West-Rural, West-Metro, and West-Metro $\times (CP/P)^3$—continue to tell the now-familiar story of faster growth in the six better developed western states vis-à-vis the five least developed ones. Each control combination shown in table 5–2 gives West-Rural a negative partial, and the last two are significant at the 5 percent confidence level. Each combination gives West-Metro an r that is both positive and significant, generally at the 1 percent level. West-Metro $\times (CP/P)^3$, which weights the West-Metro states according to degree of urbanization, has even higher r's—consistently. The last column presents a significantly negative partial for West-Rural coupled with a significantly positive one for West-Metro; the difference between them is .71.

What is the most logical explanation? Industry is attracted to the West by strong markets. But some firms are reluctant to go to the least developed states. They prefer to locate where regional (or subregional) markets are big enough to support a decent-sized plant, or where the plant will be close to the region's population center of gravity (to minimize shipping costs), or where the external economies and urban amenities of major metropolitan areas are available. Some of the new industry is therefore diverted from the least developed states to those that have crossed the developmental threshold.

About agglomeration there is not much to say. The MB dummy does show a +.34 partial r in the first control column. But this is obviously spurious in the sense that MB has become a proxy for Y/P. We saw in table 5–1 how MB moves up and down with Y/P and how MB went from negative to +.10 when Y/P went to +.48. Now Y/P reads +.58; and a wage control has been added, so that MB can more readily follow Y/P up the ladder without being pushed back by the Manufacturing Belt's high wages. If the proxy relationship is destroyed by partialing out Y/P in addition to E/M and (T - 9)/W, the MB dummy drops to +.08 (not shown). And in the second column, where Y/P and (T - 9)/W but not E/M are controlled, MB goes to -.62. Could MB go almost as far as E/M (-.65) if MB were forced to compromise between the negative push of industrial supply and a positive pull from agglomeration?

Strong Controls

Many combinations of three or more variables held constant produced high partial *r*'s, often for variables not originally significant. Five combinations offering high partials for one variable or another—sometimes several variables—are presented in table 5-3. The last four combinations are variations on the theme of simultaneous control of $(T - 9)^{1.5} \times (Y^{0.8}/P)$, T, E/M or P/M, and Y/M, a group around which many of the best multiple correlation combinations are built.

Wages and Unionization.   To see how the wage and unionization variables are doing, we must look primarily at the first three columns of table 5-3; in the other two (T – 9)/W is controlled. Both $1/W^2$ and $1/U^2$ have partials exceeding the 1 percent significance level in each of the first three columns. The controls used in column two send $1/U^2$ to +.48 and $1/W^2$ to +.47. To get this far it has been necessary to do a fairly thorough job of accounting for the dominant influences—markets and climate: the control set includes four market variables and three representing climate, including two climate-weighted market variables. The third of the four leading influences—the threshold factor—has also been held constant; 1/(E/M) is a threshold variable.

The table 5-3 findings also bolster the conclusion that there is interaction between climate and wages. In all three columns (T – 9)/W has higher partials than $1/W^2$. The second column gives (T – 9)/W a +.60 to +.47 advantage over $1/W^2$. Here—and in the next column as well—T is held constant, so we know that (T – 9)/W is not primarily a proxy for T. Although there are situations where $1/W^2$ either outperforms or comes close to (T – 9)/W, the situations depicted in the table are the most typical: strong controls give (T – 9)/W higher partials than $1/W^2$. Moreover, as implied in the last two columns, (T – 9)/W is generally more effective as a control variable. Once more it appears that low wages are less of an attraction in Maine and North Dakota, where winter is a bit chilly, than in Tennessee, Alabama, and Florida (all of which have higher wage levels than Maine).

Considering that $1/U^2$ has slightly higher partials than $1/W^2$ in two control columns, it might seem that unionization is carrying most of the load. But further analysis indicates that $1/U^2$ is being led by $1/W^2$, assisted by $(F/M)^3$ and to a limited extent by E/M (when not held constant). That is, unions are strong where wages are high, surplus labor is scarce, and industry is well developed. Where the opposite conditions obtain, unions tend to be weak. The wage influence is less dependent on ties with surplus labor; and, because wages are high in the West, wages cannot be a proxy for underindustrialization. Therefore, strong controls put $1/W^2$ ahead when $(F/M)^3$ or, sometimes, an E/M variable is among the controls.

Regarding E/M, the first column has it controlled and, despite noncontrol

Table 5-3
Partial Correlations of Selected Variables with 1947–63 Per Capita Growth: Strong Controls (Three to Six Variables Held Constant)

Selected Independent Variables	Simple r with Growth	E/M, Y/P, $Lat \times Lg^3$	Variables Held Constant ("Partialled Out") $1/(E/M)$, $Lat \times Lg^3$, $(Y/M)^2$, $(E/M)^2$, T, $T(T^{0.8}/P)$	$1/(E/M)$, $Lat \times Lg^3$, Y/M, P/M, T, $T(Y^{0.8}/P)$	$(T-9)/W$, $Lat \times Lg^3$, $(Y/M)^2$, $(E/M)^2$, T, $T(Y^{0.8}/P)$	$1/(E/M)$, $(T-9)/W$, $(Y/M)^2$, $(E/M)^2$, T, $T(Y^{0.8}/P)$
(MULTIPLE R)		(.588)	(.829)	(.819)	(.802)	(.819)
Labor						
$1/W^2$	+.03	+.40	+.47	+.38	−.03	+.00
$1/U^2$	+.25	+.39	+.48	+.42	+.12	+.20
$(T-9)/W$	+.40	+.59	+.60	+.47	···	···
$(F/M)^3$	+.14	+.42	+.49	+.61	+.30	+.23
Threshold						
$1/(E/M)$	+.00	−.41	···	···	−.66	···
West-Rural Dummy	−.06	−.37	−.10	−.16	−.47	−.07
West-Metro Dummy	+.47	+.26	+.10	+.11	+.45	+.50
West Dummy	+.32	−.16	−.00	−.05	−.06	+.40
W-Metro × $(CP/P)^3$	+.51	+.31	+.24	+.28	+.60	+.63
West × CP/M	+.44	+.23	+.13	+.17	+.46	+.55
Other						
$(50 - Lat)\,(Lg - 65)^3$	+.49	···	···	···	···	+.63
$MB \times E/M$	−.45	−.29	−.19	−.38	+.04	−.18
$CP/P > 57.7\%$ Dummy	+.01	+.27	−.00	+.04	+.40	+.17

Abbreviations: Lat = Latitude, Lg = Longitude, $Lat \times Lg^3 = (50 - Lat)\,(Lg - 65)^3$, Y = Income, P = Population, E = Manufacturing Employment, M = Square Miles, T = Temperature, $T(Y^{0.8}/P) = (T - 9)^{1.5} \times (Y^{0.8}/P)$, W = Wages, U = Unionization, F = Farm Population, West-Rural = 5 least developed western states, West-Metro = 6 most developed western states, CP = Urban (City) Population, West = all 11 western states, MB = Manufacturing Belt dummy (13 states), $CP/P > 57.7\%$ = 20 urban states of $(F/M)^3$, $1/W^2$ leads $1/U^2$. In the third column, where E/M is not controlled, $1/U^2$ is ahead by four, +.42 to +.38. When E/M is brought into the control combination (not shown), the difference becomes negligible: $1/U^2$ leads by +.471 to +.464.

Labor supply is more important than industrialization as a behind-the-scenes force boosting unionization to significance. Here is what happens to the wage and unionization partials in the in the first three columns of table 5-3 when $(F/M)^3$ is controlled:

	Column 1		Column 2		Column 3	
	Before	After	Before	After	Before	After
$1/W^2$ (or $\sqrt{W}$)	+.40	(−.40)	+.47	+.46	+.38	+.40
$1/U^2$ (or $\sqrt{U}$)	+.39	(−.28)	+.48	+.36	+.42	+.24
$(T-9)/W$	+.59	+.51	+.60	+.60	+.47	+.48

The above partials (square roots are substituted for reciprocals when the former yield higher r's) show that the wage partials are virtually unaffected by control of $(F/M)^3$ and sometimes increase. Under column 1, $(T-9)/W$ does drop from +.59 to +.51, but this is because $(F/M)^3$ partly duplicates T, which goes from +.53 to +.45. With unionization, though, the story is different: the partials decline sharply.

Using more stringent controls, the best twelve-variable combination (table 5-6) further illustrates unionization's dependence on other labor influences for significance. Here are the partial r's resulting (a) when ten variables—all but the two labor variables—are controlled, (b) when $(F/M)^3$ is also controlled, and (c) when $1/W^2$ and $1/U^2$ alternate as the twelfth control variable:

	Step 10	Step 11: $(F/M)^3$	Step 12: $1/W^2$	Alt. 12: $1/U^2$
$(F/M)^3$	+.58	....	....	....
$1/W^2$	+.59	+.75	....	+.73
$1/U^2$	+.42	+.31	−.15	....
$(T-9)/W$	+.64	+.77	+.29	+.75

Incidentally, the last control combination, which includes both $(F/M)^3$ and $1/U^2$, gives $(F/M)^3$ an F (significance) value of 12.74 but $1/U^2$ an F of 3.83. Clearly, unionization is a proxy for labor supply and wages; they are not proxies for unionization.

Labor Supply.   In the previous table, where only two or three variables were held constant at a time, $(F/M)^3$ reached significance but usually did not do as well as $1/W^2$ and $1/U^2$. And indeed it usually does not do as well—not with per capita growth anyway. Yet often enough we find $(F/M)^3$ ahead of the others. It was ahead in table 5-2 when it reached +.39. The first three columns of table 5-3 again show $(F/M)^3$ in first place. Its partials are +.42, +.49, and +.61, all of which are better than the partials for $1/W^2$ and $1/U^2$. These $(F/M)^3$ partials, particularly the last one, confirm the earlier finding that the labor supply influence is substantially independent of the wage influence. Equally important, the highest reading (+.61) gives us a figure that is significant far beyond the 1 percent confidence level.

Still higher partials can be reached but require more control variables. If every variable except $(F/M)^3$ from the best twelve-variable combination (table 5-6) is held constant, $(F/M)^3$ hits +.74. In this situation it clearly does not depend upon the wage influence, for $(T - 9)/W$ is held constant. In fact, $(T - 9)/W$ actually raises $(F/M)^3$ from +.58 to +.74 when the former is entered eleventh in the control set.

An analysis of residuals was again used to check the labor supply interpretation of $(F/M)^3$. When this was done under absolute growth with $(F/M)^4$, the largest reductions in residual (unexplained) growth came from (a) increases in predicted growth in North Carolina, Tennessee, and South Carolina and (b) cutbacks in the growth predictions for Pennsylvania, Louisiana, Alabama, and Massachusetts. This time, when $(F/M)^3$ was entered behind the six variables that push it to +.61 in table 5-3, the leading reductions in residuals come from (a) higher predicted growth for North Carolina, Tennessee, Delaware, and South Carolina and (b) a lower prediction for Louisiana. North Carolina still had the biggest improvement; Tennessee still ranked second.

When $(T - 9)/W$, which gives Kentucky a wage penalty, was added to the control set before $(F/M)^3$ entered, a previous overcorrection for Kentucky was wiped out and it became the state with the biggest improvement. Now the major reductions in residual growth were from (a) higher predictions for Kentucky, Tennessee, Maryland, and North Carolina and (b) lower predictions for Louisiana and Rhode Island; South Carolina fell to tenth and Delaware to fifteenth. Other control combinations kept pointing to higher growth in Kentucky, Tennessee, the Carolinas, and sometimes Maryland; Louisiana was the only consistent growth loser. Sometimes but not consistently the textile-loss states of Massachusetts, Rhode Island, and Pennsylvania were among the states with the biggest reductions in residual growth (their predictions were lowered). What we see, then, is a fairly consistent picture—consistent enough for r's in the +.45 to +.65 range—of faster growth in the Upper South, that is, in surplus labor states located fairly close to the Manufacturing Belt.

Thresholds: Theoretical Considerations.   Until now we have discussed the hypothetical threshold factor largely in terms of two dummy variables, West-Rural (five states) and West-Metro (six states). It has not been shown how these dummies came into existence and why particular states were blocked in. The story begins with the first variable listed under the threshold heading in table 5-3. This variable, $1/(E/M)$, is shown reaching a partial r of -.41 in the first control column and one of -.66 in the fourth column. Comparable partials for other density reciprocals, such as $1/(P/M)$, could have been shown. These density reciprocals, not the dummy variables, are the basic threshold variables.

How did these variables evolve? What happened was that when the per capita and percentage growth experiments were being undertaken, the reciprocals of density variables began to display peculiar behavior. The density variables— P/M, E/M, and so on—were originally intended for use in evaluating markets. They were supposed to and did have negative r's, indicating high growth rates in the less developed parts of the country—primarily the West. The reciprocals were opposite in sign (positive). But after a few market variables were held constant, the reciprocals became significantly *negative*. Thus in table 5-3, $1/(E/M)$ becomes significantly negative when three market variables are held constant.

Since a negative r for a reciprocal is like a positive r for the parent variable (with rare exceptions), the picture was one of fast *residual* growth (unexplained by markets) in the more developed states, slow growth in the less developed states.

The negative r's for the reciprocals did not look spurious: they were sometimes far too high to be accidental; and they arose consistently, under a wide variety of control combinations, both with per capita and percentage growth. Neither were proxy relationships evident: the reciprocals did not tend to climb behind some other variable and to follow it up and down; they often had the highest r's in the correlation matrix. A better posssibility was agglomeration. But this would mean high residual growth in the Manufacturing Belt, whereas the density reciprocals often became significantly negative at times when the MB dummy and MB-weighted variables were also negative.

Mathematical considerations suggested a threshold influence. Reciprocals, like roots and logs, reduce the relative differences among extremely high values and exaggerate the differences among the lowest values (for the basic variable). The low-valued cases—the states with the lowest density in this instance—thus tend to carry the correlation. This is especially true when the range of values takes the highest far above zero and the lowest down close to zero. Any very high value divided into one is a number close to zero. Rhode Island's 122.5 manufacturing employees per square mile translates into a $1/(E/M)$ of $1/122.5 = 0.01$. But out West, we get reciprocals such as 0.91 for Oregon, 9.26 for Montana, 16.13 for Wyoming, and 37.04 (or $1/0.027$) for Nevada. In other words, the high density states become relatively constant in value—very nearly zero— but the low density states assume high and quite disparate values. The reciprocals can discriminate (*a*) among the low density states and (*b*) between high and low density states but not (*c*) within the high density subset. The r is therefore determined mostly by variations within the low density range. Ultra-low density, it seemed, was a case of too much of a good thing.

Thresholds: Residuals and Dummies.   An analysis of residuals was undertaken to see if the threshold explanation had empirical support. The six variables heading the fourth control column in table 5-3 were used to get "before" residuals (by means of a multiple regression equation), and then $1/(E/M)$ was added to get "after" residuals. The findings verified that a western phenomenon was being detected. Nevada, California, Wyoming, and New Mexico—in that order—had the four largest reductions in unexplained growth. Seven of the eleven largest reductions in residual growth, and eight of the fifteen largest, belonged to western states. Of the eleven western states, only Idaho, Oregon, and Arizona did not improve.

Metropolitan areas seemed to be involved. The previously *under*estimated western states that improved through higher growth predictions were California, Utah, Colorado, and Washington—states with major metropolitan areas. Another "metro" state, Arizona (Phoenix), almost jointed this group: it had been underestimated but was overcorrected by $1/(E/M)$. The previously *over*estimated western states that improved via decreases in predicted growth were states that lack major metropolitan areas—Nevada, Wyoming, New Mexico,[1] and Montana.

New Mexico is the highest in population and population density of the previously overestimated states; Utah is the lowest of the underestimated states. This suggested a density threshold lying between New Mexico's and Utah's. But such a line would group Arizona with New Mexico. This is illogical, because (*a*) Arizona was originally underestimated, requiring no negative correction, and (*b*) Arizona has Phoenix, a larger metropolitan area than Salt Lake City in the above-threshold group. The problem was handled by separating the states into those above and those below 685,000 population (1950); Arizona is above. Three dummy variables were then created to test this threshold: a West dummy valued at one for the eleven western states and zero elsewhere; the West-Rural dummy giving the unitary value to Montana, Idaho, Wyoming, New Mexico, and Nevada; and the West-Metro dummy identifying Colorado, Utah, Arizona, Washington, Oregon, and California.

The dummy variables strongly support the threshold interpretation of $1/(E/M)$ and other density reciprocals. We have already examined many partials for West-Rural and West-Metro. Table 5-3, in the two columns where $1/(E/M)$ is not controlled, offers two more comparisons. This time the West dummy is also shown and becomes the starting point for the analysis. In the first column, with three market variables controlled, residual growth has become slightly unfavorable to the West (-.16); this is due to the eastward pull of labor. But this slight negativity is really a combination of positive tendencies in the West-Metro states (+.26) and negative tendencies in the West-Rural states (-.37). In the fourth column the West dummy is almost neutral (-.06). Again, however, this is not the result of a uniform tendency within the West. The West-Metro states show very significantly positive growth (+.45); the West-Rural states are very

significantly negative (-.47). West-Rural's climb from -.37 to -.47 echoes
$1/(E/M)$'s climb from -.41 to -.66.

Thresholds: Further Testing. A final group of experiments removed all
doubt that $1/(E/M)$ and the other reciprocals detect a western influence, one that
is largely confined to the five least developed states. If $1/(E/M)$ and its relatives
differentiate primarily among the western states, they should predict about as
well if denied any ability whatsoever to differentiate among eastern states. They
can be denied this ability if all eastern states are given the same value, zero
(they are already just a fraction above zero). To give all the eastern states values
of zero without affecting the value of $1/(E/M)$ for the western states, we simply
multiply $1/(E/M)$ by the West dummy. We can even go a little farther and
assign zero not only to the thirty-seven eastern states but to the six West-Metro
states as well. In this case we multiply by the West-Rural dummy to get forty-
three states valued at $0 \times 1/(E/M) = 0$ and five valued at $1 \times 1/(E/M) = 1/(E/M)$.

Dummy-weighted variables were constructed from $1/(E/M)$ and $1/(P/M)$.
In addition, to see whether the absolute level of development was as significant
as density, weighted variables using $1/E$ and $1/VA$ were also created. These
variables were tested under many different control combinations. The results
were always about the same insofar as the weighted and unweighted reciprocals
always had very similar partials; either could be higher. The control combination
in table 5-3 that sends $1/(E/M)$ to -.66 gives partials of -.60 for West $\times 1/(E/M)$,
-.59 for West-Rural $\times 1/(E/M)$, and -.59 for West-Rural $\times 1/E$. A more elaborate
control set using eleven of the twelve variables from the best twelve-variable
combination (table 5-6)—all but the threshold variable—yields these partials:

West-Rural	= -.53	West-Metro	= +.42
$1/(E/M)$	= -.80	$1/(P/M)$	= -.77
West $\times 1/(E/M)$	= -.80	West $\times 1/(P/M)$	= -.75
West-Rural $\times 1/(E/M)$	= -.78	West-Rural $\times 1/(P/M)$	= -.74
West-Rural $\times 1/E$	= -.78	West-Rural $\times 1/VA$	= -.78

Several points should be made. First, the threshold variables can attain
partial r's too significant to be challenged: a partial of -.80 in this context is not
due to chance. Second, the West-Rural dummy's partial continues to follow
those of the reciprocals: $1/(E/M)$ is definitely connected with the West-Rural
states. Third, $1/(E/M)$ and $1/(P/M)$ show no significant ability to describe
nuances of residual growth among the eastern states: West $\times 1/(E/M)$ has the
same partial as $1/(E/M)$ itself, and we know that West $\times 1/(E/M)$ cannot differentiate among the eastern states. Fourth, $1/(E/M)$ and $1/(P/M)$ can hardly
even discriminate within the West-Metro group: West $\times 1/(E/M)$, which dummies
in the six West-Metro states, has a partial just two points higher than West-Rural
$\times 1/(E/M)$'s (-.80 compared to -.78). Fifth, the absolute variables (e.g., $1/E$)

predict about as well as the relative ones. This indicates that we are looking at development in the abstract and not at density per se.

The conclusion that $1/(E/M)$ is not describing negative residual growth throughout the West but only in the least developed western states leads to a related one: the threshold factor has two sides, so that growth in underdeveloped states that have crossed the threshold continues to be proportional to development. This conclusion was anticipated in the earlier findings for absolute growth.

The last two threshold variables in table 5-3, West-Metro $\times$ $(CP/P)^3$ and West $\times$ CP/M, provide new evidence. West-Metro $\times$ $(CP/P)^3$ gives the most weight—the highest values—to the West-Metro states with the highest urban population percentages. By doing so, it acquires consistently better partials than West-Metro alone has.

The remaining threshold variable is West $\times$ CP/M. Y/M, P/M, or E/M could be substituted for CP/M with very little change in the partials. But the fact that the positive side of this influence continues to show up best in a variable employing CP suggests that major metropolitan areas are crucial. At any rate, a point to be stressed is that the national pattern of faster growth in the least developed states doesn't hold within the western subset. That is, the western states as a group do have faster growth than the eastern states, but within the West it is the *most* developed states that grow fastest. For example, if we go back to simple r's, CP/M is negative at $-.41$, but West $\times$ CP/M reads $+.44$—quite a contrast.

Even more remarkable, this pattern of faster growth in the more developed western states is so strong that West $\times$ CP/M can go to $+.46$ in the fourth column despite the negative pull of the five West-Rural states, which are covered along with the West-Metro states. When the negative pull of the West-Rural states is eliminated by holding constant $1/(E/M)$, as shown in the last column of table 5-3, West $\times$ CP/M goes on up to $+.55$.

In summary, there is persuasive evidence that the most developed of the least developed states are growing fastest. Although underdevelopment is basically a powerful stimulus to growth, too much underdevelopment weakens the stimulus. Some firms evidently find Albuquerque, Cheyenne, Great Falls, and Las Vegas too small. Much more attractive are places such as Denver, Salt Lake City, Phoenix, Seattle, San Francisco, and of course Los Angeles.

Other Influences. Table 5-3 also conveys evidence concerning markets, climate, agglomeration, and urban attraction. The last column of the table provides the strongest evidence yet that spatial isolation, as a particular facet of the market influence, affects growth. In this column three market variables—an industry (supply) variable, a demand variable, and a market-climate interaction variable—are controlled; so are temperature, wages, and a threshold variable. Despite the extensive market controls, Lg goes to $+.49$ and $(50 - Lat)(Lg - 65)^3$ climbs to $+.63$. The controls allow us to be reasonably certain that the effect of isolation per se is being captured and that the contour variable is not just a proxy for supply-demand ratios or the market-climate interaction effect. But if these controls aren't convincing enough, we can move on to the best twelve-variable combination (table 5-6). If $(50 - Lat) (Lg - 65)^3$ is held back until step twelve in this set—if eleven other variables including four market variables are held constant—it goes to +.78.

Climate continues to refute the argument that it is a proxy for something else. As said before, markets is the only other influence strong enough to have even an outside chance of shaping the partials for the climate variables; labor could at best play a supporting role. But when the three market variables heading the first control column are held constant, T moves from its simple r of +.47 to a partial r of +.53 (not shown). It is interesting to see what happens when this combination is extended to eight variables but with Lg replacing $(50 - Lat)$ $(Lg - 65)^3$ so that no control variable embodies climate. With five market variables—E/M, P/M, Y/M, Lg, and Y/P—partialed out, T stands at +.60. When two labor variables—$1/W^2$ and $(F/M)^3$—added to the control set, T drops only to +.57. Using a threshold variable, $1/(E/M)$, as an eighth control leaves T at +.56 (and 50 - Lat at +.57). Even after being partly duplicated by labor and thresholds, T can still explain 31 percent of the residual variance and 13 percent of the total variance. (Before labor and thresholds were controlled, it could explain 23 percent of total variance.)

But T does not by itself account for all of the climate influence. If T now enters the control set, three climate-weighted variables can still make additional contributions to the explanation of growth. Consider this sequence:

Step	Variable	Partial r	ΔR^2
10	$(T - 9)^{1.5} \times (Y^{0.8}/P)$	+.61	.109
11	$(50 - Lat) (Lg - 65)^3$	+.42	.029
12	$(T - 9)/W$	+.36	.020

Per capita income was doubly controlled (Y/P and the combination of P/M and Y/M) before step ten, and T was also controlled. Yet step 10 has $(T - 9)^{1.5}$ $\times (Y^{0.8}/P)$ entering with a partial of +.61 and explaining another 11 percent of the variance. All told, after eight wage, labor, and threshold variables were held constant, T was still able to explain 13 percent of the variance, and three other variables with climate weighting could explain another 16 percent—a total of 29 percent.

With agglomeration the situation is reversed: no control pattern seems capable of exposing latent significance. Certainly this is true when we adopt the narrower definition of agglomeration, which sees agglomeration as a magnet attracting industry to the Manufacturing Belt. In table 5-3, MB $\times$ E/M shows consistently negative partials, except for one of +.04. If we hold constant every-

thing in the best twelve-variable combination (table 5.6), MB $\times$ E/M reads
-.16 and MB is a point behind at -.15.

Somewhat related to agglomeration, and also to the threshold influence, is
the urban attraction. It was brought to light in the last chapter by the rural-urban
variable $(F/P)^4$ and secondarily by the VA dummy. (The latter is really too
ambiguous to be regarded narrowly as an agglomeration variable.) Per capita
growth also shows signs of influence from an urban attraction. Two rural-urban
variables, $1/(CP/P)$ and a CP/P dummy variable, will be seen shortly in some of
the best multiple correlation combinations. One of these, the dummy, is also
seen in table 5-3. The dummy is valued at one in twenty states with 1950 urban
percentages exceeding 57.7 (the lower limit for the Manufacturing Belt states)
and at zero in the other twenty-eight states. In table 5-6 it becomes significant at
+.40 in the situation where the threshold influence is brought out. But it will
again become significant in table 5-5 when $1/(E/M)$ is controlled. As will be
explained in more detail when we get to table 5-5, the dummy describes high
residual growth in urban states outside the Manufacturing Belt: Utah, Washington, Texas, Florida, and Colorado (in order of importance).

Multiple Correlations

Turning now to the best Rs (multiple correlations), we can again learn more
about what must go into a comprehensive explanation of growth by observing
which variables combine to yield the highest Rs. As said before, high Rs weed
out variables which duplicate one another; secondary and tertiary variables come
to the fore. Tables 5-4, 5-5, and 5-6 summarize the combinations producing
the highest Rs reached by per capita growth with any number of independent
variables from two to twelve. The column headings are explained in chapter 4 in
the "Multiple Correlation Tables" subsection.

Two to Six Variables

Table 5-4 displays the combinations giving the highest Rs attainable for
anywhere from two to six variables. Markets and climate continue to overshadow
the other locational influences. But the threshold influence soon becomes
visible, if still a bit tangled up with markets. The labor influence can also be seen
and even has two variables in the best six-variable combination.

Best for Steps 2-3. The best two-variable combination and the other
leading combinations all build upon the variable with the highest simple r. This
is the market-climate variable $(T - 9)^{1.5} \times (Y^{0.8}/P)$, which has an r of +.59.
Quite appropriately, it is joined at step 2 by $(E/M)^3$, whose simple r of -.46 is

Table 5-4

Multiple Correlations for 1947-63 Per Capita Growth: Best Combinations for Two to Six Variables

Step	Variable Entered	r or Partial r at Entry Step	R	R^2	$F(= T^2)$ to Remove
Best for Steps 2-3					
1	$(T-9)^{1.5} \times (Y^{0.8}/P)$	+.59	.589	.347	26.69
2	$(E/M)^3$	-.56	.742	.550	21.95
3	West-Metro $\times (CP/P)^3$	+.46	.803	.645	11.50
Best for Step 4					
1	$(T-9)^{1.5} \times (Y^{0.8}/P)$	+.59	.589	.347	23.55
2	$(P/M)^2$	-.50	.716	.513	19.82
3	$(Y/M)^2$	+.43	.777	.604	15.06
4	West-Metro $\times (CP/P)^3$	+.48	.833	.694	18.79
5	$1/U^2$	+.36	.856	.733	6.31
Best for Steps 5-6					
1	$(T-9)^{1.5} \times (Y^{0.8}/P)$	+.59	.589	.347	35.95
2	P/M	-.47	.703	.494	43.57
3	Y/M	+.45	.773	.598	38.22
4	$(F/M)^3$	+.47	.829	.687	20.00
5	West-Metro $\times (CP/P)^3$	+.52	.879	.773	22.75
6	W	-.36	.896	.803	6.16

Abbreviations: T = Temperature, Y = Income, P = Population, E = Manufacturing Employment, M = Square Miles, West-Metro = Metropolitan West dummy (1 = Colorado, Utah, Arizona, Washington, Oregon, California; 0 = other 42 states), CP = Urban (City) Population, U = Unionization, F = Farm Population, W = Wages

highest for the unweighted market variables—and indeed highest for any unweighted variable except T (+.47). Since $(T-9)^{1.5} \times (Y^{0.8}/P)$ is basically a demand variable and serves to hold per capita income (Y/P) relatively constant, it is natural that $(E/M)^3$ should move up to a partial r of -.56 when entering at step 2: $(E/M)^3$ can more readily describe the relationship between supply and demand when demand is constant. These two variables alone—$(T-9)^{1.5} \times (Y^{0.8}/P)$ and $(E/M)^3$—can explain over half the variation in per capita growth; they have an R of .742 and an R^2 of .550.

The best three-variable combination keeps the first two variables. They are joined at step 3 by West-Metro $\times (CP/P)^3$. This variable was created as a threshold variable but really combines market and threshold elements—even a little climate—until additional variables are controlled. In particular, the market variables controlled need to be augmented by an unweighted income variable (indirectly controlling E/Y) and a spatial variable before thresholds can claim heavy credit. As it is, West-Metro $\times$ $(CP/P)^3$ spotlights states that have attractive supply-demand ratios and are spatially isolated; it also picks up some of the climate influence in California and Arizona. It seems reasonable to give the threshold influence about half the credit for West-Metro $\times$ $(CP/P)^3$'s +.46 partial.

Adding this variable to the combination brings R to .803 and R^2 to .645. Just a little less than two-thirds of the variation in absolute growth has been explained—about 60 percent by markets and climate and 5 percent by the threshold factor.

Best for Step 4.   The best four-variable combination retreats to step 2 to pick up a different industry variable: $(P/M)^2$ is substituted for $(E/M)^3$. (There is a +.98 intercorrelation between E/M and P/M.) This weakens the combination for the moment but sets up an indirect control over Y/P, this time unweighted. When $(Y/M)^2$ enters at step 3, it is no longer a developmental density variable— $(P/M)^2$ has taken care of density—but describes per capita income. And the +.43 partial r for $(Y/M)^2$ describes not faster growth in the more densely developed states but faster residual growth in states where Y is high *relative to* P, that is, where Y/P is high.

At step 4 the combination returns to West-Metro $\times$ $(CP/P)^3$. But this variable is now preceded by not only the market-climate interaction variable and a supply variable but by a demand variable as well. Hence the market-threshold mixture embodied in the West-Metro dummy now leans more distinctly toward thresholds; the only important facet of markets not yet controlled is spatial isolation. Spatial isolation, we know, is still a residual influence but is now largely obscured by negative residual growth in the West-Rural states. (The West-Rural partial at step 4 is -.23.) That is, the spatial effect, insofar as it is not already explained, is now concentrated in—diverted to—the West-Metro states. The combined thrust of spatial isolation and the threshold factor drives R up to .833 and R^2 to .694. Four variables—three market variables and a market-threshold variable—can explain nearly 70 percent of the variation in per capita growth. Markets and climate account for all but about 5 percent of this.

Extended beyond step 4, "Best for Step 4" is no longer the best. Nevertheless, it is not far behind the best and it has more to tell us about what influences growth. The step 5 variable is $1/U^2$—unionization. This variable is also the step 4 variable when the best three-variable set is extended to four steps. In the present setting, its entry partial of +.36 is just a little higher than competing partials of +.32 for $(F/M)^3$ and +.31 for $1/W^2$. Earlier analyses have cast doubt on the likelihood that unionization is much more than a proxy for other influences, wages and labor supply in particular. The probable reason it now stands ahead of wages is that unionization is more closely linked to labor supply and can combine two influences in one variable.

Best for Steps 5-6. By forgetting that West-Metro $\times$ $(CP/P)^3$ is not purely a threshold variable but combines market and threshold elements, one could easily infer from the preceding combinations that the threshold factor is more important than labor. The "Best for Steps 5-6" combination restores perspective by (*a*) entering a labor variable before the threshold variable and (*b*) employing two labor variables compared to the one threshold variable.

The new combination is almost the same as the preceding one through the first three steps; only the adjustment for curvilinearity on the supply and demand variables has been altered (actually omitted). But at step 4 the labor supply variable, $(F/M)^3$, enters. Its entry partial of +.47 compares with partials of +.28 for both $1/W^2$ and $1/U^2$. This should put to rest any hasty generalizations about the relative importance of unionization that the preceding combination may have encouraged. At the same time, $(F/M)^3$ boasts a +.47 to +.36 advantage over West-Metro $\times$ $(CP/P)^3$, so we see that labor does not necessarily rank behind the threshold factor.

After four steps the present combination is still inferior to the preceding one (by a very narrow margin). When West-Metro $\times$ $(CP/P)^3$ enters at step 5, however, the new combination moves into first place. The repeated entry of this variable—in three combinations in a row now—strongly supports the threshold hypothesis. So does its very significant partial r, which is now +.52. It should be added that the only other significant variables at step 5 are other threshold variables, such as the West-Metro dummy (+.44) and West-Rural $\times$ $1/(E/M)$ (-.35).

At step 6 the basic wage variable, W, comes in. In this instance, W's partial of -.36 compares with one of +.32 for $1/W^2$. Perhaps a more important comparison, though, is that with the best unionization variable (at the moment), which is $\sqrt{U}$ and stands at -.24. Now that $(F/M)^3$ is unavailable for support, unionization has fallen behind wages. The wage variable, meanwhile, is strong enough to bring R to .896 and R^2 to .803. Eighty percent of the variation in per capita growth has been explained by means of two pure market variables, a market-climate variable, a market-threshold variable, and two labor variables.

Seven to Ten Variables

Two combinations that together cover the highest Rs obtained for sets of seven to ten variables appear in table 5-5. The new combinations are similar to the best six-variable combination to the extent of including $(T - 9)^{1.5} \times (Y^{0.8}/P)$, a supply variable, a demand variable, and $(F/M)^3$. But West-Metro $\times$ $(CP/P)^3$ is

Table 5-5
Multiple Correlations for 1947-63 Per Capita Growth: Best Combinations for
Seven to Ten Variables

Step	Variable Entered	r or Partial r at Entry Step	R	R^2	$F (= T^2)$ to Remove
Best for					
Steps 7-9					
1	P/M	$-.41$	.411	.169	17.49
2	Y/M	$+.35$	.523	.274	31.71
3	T	$+.65$	.762	.581	22.03
4	$(T - 9)^{1.5} \times (Y^{0.8}/P)$	$+.25$	.779	.607	35.36
5	$(F/M)^3$	$+.46$	.830	.689	13.41
6	West-Metro $\times (CP/P)^3$	$+.53$	.882	.778	29.40
7	$(T - 9)/W$	$+.43$	.904	.817 .	14.34
8	$1/(E/M)$	$-.41$	.921	.848	6.44
9	NE $\times$ E/M	$-.36$	.932	.869	5.57
Best for					
Step 10					
1	T	$+.46$	.465	.216	80.33
2	$(E/M)^2$	$-.48$	.627	.393	59.96
3	$(T - 9)^{1.5} \times (Y^{0.8}/P)$	$+.52$	.746	.557	106.70
4	$1/(E/M)$	$-.36$	.784	.615	57.25
5	$(F/M)^3$	$+.30$	.805	.648	23.08
6	$(50 - Lat) (Lg - 65)^3$	$+.47$	.852	.726	42.94
7	$(Y/M)^2$	$+.37$	.874 ·	.764	30.13
8	$(T - 9)/W$	$+.60$	.921	.847	36.61
9	CP/P > 57.7% (20 states)	$+.36$	.931	.867	17.21
10	NE (16 states)	$-.54$	.952	.906	15.02

Abbreviations: P = Population, M = Square Miles, Y = Income, T = Temperature, F = Farm
Population, West Metro = Metropolitan West dummy (1 = Colorado, Utah, Arizona,
Washington, Oregon, California; 0 = other 42 states), W = Wages, E = Manufacturing Employ-
ment, NE = 16 northeastern states dummy (1 = Maine, New Hampshire, Vermont,
Massachusetts, Rhode Island, Connecticut, New York, New Jersey, Pennsylvania, Delaware,
Maryland, Ohio, Michigan, Indiana, Illinois, Wisconsin; 0 = other 32 states), Lat = Latitude,
Lg = Longitude, CP/P > 57.7% = urban states dummy (1 = Florida, Missouri, Texas,
Colorado, Utah, Washington, California, and all aforementioned Northeast states except
Maine, New Hampshire, and Vermont; 0 = other 28 states)

either supplemented or replaced by a different threshold variable, $1/(E/M)$, and W
is replaced by $(T - 9)/W$.

Best for Steps 7-9. The "Best for Steps 7-9" combination starts with the
best six-variable combination, substitutes T for W, and continues from there. An
entry order other than the natural one is shown for the first six variables for
illustrative purposes. P/M, representing the supply or industrial side of markets,

enters at step 1. With P/M held constant, Y/M become positive as a demand variable. It is shown entering at step 2 with a partial of +.35. Together P/M and Y/M control per capita income, or the relationship between Y and P. Controlling these important market variables strengthens rather than weakens T: its entry partial is +.65 (well above its simple r of +.47) when it joins the combination at step 3. Now that its basic elements, temperature and per capita income, are spoken for, $(T - 9)^{1.5} \times (Y^{0.8}/P)$ is temporarily a bit weak: its entry partial at step 4 is an insignificant +.25. But it will revive and in the finished combination (nine variables) is the most significant variable (see "F to Remove" column). At step 5 $(F/M)^3$ enters with a partial of +.46. It is followed by West-Metro $\times (CP/P)^3$, which is now up to +.53.

A second labor variable, $(T - 9)/W$, comes in at step 7. Its entry partial of +.43 is just a little better than the -.42 partial held at this step by the basic wage variable, W, but with additional variables held constant the separation would be wider. A more interesting comparison is that between W (-.42) and the best unionization variable, $\sqrt{U}$, which is insignificant at -.25. Again we see that holding $(F/M)^3$ constant takes the steam out of unionization. And when $(T - 9)/W$ enters, $\sqrt{U}$ falls to -.04. This deepens the suspicion that $1/U^2$ was largely a joint proxy for $1/W^2$ and $(F/M)^3$ when it entered the earlier combinations.

Step 8 brings in a second threshold variable, $1/(E/M)$. This variable held a partial of -.42 at step 6, fell off to -.37 when West-Metro $\times (CP/P)^3$ entered, and is now back up to -.41. Its inclusion creates an eight-variable combination consisting of three market variables (one of them weighted by temperature), a climate variable, two labor variables, and two threshold variables (one of which embodies market elements).

The market influence is still not adequately represented: at step 9 another supply (industrial) variable enters. This is NE $\times$ E/M, in which NE is a dummy variable representing sixteen northeastern states—the Manufacturing Belt states plus northern New England. NE $\times$ E/M was designed as an agglomeration variable. Significant *positive* r's between it and growth would support the agglomeration hypothesis, which says that industry attracts industry. But in practice, NE $\times$ E/M has become an antiagglomeration variable: it shows that there is no detectable agglomeration attraction, at least not as far as the Northeast is concerned. The -.36 partial for NE $\times$ E/M (backed up by ones of -.34 for MB $\times$ E/M and -.33 for E/M) says that residual growth is poorest in the most industrialized part of the country. The new supply variable supplements P/M and raises R to .932. This R and its R^2 of .869 are the best for any nine-variable set.

If the combination were extended to ten steps, the next variable to enter would be a spatial variable—(55 - Lat) (Lg - 50). At step 10 it has a partial r of +.39. It can bring R to .942 and R^2 to .887, but this is not as good as what the next combination provides.

Best for Step 10. The best ten-variable combination returns to a variant of
E/M as its main industrial variable. This variant, $(E/M)^2$, is shown entering
behind T at step 2, where its -.48 partial r gives further emphasis to the independence of markets and climate. Controlling these two variables has little adverse
effect on $(T - 9)^{1.5} \times (Y^{0.8}/P)$: it enters third with a partial of +.52.

Step 4 illustrates how quickly the threshold variables become significant.
Although just two market variables and temperature have been controlled,
$1/(E/M)$ has already become significant at -.36. Actually, West-Rural $\times 1/(E/M)$
is slightly more significant at -.37, but in the long run $1/(E/M)$ is a shade better
for this combination. The -.36 partial is not terrible impressive, because $1/(E/M)$
has been entered a little early. If it is held back until step 7, it climbs to -.57.
This becomes -.73 at step 8—adequate proof of the variable's significance.

The step 5 variable, $(F/M)^3$, is barely significant (at the 5 percent confidence level) when it enters. Again, this is because it has been forced in early: it
sets up the next variable. A high statistical F value in the last column firmly
establishes that $(F/M)^3$ eventually becomes more significant. In fact, it quickly
goes up to +.46 if moved back one step. (Labor supply is pulling growth eastward
while spatial isolation pulls it westward; hence the step 5 and 6 variables tend to
neutralize each other, and one must be partialed out to set up the other.)

Spatial isolation has not been directly represented in the preceding combinations, except for sneaking in after the bell in "Best for Steps 7-9." This
lack of representation is misleading, since many high scoring combinations for
per capita growth included a contour (latitude-longitude) variable. But the
preceding combinations have stressed the West-Metro type of threshold variable,
and it involves overlap with spatial isolation—particularly with respect to
Washington, Oregon, California, and Arizona. Combinations featuring the West-
Rural type of threshold variable (i.e., density reciprocals) crave spatial variables.
Consequently, step 6 shows $(50 - \text{Lat}) (\text{Lg} - 65)^3$ entering with a partial r of
+.47. This partial would be +.71 if entry were deferred until step 8.

The next two variables are from previous combinations. Representing
consumer demand, $(Y/M)^2$ cooperates with $(E/M)^2$ to indirectly control a supply-
demand ratio, E/Y. The +.37 partial for $(Y/M)^2$ says that growth is faster where
Y is high relative to E. At step 8 (T - 9)/W enters, having reached +.60. This is
identical to the +.60 partial shown for (T - 9)/W in table 5-3 and is obtained
from the same control combination, except that $(F/M)^3$ has been added;
controlling $(F/M)^3$ doesn't hurt (T - 9)/W.

Step 9 reintroduces the urban attraction that came to light in the "Best for
Step 10" combination for absolute growth. This time the variable that enters
is the CP/P dummy (urban population percentage exceeds 57.7 percent), previously seen in table 5-3. The dummy's entry partial is a relatively low +.36. But
it would be a more respectable +.45 if entry were deferred until step 10. To
see what the dummy was picking up, an analysis of residuals was undertaken;
the dummy was entered at step 10 for before-and-after comparisons. Eight states

had relatively large reductions in residual growth. Five urban states—Utah, Washington, Texas, Florida, and Colorado (in that order)—improved via higher predicted growth; three rural states—Arizona, Oregon, and West Virginia—improved through lower growth predictions. California also improved but placed relatively low. The findings are partly suggestive of a refinement in the threshold pattern: urbanization is superimposed on developmental density as a threshold criterion. Faster growth in some of the more developed states outside of the West (but also outside of the Manufacturing Belt) is also indicated.

Step 10 brings in the NE (Northeast) dummy. This gives us a variable very much like NE × E/M, which came in at step 9 in the preceding combination. NE is very easy to understand when viewed in relation to the CP/P dummy. When the CP/P dummy comes in at step 9, the NR dummy jumps from -.30 to -.54. The CP/P dummy claims, "Residual growth is faster in the most urbanized states." The NE dummy counters, "But not in the Northeast." In other words, the urban attraction does not extend (not appreciably, anyway) to the highly urbanized Northeast; it does not apply where rural and urban states are not intermixed; it applies to the rural-urban checkerboard regions, where regional industry can be diverted from rural to urban states. Another feature of NE is its refutation of agglomeration: even before the CP/P dummy enters, NE's step 9 partial of -.30 is declaring that residual growth is poor in the industrially over-supplied Northeast. With this taken into account, we have a ten-variable combination explaining over 90 percent of the variation in per capita growth.

Eleven or Twelve Variables

Per capita growth is a little harder to predict than absolute and percentage growth. Additional variables are therefore required to obtain a per capita growth combination that approximates the explanatory power of ten-variable combinations for the other growth variables. Table 5-6 provides a twelve-variable combination that cuts unexplained growth down to 7 percent.

With respect to the first ten variables, the present combination differs from the preceding one only in that two of the variables are modified (but not basically changed). First, West × 1/(E/M) replaces 1/(E/M). This emphasizes the point that 1/(E/M) cannot discriminate among nonwestern states. Second, 1/(CP/P)—the reciprocal of urban population percentage—replaces the CP/P dummy. (But the CP/P dummy comes back in at step 12.)

In addition to modifying the threshold and urban attraction variables, table 5-6 reshuffles the order of entry. The new arrangement shows how certain variables react to new control combinations. The spatial variable, $(50- \text{Lat})$ $(\text{Lg} - 65)^3$, can enter at step 4 with a partial of +.42 even though industrialization, the E/Y supply-demand ratio, and temperature have been controlled—which reiterates that spatial isolation is more than a proxy for the influences

Table 5-6
Multiple Correlations for 1947-63 Per Capita Growth: Best
Combination for Eleven or Twelve Variables

Step	Variable Entered	r or Partial r at Entry Step	R	R^2	$F (= T^2)$ to Remove
1	$(E/M)^2$	-.46	.457	.209	12.18
2	$(Y/M)^2$	+.21	.494	.244	28.52
3	T	+.49	.652	.425	93.32
4	$(50 - Lat) (Lg - 65)^3$	+.42	.726	.527	54.11
5	$(T - 9)^{1.5} \times (Y^{0.8}/P)$	+.40	.776	.602	112.85
6	West $\times$ 1/(E/M)	-.45	.827	.684	63.13
7	$(T - 9)/W$	+.53	.879	.773	51.71
8	$(F/M)^3$	+.49	.910	.828	41.76
9	1/(CP/P)	-.48	.932	.869	15.52
10	NE (16 states)	-.47	.947	.897	15.68
11	$(P/M)^2$	-.43	.957	.916	9.31
12	CP/P > 57.7% (20 states)	+.36	.963	.927	5.19

Abbreviations: E = Manufacturing Employment, M = Square Miles, Y = Income, T = Temperature, Lat = Latitude, Lg = Longitude, P = Population, West = western states dummy (1 = Montana, Idaho, Wyoming, Colorado, Utah, New Mexico, Arizona, Nevada, Washington, Oregon, California; 0 = other 37 states), W = Wages, F = Farm Population, CP = Urban (City) Population, NE = 16 north-eastern states dummy (see table 5–5 abbreviations), CP/P > 57.7% = urban states dummy (see table 5–5 abbreviations)

held constant. At step 5, $(T - 9)^{1.5} \times (Y^{0.8}/P)$ still has a partial of +.40 despite extensive market and climate controls which precede it. The threshold variable, allowed to enter two steps later than in the preceding combination, now has a more significant entry partial (-.45). Similarly, $(T - 9)/W$ loses by being moved forward a step, and $(F/M)^3$ profits from being moved back three.

The new urban attraction variable, 1/(CP/P), has a good partial of -.48 when it enters at step 9. It has an even better partial of -.63 if it trades places with the NE dummy. (Think of these as positive partials for CP/P: high urbanization goes with high growth.) To allow further pursuit of the substance of the urban attraction, another analysis of residuals was made; 1/(CP/P) was entered at step 10 for this purpose. The three largest reductions in residual growth came from a higher prediction for Minnesota and lower predictions for the neighboring Dakotas. Similarly, Vermont and New Hampshire were tied for seventh, with New Hampshire (urban) gaining at the expense of Vermont (rural). Other important improvements due to higher growth estimates involved Utah (Salt Lake City), Missouri (Kansas City, St. Louis), and Colorado (Denver). Mississippi and West Virginia were the other leaders among states that improved through lower growth predictions. What we see is a general picture showing industry favoring those states outside of the Manufacturing Belt which have major metropolitan areas. States that are highly rural *compared to neighboring states* have trouble attracting industry.

Step 10 repeats with emphasis a lesson from the "Best for Step 10" combination. The NE dummy is insignificant at -.12 at step 9. But with the inclusion of $1/(CP/P)$ in the combination, NE shoots up to -.47. The message is clear: the urban attraction is of no benefit to the Manufacturing Belt. Subtractions must be made from northeastern growth to offset overestimating caused by $1/(CP/P)$.

Another market variable, $(P/M)^2$, has been climbing slowly. At step 11 it enters with a partial of -.43. The "F to Remove" value for $(E/M)^2$ falls from 54.74 to 10.93 when $(P/M)^2$ enters—because $(P/M)^2$ is now available to represent industry if $(E/M)^2$ is removed.

The urban attraction is strong enough to require more than one variable. Even though $1/(CP/P)$ has already entered the combination, the CP/P dummy comes in at step 12. Its +.36 partial pumps a little extra growth into the urban states. This raises R to .963 and R^2 to .927. About 93 percent of the variation in per capita growth has been explained.

Comparative Ratings

Markets and climate are again far ahead of the other influences, and markets again ranks first. The only significant simple r's come from market and climate variables. (The West-Metro dummy, though quite significant, describes markets until other market variables are controlled.) The only partial r's to climb well beyond the 1 percent significance level when three or less variables are controlled belong to market and climate variables. A market-climate and a pure market variable—$(T - 9)^{1.5} \times (Y^{0.8}/P)$ and $(E/M)^3$—give the highest R obtainable with two variables. The best ten-variable R is supported by six market and climate variables (including the NE dummy, which functions here as a supply variable). The two—sometime three—most significant variables in each of the best combinations represent markets and climate. Markets alone explains 35. to 55 percent of the variation in per capita growth. Climate explains 15 to 30 percent.

Labor and thresholds are almost even, but labor ranks third—based on the combined strength of wages and labor supply. This time some labor variables reach the 1 percent significance level with only a spatial isolation variable held constant. Holding constant isolation, per capita income, and industry brings a well-rounded set of significant labor partials. The best Rs for six or more variables incorporate two labor variables—$(F/M)^3$ and either W or $(T - 9)/W$. Labor explains 7 to 15 percent of the variance.

Thresholds ranks fourth. Like labor, thresholds produces significant partials with just a spatial variable constant. However, the threshold r's run a few points lower. When per capita income and industry are also controlled, some threshold partials rival those of labor. The best Rs for three or more variables are all based on combinations that include either the market-threshold variable West-Metro $\times$ $(CP/P)^3$ or a pure threshold variable such as $1/(E/M)$; the best eight-variable R has both. Thresholds takes credit for 6 to 14 percent of the variation in per capita growth.

The resource influence ranks fifth, down a notch from where it stood under absolute growth. The benchmark method of estimating the resource share of the variance puts the resource contribution at slightly over 7 percent; the residual method says 8 percent. Because indirect evidence is being used, the allowance for error must be generous: a minimum-maximum range of 1 to 15 percent is not unreasonable.

Sixth and last is the urban attraction. Strong controls are needed to produce significant partials for rural-urban variables, except where proxy relationships to per capita income are responsible. The important thing, however, is that variables such as $1/(CP/P)$ ultimately do produce very significant partials. The best combinations of ten or more variables include one or two urban attraction variables. These explain 2 to 7 percent of the variation in per capita growth.

Despite the false precision, central tendency estimates continue to add clarity to the comparisons. The six significant influences, as nearly as one can judge, make these contributions: markets, 45 percent; climate, 22 percent; labor, 11 percent; thresholds, 10 percent; resources, 8 percent; and the urban attraction, 4 percent. There is still no evidence that agglomeration (in the Manufacturing Belt sense of the term) is significant.

6

Percentage Growth: Partial and Multiple Correlations

Firm support for the findings and conclusions of the two preceding chapters comes from the third dependent variable, 1947–63 percentage growth in manufacturing employment (absolute growth divided by 1947 manufacturing employment). Markets emerges as a much stronger influence than it was with per capita growth; climate tightens its grip on second place. Labor, thresholds, resources, and the urban attraction again rank third through sixth, respectively, just as with per capita growth. And, creating complete agreement between the findings of the two growth rates, agglomeration once more fails to show any evidence of significance.

Partial Correlations

The percentage growth findings unfold in a pattern very similar to that seen earlier. Minimal controls provide only tentative evidence that labor and thresholds are significant but greatly bolster the significance of markets and climate. Moderate controls, by following control patterns basically the same as those used with per capita growth, give us a clear view of the labor influence (in all facets) and sharpen the still-blurred outline of the threshold influence. Strong controls yield highly significant partials for a variety of labor and threshold variables.

Minimal Controls

Although some of the control variables have been changed to ones better correlated with percentage growth, table 6-1 employs essentially the same controls used in table 5-1 (per capita growth). That is, the six control columns are headed by the best climate variable (T^2), the best demand variable (F/P), one of the better industry variables ($\log F/M$), the best industry variable ($\sqrt{E/P}$), a combination of the best climate and the best overall market variable (T^2 and $\sqrt{E/Y}$), and the best temperature-weighted market variable—$(T - 9)^{2.5}$ $\times [(Y/M)^{0.65}/(E/M)]$. (The last, remember, is not as complicated as it looks but is just a refined version of $T \times Y/E$.)

149

Table 6-1
Partial Correlations of Selected Variables with 1947–63 Percentage Growth: Minimal Controls (One or Two Variables Held Constant)

Selected Independent Variables	Simple r with Growth	T^2	F/P	Log F/M	$\sqrt{E/P}$	T^2 $\sqrt{E/Y}$	$T(Y^{0.65}/E)$
MULTIPLE R		(.449)	(.009)	(.561)	(.595)	(.742)	(.885)
Demand							
F/P	−.01	−.05	....	+.13	−.48	−.33	+.16
Y/P	−.06	+.13	−.09	−.27	+.21	+.17	+.07
$(T-9)^{1.5} \times (Y^{0.8}/P)$	+.65	+.57	+.66	+.67	+.66	+.50	+.07
Industry							
$\sqrt{E/P}$	−.60	−.58	−.71	−.40	....	+.15	−.36
$\sqrt{E/Y}$	−.61	−.66	−.64	−.36	−.18	....	−.40
log E/M	−.57	−.65	−.64	−.27	−.06	−.16	−.34
log F/M	−.56	−.71	−.57	....	−.33	−.45	−.26
$(T-9)^{2.5} \times \dfrac{(Y/M)^{0.65}}{E/M}$	+.89	+.85	+.89	+.84	+.84	+.77	....
$(T-9)^2/\sqrt{F/M}$	+.87	+.85	+.89	+.82	+.85	+.78	+.28
Spatial							
Lg	+.54	+.58	+.55	+.25	+.22	+.16	+.47
$(50 - Lat)(Lg - 65)^3$	+.72	+.70	+.72	+.55	+.60	+.50	+.49
Other							
T^2	+.45	....	+.45	+.65	+.45[a]	....	−.09
West-Rural Dummy	+.22	+.34	+.22	−.24	−.05	−.00	−.06
West-Metro Dummy	+.48	+.46	+.49	+.32	+.46	+.40	+.50
MB Dummy	−.41	−.33	−.50	−.26	−.33	+.08	−.29

Variables Held Constant ("Partialed Out")

[a]This partial r is for T rather than T^2.

Abbreviations: T = Temperature, F = Farm Population, P = Population, M = Square Miles, E = Manufacturing Employment, Y = Income, $T(Y^{0.65}/E) = (T-9)^{2.5} \times [(Y/M)^{0.65}/(E/M)]$, Lg = Longitude, Lat = Latitude, West-Rural = 5 least developed western states (dummy), West-Metro = 6 most developed western states (dummy), MB = Manufacturing Belt dummy (13 states)

Demand.   When we examined consumer demand in relation to per capita growth, CP/P (urban population percentage) and Y/P (per capita income) headed the list of demand variables. CP/P was treated as a demand variable because of its +.75 intercorrelation with Y/P and its ability to identify states that serve as regional market centroids, particularly states with major metropolitan areas. With percentage growth CP/P is still a good measure of consumer demand; but its opposite, F/P (farm population percentage), usually has higher r's—higher, in fact, than Y/P has. F/P is therefore substituted for CP/P in the stub column (and for Y/P in the second control column) of table 6-1. F/P's intercorrelation with Y/P is -.75, the same as CP/P's except for being opposite in sign.

As with per capita growth, the two unweighted demand variables—F/P and Y/P—are close to zero in their simple r's. This is due to conflicts with climate, industrialization, and wages, all of which have effects opposed to those of income in the Northeast (high income) and in the South (low income). The first conflict—climate—is removed by controlling T^2 (first control column). This helps a little but not much: Y/P switches from negative to positive but only reaches +.13. But when $\sqrt{E/P}$ (manufacturing employment per capita) is held constant (fourth column), Y/P goes to +.21 and F/P to a very significant -.48: excess industry no longer counters high demand in the Manufacturing Belt, and the relative lack of industry in the South no longer offsets weak demand. If T^2 and $\sqrt{E/P}$ are both controlled (not shown), Y/P jumps to +.41 and F/P moves on to -.52. (Interestingly, this two-variable control combination gives $\sqrt{E/Y}$ a partial of -.41, compared to the +.41 for Y/P: $\sqrt{E/Y}$ and Y/P become substantively identical when $\sqrt{E/P}$ is controlled.) The evidence thus indicates that strong consumer demand attracts industry when interfering influences are neutralized.

The wage conflict is not as serious: wages, unlike climate and industrialization, has only latent significance. Controlling W or $1/W^2$ therefore helps not at all, and no wage control is shown. It should be mentioned, though, that $(T - 9)/W$ gives slightly better results as a control than does T^2: $(T - 9)/W$ sends Y/P to +.15. And when we get to table 6-2, it will become apparent that the combination of $\sqrt{E/P}$ and $(T - 9)/W$ makes quite a difference.

Another warning is now required about proxies. The -.27 partial for Y/P when log F/M is controlled does not vitiate the above analysis. Log F/M has a significant (-.29) intercorrelation with Y/P, so that control of log F/M gives some control of Y/P. Y/P thus has less inclination to speak for itself and more inclination to speak for intercorrelated variables. Meanwhile, T^2, with its -.37 intercorrelation with Y/P, has climbed to +.65—low Y/P = high T^2 = growth. Also, $\sqrt{E/P}$, with its +.35 intercorrelation with Y/P, stands at -.40— low Y/P = low industrialization = growth. Finally, wages is pulling on Y/P harder than before: $1/W^2$ now has a partial r of +.21. The combined effect of three intercorrelations pulls Y/P to -.27.

The best overall variable for predicting per capita growth was the third one listed under demand, $(T - 9)^{1.5} \times (Y^{0.8}/P)$—temperature-weighted per capita income. It is not the best with percentage growth; yet it actually reaches higher simple and partial r's with percentage growth than it did with per capita growth. When its strongest element, temperature, is controlled, it slips only to +.57 (first column). When Y/P is controlled, it stays at +.65 (not shown); and when F/P is controlled, it reads +.66 (second column). Control of log F/M and $\sqrt{E/P}$ (columns three and four) is likewise harmless. The market-climate interaction effect is so strong that even when $\sqrt{E/Y}$ (which includes an income element) and T^2 are both controlled, $(T - 9)^{1.5} \times (Y^{0.8}/P)$ holds the line at +.50. It does become insignificant when another interaction variable, $(T - 9)^{2.5} \times [(Y/M)^{0.65}/(E/M)]$, is controlled; but when we get to table 6–3 we shall see additional control variables restoring it to significance.

Industry. The industry variables still describe markets but look at markets from the supply rather than the demand standpoint. More accurately, they emphasize supply but also record (directly or indirectly) the relationship between supply and demand—which is why the "industry" label is used in lieu of "supply" in table 6–1. The first two industry variables, $\sqrt{E/P}$ and $\sqrt{E/Y}$, are supply-demand ratios; $\sqrt{E/P}$ is the most effective measure of industry with percentage growth, while $\sqrt{E/Y}$ is the best all-around market variable. Log E/M, which has a +.93 intercorrelation with $\sqrt{E/P}$, replaces E/M, the best industry variable with per capita growth. The other density variable, log F/M, is a good proxy for industry and describes the demand side of markets well enough (−.29 intercorrelation with Y/P) to compensate for its inferiority to log E/M on the industry side. Two temperature-weighted variables, closely related to $\sqrt{E/Y}$ and log F/M respectively, complete the set of industry variables.

Before looking at these relative variables, we can profitably glance at an absolute measure of industry, E. With absolute growth, E went to −.76 when Y was held constant; $E^{1.5}$ hit −.87. E reached −.49 with per capita growth when Y was controlled. Now, with percentage growth, control of Y sends E to −.43 (not shown): growth continues to be faster where supply is low relative to demand. If an absolute industry variable can do this well with percentage growth, we can expect much more significant r's from the relative variables.

And more significant r's are what we get. The four unweighted relative variables—$\sqrt{E/P}$, $\sqrt{E/Y}$, log E/M, and log F/M—are all high even in their simple r's; $\sqrt{E/Y}$ reads −.61. Since they are closely related, their partials naturally dip sharply below original levels when any of them or their weighted counterparts are controlled (last four columns). But the partials that concern us are those in the first two columns. The first column controls T^2, allowing us to see that markets doesn't depend on climate for support (except where the interaction effect is concerned). On the contrary, markets and climate get in each other's way: three of the four variables show improved r's, with $\sqrt{E/Y}$ reaching

-.66 and log F/M going to -.71. (These variables improve mainly because the adverse effect of low income in the South was partly hidden by the warm climate.) The second column controls F/P, or relative demand. Manufacturing contributes to income; so there is a slight tendency for demand to move up and down with supply, obscuring the supply effect. This is why $\sqrt{E/P}$ climbs from -.60 to -.71 when F/P is partialed out. If both T^2 and F/P are controlled (not shown), the partials are -.72 for $\sqrt{E/P}$, -.70 for $\sqrt{E/Y}$, -.74 for log E/M, and -.71 for log F/M. Clearly, industry seeks an industrial vacuum.

The two temperature-weighted industry variables will be found commanding the best multiple correlation combinations later in this chapter. They are very similar to each other, having an intercorrelation of +.93. Their extraordinary predictive power is evident not only in their lofty simple r's of +.89 and +.87 but in partials falling consistently in the +.70s and +.80s. Both variables register +.85 when T^2 is partialed out. Since their market elements—$\sqrt{E/Y}$ and log F/M— have much lower partials, one can see that climate is not just an influence in its own right but also a catalyst (or inhibitor in the colder states) for markets. The same effect is seen when log F/M is partialed out: $(T - 9)^2/\sqrt{F/M}$ drops only to +.82, well above T^2's partial of +.65. Similarly, when $\sqrt{E/Y}$ and T^2 are controlled, $(T - 9)^{2.5} \times [(Y/M)^{0.65}/(E/M)]$ falls only to +.77 (column five). Also note that the R of .742 for the two weighted elements falls well short of the +.885 r for the weighted variable. (The more relevant R^2 vs. r^2 comparison is .551 vs. .783.) The conclusion that markets and climate interact is hard to avoid.

Spatial Isolation.   Table 6-1 repeats the spatial variables used in table 6-1— Lg and $(50 - Lat) (Lg - 65)^3$. To a large extent these variables are proxies for industrialization, which is why their partials get low when industry variables are controlled. But some of this lowness results because industry is, in turn, partly a proxy for spatial isolation. Isolation gets its independent significance from the fact that transport costs entailed in supplying western markets from eastern manufacturing centers increase as isolation from these centers increases.

Two of Lg's partial r's are of particular interest. The first is the +.58 partial in column one, where T^2 is held constant. If there was any suspicion that Lg's simple r of +.54 had something to do with the fact that California and Arizona (along with Florida) have benefitted most from climate, this suspicion is put to rest: Lg does not depend on climate for significance. Second, we have Lg's +.47 partial when $(T - 9)^{2.5} \times [(Y/M)^{0.65}/(E/M)]$ is held constant. The partial isn't this high simply because the weighted variable, not being a pure industrial variable, imperfectly controls the industry factor. If this were the case, Lg would remain lower than the industry variables in the table: proxies, unless they represent more than one influence, can't be more significant than the genuine articles. But Lg's partial is .07 higher than $\sqrt{E/Y}$'s, .11 higher than

$\sqrt{E/P}$'s, .13 higher than log E/M's, and .21 higher than log F/M's. It seems that Lg has something the others don't have.

The contour variable, $(50 - \text{Lat}) (\text{Lg} - 65)^3$, verifies what was observed for Lg. Despite the fact that latitude represents climate as well as north-south isolation, $(50 - \text{Lat}) (\text{Lg} - 65)^3$ remains very significant under controls involving climate. Control of T^2, for example, leaves the contour variable at +.70 (first column). Isolation also describes a lack of industry; yet control of log F/M and $\sqrt{E/P}$ is not very damaging. Even when T^2 and $\sqrt{E/Y}$—the best climate and the best market variable—are jointly controlled, $(50 - \text{Lat}) (\text{Lg} - 65)^3$ can flaunt a partial of +.50. Some of the contour variable's strength is of course due to market-climate interaction. Still, in the last column of table 6-1, where the best interaction variable is held constant, $(50 - \text{Lat}) (\text{Lg} - 65)^3$ remains very significant; its partial is +.49. Spatial isolation definitely looks like a significant influence.

Climate. Because markets appears to be the only influence strong enough to shove climate into the limelight, assuming that climate were favorably intercorrelated with markets, we must carefully review all evidence on the subject. Thus far we have noted a slight tendency for the market variables to improve in their partials when T^2 is held constant—which is not what would happen if temperature could describe markets. Now, if we use the alternative approach of holding market variables constant, the conclusion is the same. In the second, third, and fourth control columns of table 6-1, a market variable but not temperature is controlled. The result: T^2 shows partials that equal or exceed its simple r of +.45. In fact, T^2 climbs to +.54 with $\sqrt{E/Y}$ controlled (not shown), to +.56 with log E/M controlled (not shown), and to +.65 with log F/M controlled.

T^2's leap to +.65 when log F/M is controlled could be due partly to random interference between markets and climate. But I suspect that another factor is largely responsible. Log F/M inaccurately measures industrialization in the South. As a developmental measure, log F/M should describe the progressive thinning out of industry as one goes from Northeast to South to West. Actually, log F/M admirably describes the contrast between Northeast and West; but it less aptly describes the South's lack of industry vis-à-vis the Northeast. A warm climate and adequate rainfall give the South a very dense farm population—too dense to reflect the decline in industrial density. (This is why $\sqrt{E/P}$ falls only to -.40 when log F/M is held constant.) Because log F/M fails to pick up some of the market-based growth in the South, *residual* market-based growth now favors the South more than the West. T^2, high in the South, picks some of this up. Hence if $\sqrt{E/P}$ is partialed out along with log F/M, T^2 slides back from +.65 to +.60.

Before leaving the subject of climate, we should take a quick look at the relationship between wages and climate. With per capita growth the temperature variable was helped (barely) rather than hurt when a wage variable was controlled. The same is true for percentage growth. When $1/W^2$ is partialed out, T^2 goes from +.45 to +.49. If $1/W^2$ and $\sqrt{E/P}$ are jointly controlled, T^2 again goes to +.49. Following log F/M as a second control variable, $1/W^2$ brings T^2 down from +.65 to +.63—hardly enough to support the theory that climate is a proxy for wages. In more advanced control situations, where labor has become a significant influence, there is some duplication (not a great deal). But the simple r for T^2 and the partials shown in table 6-1 definitely are not based on duplication by climate of the wage influence.

Other Influences.   Labor has been omitted from table 6-1 in order to permit better coverage of other influences. Only one of the controls used in the table—log F/M—does much to help labor, and the labor partials it creates are only marginally significant. Nevertheless, there are a few variables that, held constant, can bring out labor's significance; and we should not move on to moderate controls without seeing what simple controls can do. Here are the best possibilities:

	Simple r with Growth	Variables Held Constant		
		log F/M	Lg	$(50 - Lat)(Lg - 65)^3$
$\sqrt{W}$	+.09	-.18	-.22	-.32
$\sqrt{U}$	-.18	-.31	-.41	-.40
$(F/M)^3$	-.16	+.30	+.05	+.13

Once again labor is hard to see because its eastward pull (southeastward, that is) on growth is impotent against the powerful westward pull of markets. A spatial variable or a reasonably good substitute must be used to control western growth. (Log F/M makes a good substitute because of its -.70 intercorrelation with Lg.) The results are again deceptive in placing unionization in the lead: the wage influence is still obscured by conflicts with per capita income and industrialization. But this is a subject that must be reserved for the following section.

Turning now to the threshold factor, we find that in every situation the West-Rural states show slower growth than the West-Metro states. Four of the six control columns have negative partials for West-Rural against significantly positive ones for West-Metro. But it is still too early to be sure that the West-Metro advantage is due to thresholds. The West-Metro states, which include Washington, Oregon, and California, are generally more isolated; they also have a net advantage in climate. Spatial and climate controls—here log F/M is a spatial proxy—give these alternative results:

	log F/M	Lg	T^2 log F/M	T^2 Lg	(50 − Lat) × (Lg − 65)³
			Variables Held Constant		
West-Rural	−.24	−.03	−.24	+.09	−.06
West-Metro	+.32	+.22	+.23	+.16	+.01

Log F/M is a less efficient measure of isolation. Perhaps for this reason the log F/M controls retain fairly sharp contrasts between West-Rural and West-Metro. When the stronger spatial control, Lg, is used, though, the West-Metro advantage is much smaller.

Absolute and per capita growth provided no evidence that agglomeration is a genuine influence; percentage growth offers similar findings. The MB dummy is significantly negative in its simple r (−.41), even more negative when demand is held constant (−.50), and generally negative in its other partial r's. It becomes positive only when industry is held constant and Y/P approaches or attains significantly positive partials. Then MB becomes a proxy for Y/P, which is always about twice as high in its partials. In other words, rather than clustering in the Manufacturing Belt, new industry is dispersing; industry is becoming more evenly distributed.

Moderate Controls

Even higher partial r's are obtained for previously significant variables, and additional variables become significant, when two or three variables are simultaneously partialed out. The moderate control combinations in table 6-2 substantiate this point. These combinations are basically the same as those used for per capita growth in table 5-2; but (a) $\sqrt{E/P}$ is substituted for E/M and $(E/M)^3$ as the industry control, (b) F/P is substituted for Y/P as the demand control, and (c) the combination of $\sqrt{E/P}$ and F/P—roughly equivalent to E/P and Y/P—is substituted for the combination of P/M (industry) and Y/M (Y/M controls Y/P when P/M is held constant). The control modifications were made simply because they gave better results—higher partials. But log E/M and Y/P can also be used for controlling industry and demand with relatively little change in the partials.

Demand.   High per capita income and advanced urbanization—these represent consumer demand—logically should attract industry if other factors are equal. But, we have seen, the favorable demand conditions are buried

Table 6-2
Partial Correlations of Selected Variables with 1947-63 Percentage Growth: Moderate Controls (Two or Three Variables Held Constant)

Selected Independent Variables	Simple r with Growth	Variables Held Constant ("Partialed Out")				
		$\sqrt{E/P}$ $(T-9)/W$	F/P $(T-9)/W$	F/P $\sqrt{E/P}$	F/P Lg	$\sqrt{E/P}$ F/P Lg
(MULTIPLE R)		(.650)	(.340)	(.711)	(.548)	(.712)
Demand						
F/P	-.01	-.59	· · ·	· · ·	· · ·	· · ·
Y/P	-.06	+.47	+.12	-.22	-.35	-.27
Industry						
$\sqrt{E/P}$	-.60	· · ·	-.76	· · ·	-.54	· · ·
$\log F/M$	-.56	-.56	-.72	+.04	-.29	+.07
$(T-9)^2/\sqrt{F/M}$	+.87	+.83	+.89	+.79	+.85	+.79
Lg	+.54	+.34	+.65	+.06	· · ·	· · ·
Labor						
$1/W^2$	-.06	-.38	-.33	+.32	+.41	+.41
$\sqrt{U}$	-.18	+.14	-.08	-.23	-.54	-.35
$(F/M)^3$	-.16	-.27	-.37	+.38	+.13	+.39
Other						
T^2	+.45	+.37	+.42	+.48	+.52	+.49
West-Rural Dummy	+.22	+.04	+.31	-.22	-.04	-.24
West-Metro Dummy	+.48	+.50	+.50	+.32	+.19	+.37
West-Metro × CP/E	+.66	+.69	+.69	+.57	+.52	+.67
MB Dummy	-.41	+.20	-.48	-.06	-.31	-.06

Abbreviations: T = Temperature, W = Wages, E = Manufacturing Employment, P = Population, F = Farm Population, Lg = Longitude, M = Square Miles, U = Unionization, West-Rural = 5 least developed western states, West-Metro = 6 most developed western states, CP = Urban (City) Population, MB = Manufacturing Belt dummy (13 states) under cold climates (Manufacturing Belt), relative overindustrialization (Manufacturing Belt), and high wages (Manufacturing Belt and West)—all of which hamper growth. Table 6-1 showed two demand variables, F/P and Y/P, moving toward or actually achieving significance when T^2 or $\sqrt{E/P}$ were controlled; better results obtained through joint control of T^2 and $\sqrt{E/P}$ were also mentioned. Table 6-2 goes another step and controls all three interfering influences at once. For this purpose, the climate and wage influences are combined in one variable, $(T - 9)/W$. Column one of the table shows that, with $\sqrt{E/P}$ and $(T - 9)/W$ held constant, F/P goes to -.59 and Y/P to +.47. The negative partial for F/P can be viewed as a positive one for CP/P, which actually stands at +.49.

What happens if log E/M replaces $\sqrt{E/P}$ as the industry control—if log E/M and $(T - 9)/W$ are held constant (not shown)? In this case, F/P goes to -.57, almost as high, and Y/P again reaches +.47. CP/P hits +.55. Any way you look at it, consumer demand attracts industry.

The earlier discussion indicated what happens when wages is left out of the control set (T^2 and $\sqrt{E/P}$ held constant): Y/P goes to +.41 and F/P to -.52. But what happens if wages is included and climate left out? If $1/W^2$ and $\sqrt{E/P}$ are the control variables, Y/P can only get to +.21, but F/P reaches -.55.

The consistently better performance of F/P comparison with Y/P indicates that substantive nuances that go with urbanization are important to manufacturing growth. These nuances are subsumed under what is being called the urban attraction. Whatever its ultimate nature, the urban attraction is what makes urban states more attractive even after differences in per capita income among the states have been accounted for (along with differences in climate, industry, and labor factors).

Industry. High as they are, the simple and partial *r*'s already examined for the industry variables do not fully describe the effect of differences in industrialization on differences in growth. The main problem is that the heavily industrialized (excess supply) states of the Manufacturing Belt have a compensating advantage in being highly urbanized and endowed with high per capita income: we saw that $\sqrt{E/P}$ goes from -.60 to -.71 when F/P (representing rural-urban mix and demand) is controlled. A second problem is that the paucity of industry in the West is slightly offset by the West's high wages. A third problem, not too important, is that the northern part of the West is hurt and the southern part helped by climate, so that growth runs higher or lower than what industrialization would dictate. Demand, wages, and climate must be controlled.

Adequate control over the interfering influences can be established by using just two variables, a demand variable—Y/P, CP/P, or F/P—and a temperature-weighted wage variable, $(T - 9)/W$. With per capita growth Y/P was the most significant demand variable and was used for illustrative purposes (table 5-2): control of Y/P and $(T - 9)/W$ boosted the best industry variable, E/M, from a simple r of $-.45$ to a partial r of $-.65$. Percentage growth gives comparable results. This time, though, F/P is the strongest demand variable; F/P and (T − 9)/W becomes the control combination. Table 6-2 shows the industry variables responding favorably to this combination: Lg goes from +.54 to +.65, $\sqrt{E/P}$ from $-.60$ to $-.76$, and log F/M from $-.56$ to $-.72$. Two other industry variables used in table 6-1 but not shown in table 6-2 also improve: $\sqrt{E/Y}$ goes from $-.61$ to $-.75$ and log E/M from $-.57$ to $-.77$.

One of the industry variables, log F/M, becomes rather prominent later in this chapter as adapted for use in the weighted variable $(T − 9)^2/\sqrt{F/M}$. This makes it important to understand what log F/M describes. It includes three elements: demand, supply, and spatial isolation. Observe the $-.56$ partial for log F/M in the first column. It occurs where supply ($\sqrt{E/P}$) has been held constant but spatial isolation and demand are significant: Lg reads +.34 and Y/P reads +.47. Since log F/M is stronger than either of the other variables, it looks like its strength derives from an ability to combine spatial isolation and per capita income: states with low farm population densities are western and tend to be more urbanized, which means higher per capita income. In the third column, supply and demand are held constant and Lg is not significant (because the labor variables are maturing and pulling growth eastward). With none of the three elements operating, log F/M falls to +.04. In the fourth column F/P and Lg are controlled but not $\sqrt{E/P}$. Log F/M's $-.29$ partial now reflects that of $-.54$ for $\sqrt{E/P}$. In the last column all three market influences—supply, demand, and isolation—are controlled; log F/M reads +.07.

This brings us to the weighted version, $(T − 9)^2/\sqrt{F/M}$. It rewards states that combine the virtues of low farm population density and warm climate (with low density further combining spatial isolation and strong supply-demand ratios). In table 6-1 this variable displayed great strength: it ranged from +.78 to +.89, except when another temperature-weighted market variable was held constant. Now, in table 6-2, the performance is repeated. This time the partials range from +.79 to +.89. Yet in every column at least one and sometimes two or three market variables are controlled. (The +.79 readings occur in the two columns where both supply and demand—$\sqrt{E/P}$ and F/P—are controlled and log F/M moves close to zero.) It is increasingly apparent that the market influence interacts with climate to produce an influence that market variables alone cannot describe.

Labor. The next three variables in table 6-2—$1/W^2$, $\sqrt{U}$, and $(F/M)^3$— represent labor. A reciprocal continues to provide the best adjustment for curvilinear correlation in the case of wages, but for unionization the square root now works best and is shown; $(F/M)^3$ is still the labor supply variable. Only the last three columns of the table merit consideration in relation to labor: a labor variable, (T − 9)/W, is held constant in the first two columns, causing the other labor variables to become proxies. (For example, $1/W^2$ becomes a proxy for Y/P in the first column, where Y/P goes to +.47; it is a proxy for Lg in the second column, where Lg reaches +.65 and low wage rates can describe comparatively slow growth in the East.)

We saw earlier that the most effective one-variable control arrangement for labor involved holding Lg constant. Controlling Lg tones down the fast growth in the West. This allows the labor-oriented growth in part of the East (the South) to register better in comparative terms. With Lg partialed out, unionization is the most significant labor influence; per capita and percentage growth agree on this point. But as pointed out before, this is misleading: the wage influence is still partly obscured by the tendency of high wages to describe high demand, and unionization is still tending to act as a proxy for supply. Thus with per capita growth, wages moved ahead of unionization as the most significant labor influence when Y/P and $(E/M)^3$ were controlled.

Percentage growth verifies the per capita growth findings. We saw that when Lg alone is controlled, $\sqrt{U}$ has a .19 advantage over the closest wage variable: $\sqrt{U}$ is -.41 and $\sqrt{W}$ is -.22. But in column four of table 6-2, controlling F/P (demand) in addition to Lg cuts this advantage to .13: $\sqrt{U}$ reads -.54 and $1/W^2$ reads +.41. Unionization still looks like a potent influence, though—because it is closely linked with $\sqrt{E/P}$, which now has an identical -.54 reading. Unions tend to be strong where industry is strong, weak where industry is weak; but wages, while high where industry is strong, are again high in the West, where industry is weak. Unionization has become a three-way proxy for wages, industrialization, and labor supply. In the last column, $\sqrt{E/P}$ is also held constant and the truth comes out: $\sqrt{U}$ plummets from -.54 to -.35. Wages, however, is not affected: $1/W^2$ stays at +.41 and becomes the new leader.

The industrialization prop has been removed, but labor supply and wages continue to lend support to unionization. If we now remove the labor supply prop by controlling $(F/M)^3$—four variables held constant—$\sqrt{U}$ continues down to -.28, but $1/W^2$ just steps from +.41 to +.40. Finally, if $1/W^2$ is used as a fifth control variable, $\sqrt{U}$ topples to -.14. These findings do not rule out the possibility that unions have some effect on manufacturing growth. But any such effect is severely limited, is substantially less than the effect of wages, and can be adequately (if indirectly) described by wages and labor supply.

The above conclusion is verified from another direction by the r's in the third column. It was said that demand and industry counter the wage influence and create the illusion that unionization is more significant than wages. Column three shows what happens when just these two influences, represented by F/P and $\sqrt{E/P}$, are neutralized. What happens is that $1/W^2$ becomes significant (+.32) but not $\sqrt{U}$ (-.23). If $(F/M)^3$ is partialed out third (not shown), $1/W^2$ declines five points to +.27 and $\sqrt{U}$ declines nine to -.14. Wages is now well ahead of unionization, although fast growth in the West still belittles the eastern influence of wages. This problem is removed by reintroducing Lg as control variable number four. We are back to the partials of +.40 for $1/W^2$ and -.28 for $\sqrt{U}$.

Let us turn now to labor supply. A dense farm population, indicative of abundant surplus labor, appears to stimulate growth. The analyses of both absolute and per capita growth revealed significant partials for $(F/M)^3$ and $(F/M)^4$ whenever both demand and industrialization were held constant. With per capita growth, the supply-demand control combination used in table 5-2 sent $(F/M)^3$ to +.39. The equivalent control combination for percentage growth is F/P and $\sqrt{E/P}$ (column three). This time $(F/M)^3$ goes to +.38; labor supply is again significant at the 1 percent confidence level. And if we move on to the last column, where Lg is added as a third control, $(F/M)^3$ goes up a point to +.39. Could this be the result of a proxy relationship with wages? When $1/W^2$ is added as a fourth control (not shown), $(F/M)^3$ simply goes back to +.38. With unionization? It now stands at -.22; $\sqrt{U}$ is the proxy.

Other Influences. Climate, the threshold factor, and agglomeration are the remaining influences covered in the table. Climate is by far the most important. T^2 shows significant partials even in the first two columns, where $(T - 9)/W$ is controlled. The +.37 partial in the first column is quite impressive: it occurs in the face of an adverse intercorrelation with Y/P, which has become very significant (+.47) and is pulling down on southern growth (Y/P is lowest in the South). In the last three columns, where $(T - 9)/W$ is not controlled but an income variable (F/P) is, the partials for T^2 are higher than its simple r. These partials are helped some by the emergence of labor as a significant influence but do not depend on labor: adding $1/W^2$ to the control variables in the last column leaves T^2 with a partial of +.38. (This is more duplication between labor and climate than usually found. The control combination of log F/M, $1/W^2$ and $(F/M)^3$, for example, gives T^2 a partial of +.61, barely lower than the +.65 resulting when log F/M alone is controlled.)

In the preceding chapter, table 5-2 had T reaching +.65 when P/M and Y/M were used to control industry and income; this partial explained 31 percent of the total variance. With percentage growth the control combination of log P/M and log Y/M gives identical results: T goes to +.65 and can explain 31 percent of the total variance. There can be no question of support from labor, for in this instance all of the labor variables are hovering near zero. Neither is a cold climate speaking for overindustrialization in the Manufacturing Belt: industry is well controlled and the MB dummy reads -.09.

The threshold analysis again begins with a comparison of the West-Rural and West-Metro dummies. West-Metro continues its perfect record of superiority, begun with absolute growth back in table 4-1. The most comprehensive control combination (last column) shows West-Metro at +.37 and West-Rural at -.24—a considerable difference. The control combination of log F/M and $\sqrt{E/P}$, not shown, gives West-Metro a +.38 to -.30 advantage.

Table 6-2 also introduces a new threshold variable. One recalls that West-Metro $\times$ CP generated high r's with absolute growth and that West-Metro $\times$ $(CP/P)^3$ did the same with per capita growth. These variables seemed to describe a link between progressively higher growth and progressively higher development in the West-Metro group, when development was viewed in terms of urbanization. With percentage growth this finding was not confirmed: variants of West-Metro $\times$ CP/P generally did about the same as West-Metro itself. This seemingly reflects the arithmetic advantage held by states with low E values—low E goes with low CP/P—when percentage growth is computed. Nevertheless, when West-Metro was weighted by a demand-supply ratio based on CP, namely, CP/E, better results *were* obtained. The weighted variable, West-Metro $\times$ CP/E, appears at the bottom of the table. Its r's are substantially better than the West-Metro r's; growth is proportional to strength of market within the West-Metro group. This hints—only hints—that levels of urbanization continue to influence growth after the threshold is crossed.

Agglomeration takes us back to the MB dummy. If there is an agglomeration influence, the MB dummy should have some significantly positive r's. These should not rest on proxy relationships. MB does offer one positive r (+.20); but it is not significant, and it rests on a proxy relationship to Y/P. If Y/P is added to the control variables in the first column, the dummy becomes negative (−.01). All of the other partials for MB are likewise negative. The one deserving the most attention is the −.48 partial in the second column. Here one influence that is favorable to the Manufacturing Belt, demand, and two unfavorable influences, climate and wages, are set aside. This affords an unusually good view of whether old industry attracts or repels new industry. It repels. A slightly different dummy, NE (Northeast), goes to −.57 under the same controls by taking in the three northern New England states in addition to the states of the Manufacturing Belt.

Strong Controls

High partial r's for variables with latent significance or that temporarily lost significance were obtained under many different strong control combinations. The best results (and the strongest controls) resulted when the controls were built around a combination of (1) a temperature-weighted market variable, (2) temperature itself, and (3) a supply-demand ratio. In other words, the two dominant influences—markets and climate—had to be well controlled. The three central variables required supplementation by spatial, per capita income (weighted), labor, and threshold variables.

Markets.   Two market variables appear in table 6–3. The first, $(T - 9)^{1.5} \times (Y^{0.8}/P)$ will be remembered as the variable with the highest simple r opposite per capita growth. With percentage growth it again has a highly significant simple r (+.65). But it falls into limbo in the first control column when two other market variables placing considerable emphasis on income are partialed

Table 6-3
Partial Correlations of Selected Variables with 1947–63 Percentage Growth: Strong Controls (Three to Six Variables Held Constant)

Selected Independent Variables	Simple r with Growth	$\dfrac{E/Y}{T^2}$ $(T-9)^2\sqrt{F/M}$	Lat × Lg $T(Y^{0.8}/P)$ $1/(P/M)$ $\dfrac{E/Y}{T^2}$ $(T-9)^2\sqrt{F/M}$	Lat × Lg $(T-9)^2/W^2$ $T(Y^{0.8}/P)$ $\dfrac{\sqrt{E/P}}{T^2}$ $(T-9)^2\sqrt{F/M}$	Lat × Lg $(T-9)^2/W^2$ $1/(P/M)$ $\dfrac{\sqrt{E/P}}{T^2}$ $(T-9)^2\sqrt{F/M}$	$(F/M)^3$ $(T-9)^2/W^2$ $1/(E/M)$ $\dfrac{\sqrt{E/P}}{T^2}$ $T(Y^{0.65}/E)$
		Variables Held Constant ("Partialed Out")				
(MULTIPLE R)		(.909)	(.924)	(.928)	(.948)	(.906)
Markets						
$(T-9)^{1.5} \times (Y^{0.8}/P)^3$	+.65	–.02	····	····	+.56	+.52
$(50 - Lat)(Lg - 65)^3$	+.72	+.01	–.21	–.06	+.09	+.60
Labor						
$1/W^2$	–.06	+.38	+.57	+.05	–.14	–.08
$\sqrt{U}$	–.18	–.33	–.43	–.08	–.12	+.06
$(T-9)^2/W^2$	+.32	+.47[a]	+.71	····	····	····
$(F/M)^3$	–.16	+.36	+.50	+.19	+.31	····
Threshold						
$1/(E/M)$	+.41	–.31	+.00	–.67	–.14	····
$1/(P/M)$	+.41	–.34	····	–.71	····	+.33
West-Rural Dummy	+.22	–.23	+.02	–.41	+.12	–.18
West-Metro Dummy	+.48	+.18	–.02	+.33	+.17	+.55
W-Rural × $1/(E/M)$	+.30	–.32	–.07	–.65	+.02	–.06
W-Rural × $1/(P/M)$	+.26	–.37	–.18	–.67	+.07	+.07
W-Metro × CP/E	+.66	+.37	+.18	+.52	+.25	+.58

[a] This partial r is for $(T-9)/W$.

Abbreviations: T = Temperature, F = Farm Population, M = Square Miles, E = Manufacturing Employment, Y = Income, P = Population, Lat × Lg = (50 − Lat) (Lg − 65), Lat = Latitude, Lg = Longitude, W = Wages, $T(Y^{0.65}/E) = (T-9)^{2.5} \times [(Y/M)^{0.65}/(E/M)]$, U = Unionization, West-Rural = 5 least developed western states (dummy), West-Metro = 6 most developed western states (dummy), CP = Urban Population out. This is deceiving; $(T - 9)^{1.5} \times (Y^{0.8}/P)$ still has latent significance. In the last two columns it shows partials of +.56 and +.52. The comparable partials for unweighted Y/P (not shown) are +.28 and +.44. If all other variables in the best ten-variable combination (table 6-5) are partialed out, $(T - 9)^{1.5} \times (Y^{0.8}/P)$ hits +.60; Y/P lags behind at +.42. It is again apparent that per capita income (consumer demand) influences growth and that a market-climate interaction effect exists.

The second market variable tested in the table is $(50 - Lat)(Lg - 65)^3$. This is a spatial isolation variable that, by cubing the longitude element, gives longitude (east-west) much more weight than latitude. Despite a simple *r* of +.72, it is down to +.01 in the first column: two other market variables are controlled, allowing labor to become significant and pull residential growth to the East. Poor residual growth in the subthreshold states also hurts, as does the ability of $\sqrt{F/M}$ to duplicate longitude. But in the last column—spatial variables are controlled in the intermediate ones—$(50 - Lat)(Lg - 65)^3$ revives, going to +.60. The secret of its renewed success is that both the eastward pull of labor and the threshold problem have been controlled; additionally, $(T - 9)^2/\sqrt{F/M}$ has been replaced by $(T - 9)^{2.5} \times [(Y/M)^{0.65}/(E/M)]$, which has less tendency to duplicate longitude.

Since two market variables and climate are also controlled, supply-demand and climate proxy relationships cannot very well lie behind this +.60 partial. Nor is it a case of $(T - 9)^{1.5} \times (Y^{0.8}/P)$ not having been controlled: when the weighted income variable becomes a seventh control, $(50 - Lat)(Lg - 65)^3$ moves ahead to +.66. If entered last in the best ten-variable combination—nine variables held constant—the contour variable reaches +.81. Lg reaches +.55. The evidence strongly implies that northeastern manufacturers find it hard to compete with local industry in states remote from the Northeast. This forces them either to establish branch plants to serve regional markets or simply to yield the more remote markets to developing regional firms.

Wages and Unionization. The first two control columns in table 6-3 feature partial *r*'s for labor variables; a wage variable is held constant in the remaining three. With just the three basic variables—$(T - 9)^2/\sqrt{F/M}$, T^2, and E/Y—held constant, wages is already significant at the 1 percent confidence level: $1/W^2$ hits +.38. Although longitude is not directly controlled, the combination of $\sqrt{F/M}$ and E/Y can do a pretty fair job of explaining east-west isolation. These variables also bring per capita income and industrialization under substantial control, thus pushing aside all three of the forces that hide the wage influence.

Because industry is adequately controlled, unionization cannot speak for it as a proxy; $\sqrt{U}$ reads −.33, five points below wages. And when $1/W^2$ joins the control set—four variables held constant (not shown)—$\sqrt{U}$ drops to −.13. This new partial in turn hinges on a further proxy relationship between $\sqrt{U}$ and $(F/M)^3$, which is still significant at +.29.

Although the column one partials are rather low, they climb steadily as more control variables are added. One difficulty is that the subthreshold states, which now show low residual growth, have low wages when compared to the other western states. Controlling a threshold variable, $1/(P/M)$, takes care of this: $1/W^2$ goes to +.47 and $\sqrt{U}$ to −.42. Per capita income and spatial isolation are imperfectly controlled, so additional increases result when $(T − 9)^{1.5}$ $\times (Y^{0.8}/P)$ and $(50 − \text{Lat}) (\text{Lg} − 50)$ are held constant. This gives us the control set shown in the second column. The wage and unionization partials become +.57 for $1/W^2$ and −.43 for $\sqrt{U}$. Unionization is now looking very much like a proxy for wages.

In the previous table, no temperature-weighted wage variable was shown. Very significant partials were available; but temperature was not controlled, and the weighted wage partials were based largely on proxy relationships to temperature per se. In table 6–3, however, T^2 is held constant, so weighted wages can be shown. The first control set gives $(T − 9)/W$ a partial of +.47, a good deal better than the +.38 partial for $1/W^2$. But the best weighted wage variable in most of the percentage growth experiments was the one featured with absolute growth—$(T − 9)^2/W^2$, or $(T − 9)^2 \times 1/W^2$. It is ahead of $1/W^2$ in the second column by a +.71 to +.57 margin. These two comparisons provide renewed evidence of the wage-climate interaction effect. Just as market-oriented firms avoid otherwise attractive states when the climate is too cold, so do labor-oriented firms avoid low-wage states with cold climates (e.g., North Dakota).

Evidence has been mounting that unionization derives its significance from an ability to combine three beneficial proxy relationships—to industrialization, to labor supply, and to wages. Industrialization is controlled in both labor columns in table 6–3, with the result that wages has better partials than unionization. Now let us do something about labor supply and see what happens. If $(F/M)^3$ is added to the six-variable combination heading the second column, we get revised partials of +.69 for $(T − 9)^2/W^2$ (down .02), +.55 for $1/W^2$ (down .02), and −.35 for $\sqrt{U}$ (down .08). Forced to limit its proxy relationships to one (wages), unionization is no longer significant at the 1 percent level, which is ± .39 when seven variables are held constant. By making $(T − 9)^2/W^2$ the eighth control variable, we can force $\sqrt{U}$ back to −.01.

One more test frosts the unionization-is-a-proxy cake. This test goes to the best ten-variable combination (table 6–5) for its control variables. That combination uses $\sqrt{E/P}$ instead of E/Y to control industrialization; hence per capita income (Y/P) is not as well controlled and the labor partials run somewhat low. But the findings nevertheless support the point being made. Here are the labor partials resulting (a) when eight variables—all but the two labor variables—

are controlled, (b) when $(F/M)^2$ is also controlled, and (c) when $1/W^2$ and $1/U^2$ take turns being the tenth control variable:

	Step 8	Step 9: $(F/M)^2$	Step 10: $1/W^2$	Alt. 10: $1/U^2$
$(F/M)^2$	+.39	....	....	....
$1/W^2$	+.33	+.47	....	+.42
$1/U^2$	+.30	+.24	-.01	....
$(T-9)^2/W^2$	+.63	+.77	+.70	+.77

The addition of $(F/M)^2$ to the control set shoves $1/U^2$ beyond the margin of significance (the 5 percent level is now ± .32). But the wage variables actually improve, denying that they are proxies for labor supply. And when $1/W^2$ is partialed out tenth, $1/U^2$ falls past zero to -.01 (the wrong sign). We must conclude that unionization is a proxy for labor supply and wages.

Temperature-weighted wages delivers a brilliant encore in the text table. It begins by displaying a partial r that is thirty points above that of the unweighted wage variable—which means an r^2 almost three times as high (.59 compared to .22). Then, when $1/W^2$ is partialed out, $(T-9)^2/W^2$ declines only to +.70. And this isn't because temperature is carrying the ball: T^2 is among the variables held constant (along with three climate-weighted market variables).

Labor Supply.   The labor supply variables—chiefly $(F/M)^3$—have been coming up quite regularly with significant partials. Table 6-2 offered one of +.39 and another of +.38; the latter was higher than anything for wages or unionization. Yet these two r's are not safely above the 1 percent level and could leave some doubt as to their legitimacy. Table 6-3 clears away this doubt. It first shows a significant partial of +.36 which, though lower than the others, comes by a different route. This makes spurious correlation unlikely. Next, the table shows a +.50 partial for $(F/M)^3$. This one *is* safely above the 1 percent level. There is also a +.31 partial for $(F/M)^3$ in the fourth column, where a wage variable has been controlled and $\sqrt{U}$ reads -.12; $(F/M)^3$ is not a proxy for wages or unionization. This +.31 partial isn't very significant, of course, but if one more control variable is used, it improves: if $(T-9)^{1.5} \times (Y^{0.8}/P)$ is partialed out seventh, $(F/M)^3$ goes to +.39 (while $\sqrt{U}$ drops to +.03).

Sometimes, particularly when many variables are controlled, $(F/M)^2$ gives better results than $(F/M)^3$. It appears in the best multiple correlation combinations for eight to ten variables (table 6-5). Entered last in the best ten-variable set, $(F/M)^2$ reaches +.66. The significance of this partial can hardly be questioned. Nor can it result from proxy relationships to wages or unionization: $(T-9)^2/W^2$ has been controlled, and $\sqrt{U}$ has a partial of -.05.

The labor supply variables measure surplus labor indirectly; they are really proxies for labor supply. This introduces the possibility of misinterpretation and makes it prudent to recheck their substance through before-and-after analyses of residual (unexplained) growth. "After" means after $(F/M)^3$ is added to a group of variables held constant. When this was done with absolute and per capita growth, the biggest reductions in unexplained growth involved higher predictions for North and South Carolina, Kentucky, and Tennessee—surplus labor states situated relatively close to the Manufacturing Belt. Kentucky, which has the highest wages and coldest climate of any southeastern state, responded to $(F/M)^3$ only after being penalized by a temperature-weighted wage variable. The question is: do we get the same results with percentage growth?

To answer this question, a new analysis compared the residuals found before and after $(F/M)^3$ was added to the six-variable control set heading the second column in table 6-3—the column in which $(F/M)^3$ reaches +.50. A second comparison was made with $(T - 9)^2/W^2$ entering before $(F/M)^3$. In the first comparison, the two biggest reductions in residual growth went to North Carolina and Tennessee—the same states that ranked one-two in the comparable analyses for absolute and per capita growth. Other leading states for which lower residual growth resulted from higher predicted growth were—in order—Mississippi, Arizona, Delaware, and South Carolina. The leading reductions in states where growth predictions were cut went to Louisiana, Rhode Island, Texas, and Massachusetts. When the experiment was repeated with $(T - 9)/W^2$ in the "before" control set, Kentucky and Tennessee were one-two; both benefitted from higher predicted growth. North Carolina remained among the leaders but fell to eighth; Arizona and Delaware also repeated. Among leaders benefitting from lower predicted growth, only Louisiana, Rhode Island, and Massachusetts repeated.

The results are far from perfect—we don't expect perfect predictions from a variable whose r is +.50—but in general the pattern fits the theory: there are deservedly lower predictions for states that have lost labor-oriented industry and deservedly higher predictions for states that have acquired labor-oriented industry. The textile shift is clearly reflected, or so it would seem. Massachusetts and Rhode Island, which had the first and third largest textile losses, are among the highest losers. North Carolina and South Carolina, with the biggest textile gains, are among the leaders and get higher predicted growth. Kentucky and Tennessee, while not textile gainers, do have abundant supplies of low-cost labor and therefore fit nicely into a surplus labor pattern. The interpretation of $(F/M)^3$ as a labor supply variable appears sound.

To this conclusion I would add a qualification. It is abundant *low-cost* labor that has attracted labor-oriented firms to southern states. There is almost certainly a wage element built into $(F/M)^3$, something that the wage variables do not adequately represent. This might be an interaction effect of a different sort: interaction between the wages of labor and the abundance of labor. Or perhaps it is interaction between wage levels and proximity to the New York garment industry; this would explain why the states closest to New York benefit most. Whether or not these explanations are the best—they do hold some truth— the point remains that the analytical distinction between wages and labor supply is artificial to a degree.

Thresholds: Preliminary Findings. In the last chapter we saw that density reciprocals such as $1/(E/M)$ and $1/(P/M)$ acquire new substance when market variables are controlled. The density reciprocals were originally intended to measure variations in development associated with strong and weak markets. The market relationship calls for positive r's between the density *reciprocals* and growth: low density = high reciprocal = high growth. But when other (and better) market variables were partialed out, the reciprocals became negative—significantly negative. Something was undermining residual growth in the most under-developed states.

Various tests showed that density had become an indicator of the presence or absence of an adequate economic base—a threshold level of development. "Threshold" does not imply that a state below the threshold cannot grow rapidly; it implies, rather, that the state must cross the threshold before it can fully exploit its market potential. That is, the state must be able to provide the labor force, skills, services, facilities, intermediate and consumer markets, and urban living conditions needed or wanted by a wide range of firms, some of which are more demanding than others. A regional market big enough for economies of scale could be critical in this respect. The per capita growth analysis indicated that the threshold influence adversely affects the five western states with the smallest metropolitan areas (if any): Montana, Idaho, Wyoming, New Mexico, and Nevada.

Does percentage growth tell the same story? It does. Table 6-3 shows two density reciprocals, $1/(E/M)$ and $1/(P/M)$, becoming significantly negative (-.31 and -.34) with just three variables held constant. Predictably, the control set includes two market variables—E/Y and the extremely powerful weighted variable, $(T - 9)^2/\sqrt{F/M}$. In the third column, where two more market variables— $(T - 9)^{1.5} \times (Y^{0.8}/P)$ and $(50 - Lat)(Lg - 65)$—and a wage variable are thrown into the mix, highly significant partials are reached: $1/(E/M)$ goes to -.67 and $1/(P/M)$ to -.71. And this is not the limit. If entered last in the best nine-variable combination (table 6-5), $1/(P/M)$ gets to -.81. The underdeveloped states are again showing poor residual growth.

Thresholds: Residuals and Dummies. The experiments used with per capita growth to verify the nature of the threshold influence were repeated for percentage growth. First came an analysis of residuals. The analysis started where $1/(P/M)$ reaches its -.71 partial in table 6-3; then $1/(P/M)$ was added to the control set. By a considerable margin, the three biggest reductions in residual growth were in Nevada, Arizona, and Wyoming—all western states. Eight of the eleven western states were among the thirteen with the largest reductions in unexplained growth; nine of the eleven western states (all but Oregon and California) had their residuals reduced. The western character of the influence is verified.

Reduced residuals resulting from cuts in predicted growth accrued to—in order of magnitude of reduction—Nevada, Wyoming, Montana, and Idaho. Interestingly enough, the low-to-high population density rankings for these states are the same: Nevada, Wyoming, Montana, and Idaho. There is perfect agreement between rank order of underdevelopment and rank order of reduction. The fifth subthreshold state, New Mexico, failed to conform insofar as it was under-predicted at the start and improved via a higher prediction. However, in a second analysis using $1/(E/M)$ and another control combination, New Mexico fell into the sub-threshold group.

Meanwhile, reduced residuals due to higher predicted growth also went to Arizona, Washington, Colorado, and Utah—all of which were identified as above the threshold. California and Oregon didn't conform. California was accurately predicted to begin with and couldn't accommodate a higher prediction (this applies only to percentage growth). Oregon, which also failed to conform in the per capita growth analysis, is sandwiched between the two most developed western states—California and Washington—and seems to lose growth to them. One might say that Oregon has a higher threshold.

The West, West-Rural, and West-Metro dummies used with per capita growth were recreated to repeat the chapter 5 tests. The simplest test was to verify the analysis of residuals by comparing West-Rural and West-Metro. We have already seen many such comparisons; table 6–3 shows a few more. The three columns where $1/(P/M)$ or $1/(E/M)$ is controlled don't count; but in the other two, West-Metro is positive and West-Rural negative. In column three, on which the analysis of residuals was based, West-Metro reads +.33 to West-Rural's -.41. Between these two readings West (not shown) is neutral; its partial is -.03. This again demonstrates that the West-Rural states are doing poorly in their residual growth but that this condition does not apply to the West as a whole.

Thresholds: Further Testing.   The next test attempted to demonstrate that $1/(E/M)$ and $1/(P/M)$ cannot discriminate among high density states and that their predictive ability therefore must rest on discrimination among the low density states. The theoretical basis for this test was described in the last chapter: the eastern state reciprocals are all equal to one over a high density value and therefore are all close to zero. The test put them at exactly zero to see if it made any difference. This was done by multiplying $1/(E/M)$ and $1/(P/M)$ by West (all eastern states valued at zero) or, alternatively, by West-Rural (all eastern *and* West-Metro states valued at zero). The resulting partials did indeed demonstrate that the reciprocals had little if any discriminatory power outside of the West.

Comparisons of partials for $1/(P/M)$, West $\times$ $1/(P/M)$, and West-Rural $\times$ $1/(P/M)$ had their partials all on about the same level; the same was true for $1/(E/M)$.

Table 6-3 compares $1/(E/M)$ with West-Rural $\times$ $1/(E/M)$ and also compares $1/(P/M)$ with West-Rural $\times$ $1/(P/M)$. In the first column the West-Rural versions do better. But in the third column the unweighted versions do better. Either way, the leader is always just a few points ahead of most. Clearly, the negative influence recorded by the density reciprocals is largely if not wholly confined to the five West-Rural states.

A more detailed picture, and one less subject to distortion from uncontrolled influences, is obtained when eight variables are controlled—all but the two West-Rural variables from the best ten-variable combination (table 6-5). These partials result:

West-Rural	= -.63	West-Metro	= +.46
$1/(E/M)$	= -.66	$1/(P/M)$	= -.61
West $\times$ $1/(E/M)$	= -.76	West $\times$ $1/(P/M)$	= -.64
West-Rural $\times$ $1/(E/M)$	= -.77	West-Rural $\times$ $1/(P/M)$	= -.69
West-Rural $\times$ $1/E$	= -.77	West-Rural $\times$ $1/VA$	= -.79

In this illustration, better results are obtained by blocking out the eastern states. This proves that the reciprocals are of no value for eastern predictions. Still better results occur when the West-Metro states are also blocked out (West-Rural replaces West as the multiplier). This proves that the reciprocals are of no net value for discriminating among states in the West-Metro group. A West-Rural influence is again evident.

The positive side of thresholds—growth proportional to development among the West-Metro states—remains to be discussed. Generally, the strong control combinations followed the lead of the moderate combinations in refusing to give variants of West-Metro $\times$ CP/P higher partials than West-Metro itself. On the other hand, West-Metro $\times$ CP/E continued to outperform West-Metro. In the third column, it shows a +.52 to +.33 advantage over West-Metro. The West-Metro states with the widest gaps between supply (E) and demand (CP) *are* growing faster. And because CP is the only demand variable that works well in the demand-supply ratio, there is an implication that growth is aided by urbanization.

Other Influences.   A few other actual or potential influences remain to be discussed in relation to strong controls. The first is climate. It is not directly tested in the table, for it is needed as a control. However, T^2 was tested against strong controls and gave a respectable performance. Four market variables—E/Y, log F/M, Y/P, and Lg—were first held constant for well-rounded control over markets (except for the interaction effect). T^2 climbed from its simple r of +.45 to a partial r of +.60—still able to explain a solid 20 percent of the total variance.

Then two labor variables—$1/W^2$ and $(F/M)^3$—were added to the controls.[1] T^2 eased back to +.59. Next, $1/(P/M)$—stronger than $1/(E/M)$ at this point—was used as a seventh control to take care of thresholds. This moved T^2 back to +.56, reflecting the fact that Montana, Idaho, and Wyoming are hampered by cold climates. With the seven variables partialed out, T^2 could explain 32 percent of the residual variance and 14 percent of the total variance. Another climate variable, 50 – Lat, had a partial of +.65, capable of explaining 19 percent of the total variance.

But this isn't all; the interaction effect must be considered. It was evaluated by using T^2 as control number eight and then letting other climate and climate-weighted variables enter the combination. They entered in this order and contributed the indicated increases to R^2:

Step	Variable	Partial r	ΔR^2
9	$(T - 9)^2/\sqrt{F/M}$	+.84	.214
10	50 – Lat	+.47	.019
11	$(T - 9)^2/W^2$	+.33	.008
12	$(T - 9)^{1.5} \times (Y^{0.8}/P)$	+.43	.012

Even with T^2, log F/M, and three other market variables controlled, $(T - 9)^2/\sqrt{F/M}$ shows a partial of +.84 and can explain 21 percent of the variance. Other climate variables make further contributions. Summing up, after seven market, labor, and threshold variables were controlled, T^2 could explain 14 percent (and 50 – Lat 19 percent) of the variance; and four additional climate and climate-weighted variables could explain another 25 percent—39 percent in all.

Unlike climate, agglomeration can't get off the ground. No agglomeration variables are shown in table 6–3; there is really nothing to show. But if MB $\times$ E/M were shown—it is probably the best agglomeration variable—the partials in the five columns would be -.18, -.22, -.12, -.03, and -.09. With ten variables held constant (table 6–5), MB $\times$ E/M reads +.02. Industry is not clustering to the Manufacturing Belt; it is dispersing.

The urban attraction, already found to be significant with absolute and per capita growth, is also significant with percentage growth. One significant and two almost-significant partials could have been shown by adding the CP/P dummy to table 6–3. This dummy values states that are more than 57.7 percent urban at one and other states at zero. It has partials of +.27, +.28, and +.36 under the last three control combinations in the table. However, at this stage the dummy seems to be largely a proxy for thresholds (middle combination) and per capita income (last two combinations). It takes one or two more control variables to remove the uncertainty. If all but the rural-urban variable in the best nine-variable combination are controlled, we get partials of +.39 for the CP/P dummy, +.40 for CP/P, -.40 for F/P, -.52 for F/CP, and -.55 for $1/(CP/P)$. If all but the rural-urban variable in the best ten-variable combination are held constant, we get partials of +.46 for CP/P, -.50 for F/P, -.62 for 1/(CP/P), and -.66 for F/CP. As before, the urban states show faster residual growth when the four leading influences—markets, climate, labor, thresholds—are set aside.

Multiple Correlations

Continuing in the format of the preceding two chapters, we are ready to inspect the best Rs (multiple correlations). These will provide a better idea of the relative shares claimed by different influences in explaining percentage growth. The Rs are summarized in two tables—6-4 and 6-5. The first presents three combinations that provide the highest Rs obtainable for two to seven variables, and the second offers two more combinations with the best Rs for eight to ten variables.

Two to Seven Variables

All of the best combinations for two to seven variables begin with (and retain as their most significant variables) three variables representing markets and climate. A labor variable—either wages or labor supply—always comes in at step four. Then comes a threshold variable. And, in the seven-variable combination, this is followed by a second labor variable and finally an urban attraction variable. We are back to the same old one-two-three-four-five ranking: markets, climate, labor, thresholds, and the urban attraction.

Best for Steps 2-3. All of the best combinations revolve around a temperature-weighted market variable, either $(T - 9)^{2.5} \times [(Y/M)^{0.65}/(E/M)]$ or $(T - 9)^2/\sqrt{F/M}$ (slightly modified in one set). "Best for Steps 2-3" uses $(T - 9)^{2.5} \times [(Y/M)^{0.65}/(E/M)]$. It is shown entering at step one, where its +.89 simple r converts to an R^2 (really r^2) of .783. The one variable explains nearly 80 percent of the variation in percentage growth.

Step 2 brings in West-Metro $\times$ CP/E. All but the six West-Metro states are valued at zero; the six are valued at CP/E. Faster growth for the most developed western states as a group is thus combined with proportionality within the group. The dummy multiplier is doing most of the work: its step two partial is +.50, compared to +.52 for West-Metro $\times$ CP/E. (Except for the consistent superiority of West-Metro $\times$ CP/E over West-Metro in other settings, this difference would appear to be spurious.) At the moment West-Metro is primarily a market variable, not a threshold variable. Mainly, it is picking up the spatial isolation facet of markets. (West-Metro is a dummy longitude variable with underpopulated states blanked out.) Isolation could almost as well be represented at

Table 6-4

Multiple Correlations for 1947–63 Percentage Growth: Best Combinations for Two to Seven Variables

Step	Variable Entered	r or Partial r at Entry Step	R	R²	F (= T²) to Remove
Best for Steps 2-3					
1	$(T-9)^{2.5} \times [(Y/M)^{0.65}/(E/M)]$	+.89	.885	.783	100.04
2	West-Metro × CP/E	+.52	.918	.843	22.23
3	E/Y	−.46	.936	.876	16.51
4	$(F/M)^4$	+.33	.943	.889	5.14
Best for Step 4					
1	E/Y	−.60	.600	.360	43.08
2	$(T-9)^2$	+.49	.718	.516	48.98
3	$(T-9)^{2.5}/\sqrt{F/M}$	+.80	.911	.830	179.24
4	$(T-9)/W$	+.61	.945	.893	36.45
5	West-Rural × 1/(P/M)	−.40	.954	.910	8.23
Best for Steps 5-7					
1	T^2	+.45	.449	.202	50.36
2	E/Y	−.63	.721	.520	63.89
3	$(T-9)^2/\sqrt{F/M}$	+.80	.909	.826	206.86
4	$(T-9)/W$	+.47	.930	.865	27.31
5	1/(P/M)	−.61	.957	.916	28.04
6	$(F/M)^3$	+.32	.962	.925	6.29
7	CP/P > 57.7% (20 states)	+.29	.965	.931	3.78

Abbreviations: T = Temperature, Y = Income, E = Manufacturing Employment, M = Square Miles, West-Metro = 6 most developed western states, CP = Urban Population, F = Farm Population, W = Wages, West-Rural = 5 least developed western states, P = Population

step two by Lg, with a partial of +.47, or by $(50 - Lat)(Lg - 65)^3$, with a partial of +.49.

With two market variables already entered—one a weighted supply-demand ratio and the second primarily a spatial variable—one might think that markets would now yield to some other influence. But at step 3 still another market variable, E/Y, enters with a −.46 partial, comfortably above the 1 percent significance level. (Another supply-demand ratio, E/P, is almost as good at −.45; $\sqrt{E/M}$ reads −.40.) In fact, no labor or threshold variable is yet significant. E/Y completes the best three-variable combination, giving it an R of .936 and an R^2 of .876.

Now is a good time to stop and ponder the similarity of the best three-variable combinations for absolute growth, per capita growth, and percentage growth. Here they are, with steps two and three transposed in the last combinations:

Absolute Growth	*Per Capita Growth*	*Percentage Growth*
$(T - 9)Y$	$(T - 9)^{1.5} \times (Y^{0.8}/P)$	$(T - 9)^{2.5} \times [(Y/M)^{0.65}/(E/M)]$
$E^{1.5}$	$(E/M)^3$	E/Y
West-Metro $\times$ CP	West-Metro $\times$ (CP/P)^3	West-Metro $\times$ CP/E

Each begins with a temperature-weighted market variable featuring income (Y), as related to the growth rate base in the cases of the two growth rates. Second comes an industry variable, which does double duty as a direct or indirect measure of the E/Y relationship. The third variable in each instance is the West-Metro dummy multiplied by urban population (CP), where CP is related to the rate base under the two growth rates. Each combination thus has the same three factors: demand, supply, and a spatial isolation. The market influence, as conditioned by climate, is so overwhelming that nothing else—except a dash of thresholds—can get in until *all three* facets of markets have had their say.

Extended to four steps, the best three-variable set is inferior to the following one—slightly. The fourth variable is a labor supply variable, $(F/M)^4$. Its entry partial of +.33 is almost equaled by partials of −.32 for $\sqrt{U}$ and +.31 for $1/W^2$. Labor has come to life.

Best for Step 4. The best four-variable combination switches to a new temperature-weighted market variable for its main component. This is $(T - 9)^{2.5}/\sqrt{F/M}$. It would normally enter first, with a simple r of +.85. It is entered third in the table, however, to illustrate the strength of the interaction effect. Even with one of the best market variables and temperature—E/Y and $(T - 9)^2$— entered first, $(T - 9)^{2.5}/\sqrt{F/M}$ shows a partial of +.80. Incidentally, $(T - 9)^{2.5} \times [(Y/M)^{0.65}/(E/M)]$ also reads +.80 but lags at the third decimal place.

So far nothing but markets and climate is represented. But now, with three market and climate variables entered, a labor variable moves up. This time it is wages: $(T - 9)/W$ enters at step 4 with an excellent partial of +.61. This is not a proxy expression of climate, held constant. Neither is it essentially an expression of wages with just a little wage-climate interaction added; $1/W^2$ is far back at +.40. Rather, the comparative r^2's of .16 and .37 for $1/W^2$ and $(T - 9)/W$ tell us that this is mostly the wage influence but that the wage-climate interaction effect is also registering. The interaction effect actually explains more (.37 − .16 = .21) than wages alone (.16) can explain.

This combination is no longer in front when extended to five steps, but it gives the next set of variables close competition. Fifth to enter is a threshold variable, West-Rural $\times$ 1/(P/M). Its entry partial of −.40 is slightly better than one of −.39 for 1/(P/M). This adds to the evidence that the density reciprocals concentrate their effect on the five most underdeveloped western states. Also, it demonstrates that the threshold effect consistently demands representation before multiple correlation combinations grow very large.

Best for Steps 5–7.   The "Best for Steps 5–7" combination begins with practically the same five variables; there are just two minor differences. First, the exponent on temperature has been reduced in the market-climate variable, which is now $(T - 9)^2/\sqrt{F/M}$. Second, the West-Rural multiplier has been dropped from the threshold variable, which becomes $1/(P/M)$. This variable shows a very high entry partial of $-.61$ as well as a higher statistical F (significance) value than $(T - 9)/W$. These conditions wrongly imply that $1/(P/M)$ should have entered fourth. Actually, $1/(P/M)$ was only up to $-.34$ at step 4 and at step 5 had the lowest significance. But when a second labor variable, $(F/M)^3$, entered at step 6, the F value for $(T - 9)/W$ dropped from 34.50 to 22.22.

Though minor, the two revisions are enough to boost the combination into first place at step five. R is $.957$; R^2 is $.916$. Better than 90 percent of the variation in percentage growth has been explained.

The sixth variable, $(F/M)^3$, seems to be of questionable significance, given that its entry partial is only $+.32$. But, as frequently happens, it becomes more significant as additional variables follow. Sometimes, when opposing forces are approaching significance—labor supply and urbanization in this instance—one must be controlled before its opposite can register. In the present combination, the next variable brings the F (significance) value for $(F/M)^3$ up close to the 1 percent mark. By giving the combination two labor variables to the one for thresholds, $(F/M)^3$ reiterates the greater significance of labor. At the same time, it brings to fruition the highest R obtainable for six variables—$.962$.

At step 7 a rural-urban variable, the CP/P dummy, comes in. It represents the twenty most urbanized states; they have higher residual growth than the rest. Like $(F/M)^3$, the dummy has significance problems. But they too can be resolved by controlling additional variables: the dummy reaches the 1 percent confidence level when $\sqrt{P/M}$ enters next, with a partial of $-.31$ (the under-development stimulus conflicts with the urban stimulus). Actually, there is enough other evidence of an urban attraction that the dummy can safely be interpreted without waiting for its F value to go up: it does represent the urban attraction. The CP/P dummy brings R to $.965$ and R^2 to $.931$.

Eight to Ten Variables

The two best combinations for eight to ten variables form table 6–5. One combination centers on $(T-9)^2/\sqrt{F/M}$, the other on $(T-9)^{2.5} \times [(Y/M)^{0.65}/(E/M)]$. The supporting cast is much the same in both combinations, however. There are five variables in common: $\sqrt{E/P}$, T^2, $(T - 9)^{1.5} \times (Y^{0.8}/P)$, $(T - 9)^2/W^2$, and $(F/M)^2$. Three other parts are shared by twins: the second group substitutes

Table 6-5
Multiple Correlations for 1947–63 Percentage Growth: Best Combinations for Eight to Ten Variables

Step	Variable Entered	r or Partial r at Entry Step	R	R^2	$F(=T^2)$ to Remove
Best for Steps 8–9					
1	$\sqrt{E/P}$	−.60	.595	.354	60.28
2	T^2	+.43	.689	.475	93.29
3	$(T-9)^2/\sqrt{F/M}$	+.82	.911	.830	140.69
4	$1/(P/M)$	−.42	.928	.861	72.93
5	$(F/M)^2$	+.40	.940	.884	24.58
6	$(T-9)^{1.5} \times (Y^{0.8}/P)$	+.33	.947	.897	18.89
7	$(T-9)^2/W^2$	+.45	.958	.918	46.80
8	$1/(CP/P)$	−.50	.969	.939	16.09
9	$(50 - \text{Lat}) (\text{Lg} - 50)^3$	+.54	.978	.956	16.04
Best for Step 10					
1	T^2	+.45	.449	.202	82.94
2	$\sqrt{E/P}$	−.58	.689	.475	50.13
3	$(T-9)^{2.5} \times [(Y/M)^{0.65}/(E/M)]$	+.80	.901	.812	145.00
4	$(50 - \text{Lat}) (\text{Lg} - 65)^3$	+.43	.920	.846	70.68
5	West-Rural $\times$ $1/(E/M)$	−.32	.929	.863	53.94
6	West-Rural $\times$ $1/(F/M)$	+.39	.940	.884	13.64
7	$(T-9)^2/W^2$	+.38	.949	.901	54.82
8	$(T-9)^{1.5} \times (Y^{0.8}/P)$	+.55	.965	.931	21.13
9	$(F/M)^2$	+.33	.969	.939	28.69
10	F/CP	−.66	.982	.965	28.58

Abbreviations: E = Manufacturing Employment, P = Population, T = Temperature, F = Farm Population, M = Square Miles, Y = Income, W = Wages, CP = Urban Population, Lat = Latitude, Lg = Longitude, West-Rural = 5 least developed western states (dummy)

West-Rural $\times$ $1/(E/M)$ for $1/(P/M)$, $(50 - \text{Lat}) (\text{Lg} - 65)^3$ for $(50 - \text{Lat}) (\text{Lg} - 50)^3$, and F/CP for $1/(CP/P)$. As the extra variable, the "Best for Step 10" set includes West-Rural $\times$ $1/(F/M)$, to be explained shortly.

Best for Steps 8–9. The highest Rs for eight or nine variables are reached with a combination that begins with the best five-variable set and modifies two variables. First, $\sqrt{E/P}$ replaces E/Y as the supply-demand (or industry) variable. Second, $(F/M)^2$ replaces $(T-9)/W$ as the labor variable. At step six $(T-9)^{1.5} \times (Y^{0.8}/P)$ comes in. What we now have is $\sqrt{E/P}$ and Y/P jointly describing what E/Y described in the best five-variable combination. The new arrangement allows industry and income to carry different weights; it also uses climate as a catalyst on the income side.

Wage variables were able to enter earlier in preceding combinations because E/Y had come first and controlled variations in per capita income. It will be recalled that low wages are self-defeating until per capita income is held constant: they undermine consumer demand. In the present combination, $\sqrt{E/P}$ cannot replace E/Y as a setup for wages. But when the per capita income variable enters at step 6, $(T - 9)^2/W^2$ comes up from +.29 (step 5) to +.45. This puts it ahead of the remaining variables and allows it to enter at step 7. The entry partial, +.45, is not overwhelming but would be much better if the westward pull of spatial isolation were not counteracting the eastward pull of low wages. If the latitude-longitude variable shown entering at step 9 had been entered at step 7, $(T - 9)^2/W^2$ would have been able to show a +.59 partial at step 8.

At step 8 a rural-urban variable, $1/(CP/P)$, enters with a partial of -.50. This is equivalent to a positive r for CP/P: high urbanization = high growth. We saw $1/(CP/P)$ once before—in the best twelve-variable set for per capita growth, where it came in at step 9 reading -.48. And it is closely related to $(F/P)^4$, which went to -.49 in the best ten-variable set for absolute growth. It is also related to the CP/P dummy, capable of reaching +.45 at step 10 in the best ten-variable set for per capita growth, and to F/CP, entered in the combination following this one.

With per capita growth, the analysis of residuals for $1/(CP/P)$ found it recording diversions of growth from the Dakotas to Minnesota; from Vermont to New Hampshire; from West Virginia and Mississippi to unknown places (presumably nearby); and from other rural states to Utah, Missouri, and Colorado. A new analysis was made for percentage growth, with $1/(CP/P)$ entering last in the best nine-variable set. The three biggest reductions in unexplained growth went to West Virginia, North Dakota, and Vermont, all of which had been overpredicted. Other previously overpredicted states among the eleven most improved were Oregon, South Dakota, and Maine; Mississippi was also overpredicted but ranked fifteenth. The urban states—underpredicted—showing the largest reductions in residual growth were Utah, Florida, Tennessee, Oklahoma, and Colorado. Minnesota and Missouri were again underpredicted but received excessive corrections. In short, the new pattern is very much like the old. Both show that industry avoids states that are more rural than other *nearby* ones.

Ninth and last to enter is $(50 - Lat)(Lg - 50)^3$. (The cubing of longitude puts most of the burden on east-west spatial isolation.) The spatial variable enters with a partial of +.54. Spatial variables generally do better than this when not combined with $(T - 9)^2/\sqrt{F/M}$, but the F/M variable duplicates much of what Lg could otherwise explain. Even so, spatial isolation demands its own variable in the long run. When it enters in the present combination, R goes to .978 and R^2 to .956. Unexplained variation in growth is down to less than 5 percent.

Step 9 is as far as this combination can go. No unused variable in the eighty-variable matrix has a partial higher than ±.20.

Best for Step 10. The biggest difference between the best ten-variable combination and the preceding one is that the ten-variable set returns to the temperature-weighted market variable used in "Best for Steps 2-3." This is $(T - 9)^{2.5} \times [(Y/M)^{0.65}/(E/M)]$, which is just a refined version of $T \times Y/E$. It is worth repeating that the simple r of +.89 for this variable exceeds that of any other variable. It so accurately predicts growth that if all of the other nine variables in the new combination are held constant, it still has a partial r of +.89. It can explain almost as much by itself as the other nine variables put together: it explains 78 percent (r^2), the other nine explain 83 percent (R^2)—with considerable duplication being evident.

Both combinations in table 6-5 follow a natural entry order after step two. Yet in the ten-variable set the spatial variable—$(50 - \text{Lat}) (\text{Lg } 65)^3$—comes in at step 4 instead of step 9. And it becomes the third most significant ("F to Remove") instead of the least significant member of the group. The explanation: $\sqrt{F/M}$ duplicated Lg in preceding combination. In other words, spatial isolation is more important than the nine-variable set seems to indicate.

"Best for Step 10" has a new threshold variable, West-Rural $\times$ 1/(E/M). It enters at step 5 with a partial r of -.32. Early entry is responsible for the low partial; it would be -.61 if the step 7 and 8 variables entered beforehand and -.77 if the step 9 and 10 variables were also moved up. Meanwhile, it is worth noting that this combination, like all of the preceding ones, cannot get to five variables without calling in a threshold variable. The particular one chosen, a variant of 1/(E/M), is of a different family than the 1/(P/M) variants seen in preceding combinations; the E/M family works best with the new step 3 variable.

The step 6 variable, West-Rural $\times$ 1/(F/M), is a counter-variable to West-Rural $\times$ 1/(E/M). It begins as an anemic threshold variable with a -.14 partial at step 5, then switches to positive when West-Rural $\times$ 1/(E/M) enters. This switch is analogous to Y/M's switch from negative to positive when E/M or P/M is controlled: Y/M ceases to describe density (or industrialization) and becomes an indirect measure of Y/E or Y/P. In the case at hand, with 1/(E/M) held constant for the West-Rural states, 1/F/M) describes F/E. F/E is much like F/P; both are related to per capita income (Y/P). The positive partial for 1/(F/M) is like a negative partial for log F/M. This means that where F is low—where F/E is low, that is—growth is high. At the same time, F/E (or F/P) is low where Y/P is high; hence we may be witnessing a per capita income effect within the West-Rural group. The high income states within the West-Rural group perhaps aren't as handicapped as the rest and were too severely penalized at step 5.

This much is theory. If the theory is correct, West-Rural $\times$ 1/(F/M) should achieve its decreases in residual (unexplained) growth through higher predictions in the high income and lower predictions in the low income West-Rural states. Their 1950 per capita incomes were as follows: Nevada, $2,021; Wyoming, $1,668; Montana, $1,622; Idaho, $1,293; and New Mexico, $1,176. An analysis of residuals, made with West-Rural $\times$ 1/(F/M) entering at step 10 ($r = +.52$), showed very big reductions in unexplained growth in New Mexico and Nevada but not much improvement anywhere else. Predicted growth was cut in New Mexico, lowest in per capita income among the five, and raised in Nevada, highest in per capita income. New Mexico, where income is undermined by large Indian and Mexican-American segments in the population, evidently has a market weakness (rural poverty) that reinforces the threshold effect; Nevada, the most urbanized West-Rural state, enjoys high consumer purchasing power as an offset to thresholds. If this is the case, West-Rural $\times$ $1/(F/M)$ can be regarded as another market variable.

At steps 7 and 8 wages and per capita income, both weighted by temperature, come in. The wage variable, $(T - 9)^2/W^2$, is actually inferior to $(T - 9)/W$ at this point—their partials are +.38 and +.44—but $(T - 9)^2/W^2$ is better in the long run. When the tendency of low per capita income to describe low wages is taken care of by controlling wages, $(T - 9)^{1.5} \times (Y^{0.8}/P)$ jumps from +.32 (step 7) to +.55 (step 8).

Labor supply—$(F/M)^2$—is the step 9 variable. Actually, this influence had started to blossom back at step 7, where $(F/M)^3$ stood at +.32. But the wage variable knocked $(F/M)^3$ down to +.22 (step 8), with the connection between surplus labor and low per capita income barring the way to significance. But with income controlled, labor supply is back, represented by a slightly different variable. It still isn't very significant, for another adverse relationship has arisen. The urban attraction is emerging—F/CP (step 10) now stands at -.33—and surplus labor must struggle to avoid becoming a proxy for rural status. If $(F/M)^2$ were entered at step 10, behind F/CP, its entry partial would be +.66.

When F/CP enters at step 10, its partial is -.66: a low ratio of farm to urban population goes with high residual growth. Other rural-urban variables are also doing well at this point: $1/(CP/P)$ reads -.62, $(F/P)^3$ reads -.50, CP/P reads +.46, and the CP/P dummy reads +.43. By joining the combination, F/CP maintains the perfect record of the urban attraction—perfect in the sense that a rural-urban variable is now included in the best sets of ten (or more) variables for absolute growth, per capita growth, and percentage growth. Its entry brings R to .982 and R^2 to .965; the unexplained variance is down to 3.5 percent.

Since F/CP has not appeared in any previous combinations, one is curious about whether it affects the same states as affected by the other rural-urban variables. In particular, does it refuse to accord urban attraction benefits to the Manufacturing Belt states? Also, does it still penalize Vermont, West Virginia, Mississippi, the Dakotas, and Oregon? And does it still reward New Hampshire, Florida, Tennessee, Minnesota, Missouri, Oklahoma, Colorado, and Utah? An analysis of residuals shows all of these states except New Hampshire, Missouri, and Colorado included among those with the twelve biggest reductions in unexplained growth. The biggest reductions coming via higher predictions go— in order of magnitude—to Utah, Florida, Minnesota, Tennessee, Oklahoma, and Georgia (thirteenth); Colorado is farther back. The biggest reductions via lower predictions go to the states of Mississippi, North Dakota, South Dakota, West Virginia, Louisiana, Oregon, and Vermont. (Louisiana's improvement may be spurious.) Growth *is* being diverted from rural to urban states *outside* of the Manufacturing Belt.

The urban attraction is not fully covered by F/CP. After F/CP enters, the CP/P dummy ("Best for Steps 5–7") still has a partial of +.32 (down from +.43), the highest for any remaining variable. If the combination is extended to eleven steps, the dummy will bring R^2 to .969, reducing the unexplained variance to 3 percent.

Comparative Ratings

As usual, markets and climate rank one-two in the comparative ratings. These influences produce the only significant simple r's: market variables climb far beyond and climate variables ten points beyond the 1 percent level. (West-Metro variables also show high simple r's but are primarily market variables until markets is well controlled.) Not counting a situation where unionization is partly a proxy for industry, no other influences can show partial r's significant at the 1 percent level until at least two variables are held constant. The three most significant variables behind the best four-variable R are a market, a climate, and a climate-weighted market variable. Six market and climate variables enter into the best ten-variable R, and three of the six have the highest F values among the ten. Markets accounts for 50 to 70 percent of the variation in percentage growth. Climate accounts for 15 to 33 percent.

Labor repeats as the third-ranked influence. Control of just two variables gives us wage and labor supply partials significant at the 1 percent level: labor supply responds to control of demand and supply, wages to control of demand and spatial isolation. The best four-variable and five-variable R's draw support from a wage variable, $(T - 9)/W$; the best R's for six to ten variables depend on a wage and a labor supply variable, usually $(T - 9)^2/W^2$ and $(F/M)^2$. Labor explains 3 to 9 percent of the variation in percentage growth.

Thresholds again ranks fourth. Unlike the labor variables, the threshold variables cannot be made significant by controlling just two variables. But a three-variable control set (table 6–5) sends $1/(P/M)$ to −.42, five points beyond the 1 percent confidence level. All of the best Rs are based on combinations having a threshold variable, or at least a combined market-threshold variable (West-Metro $\times$ CP/E) among the first five. The threshold influence accounts for 2 to 8 percent of the variance.

Resources ranks fifth with percentage growth. The benchmark estimate puts the resource contribution at 4 percent. The residual method of estimating credits resources with the 3 percent unexplained variance from the best ten-variable set (extended to eleven variables) plus 1 percent for possible duplication by climate—again 4 percent. A liberal allowance for error has resources explaining 1 to 8 percent of the variance.

The urban attraction, ranking sixth, shows early signs of significance: F/P bests Y/P as a demand variable in several contexts, indicating that the urban state advantage does not rest wholly on higher incomes. The CP/P dummy enters at step 7 in the best seven-variable combination. The best nine-variable set includes 1/(CP/P). The best ten-variable set has F/CP, whose step 10 partial of –.66 is extremely significant. The urban attraction explains 1 to 3 percent of the variation in percentage growth.

To bring everything together and provide clear comparisons, we can again disregard ranges and concentrate on central tendencies. As nearly as one can judge, markets explains around 60 percent, climate 23 percent, labor 6 percent, thresholds 5 percent, resources 4 percent, and the urban attraction 2 percent of the variation in percentage growth. Putting it a little differently, markets and climate together explain about five-sixths and everything else about one-sixth. Percentage growth, like absolute and per capita, offers no evidence of an agglomeration (Manufacturing Belt) attraction working against the decentralizing force of markets.

7

Synthesis and Conclusions

Each of the three measures of growth have produced findings bearing on several locational hypotheses. It is time to pull all related findings together to see what conclusions their synthesis can support. Do the findings tell us why one state or region grows faster than another? By and large, they do. Some of the conclusions remain tentative, but we can extract from the evidence a reasonably sharp picture of manufacturing growth. We can identify the principal factors affecting growth, assess their relative importance, and note certain ambiguities allowing some factors (low wages, underdevelopment) to simultaneously attract and repel industry.

Locational Influences

The locational influences examined in this study are (1) markets, including developmental density, (2) climate, (3) labor, (4) thresholds, or foundation levels of development, (5) resources, (6) the urban attraction, or rural-urban mix, and (7) agglomeration, or the clustering of industry. The findings leave no doubt that markets and climate are far ahead as the leading influences affecting manufacturing growth in the United States. Labor and thresholds follow as secondary influences. Resources and the urban attraction might best be labeled tertiary influences, although one could easily quarrel about where resources belongs. Agglomeration has no measurable effect on Manufacturing Belt growth.

Markets

Although climate interacts with markets to an extent that makes it hard to separate the two influences, markets is definitely in front. The market influence explains 55 to 75 percent of the variance for absolute growth, 35 to 55 percent for per capita growth, and 50 to 70 percent for percentage growth. "Markets," however, is not a single factor but four related ones: (1) absolute demand, measured by population and income and directly relevant only to absolute growth, (2) relative demand in the sense of per capita income, (3) relative supply, measurable by manufacturing employment per capita or per square mile, and (4) spatial isolation, or the distance (transport costs) of the market from northeastern manufacturing centers. Items two and three can be combined in the concept of a supply-demand ratio, specifically, the ratio of manufacturing employment to income; indeed, item three—the ratio of manufacturing employment to population—can also be viewed as a supply-demand ratio.

Absolute Demand. The absolute level (or total amount) of consumer demand affects absolute growth. One expects increases in manufacturing employment for states over a period of years to be at least moderately proportional to state population. For population represents consumers, and industry can minimize distribution costs and provide better service by locating where the consumers are. Moreover, population at the beginning of a time period influences population growth during that period: the birth rate applies to the population base. Population growth, in turn, spurs the growth of market-oriented industry.

These considerations undoubtedly explain why population (P) and income (Y) are two of the best indicators for absolute growth. The demand variables are outranked only (and barely) by January mean temperature (T): P and Y have r's of +.42, compared to +.45 for T^2. (A reminder: for forty-eight cases an r of ±.36 can occur by chance only 1 percent of the time, and one of ±.28 is significant at the 5 percent level.)

Although the r's of +.42 explain only 18 percent (r^2) of the variance, demand's pull is really stronger than appears. One problem is that the most populous states tend to be the most industrialized: supply is linked to demand. Therefore, if $E^{1.5}$ (manufacturing employment) is held constant, P and Y soar to +.82 and +.89 respectively. Another problem is that P and Y don't take the market-climate interaction effect into account: $(T - 9)^{2.5} \times Y$ has an r of +.92.

Relative Demand. As just observed, income describes purchasing power more accurately than does population. This brings us to the next facet of markets—relative demand. The reason for income's better performance is that it is not strictly a measure of absolute demand. It is a combination of absolute and relative demand, or population and per capita income: $Y = P \times Y/P$. In truth, consumer demand depends not only on how many consumers there are but on how much they have to spend. Affluent consumers are better than poor ones.

Looking again at absolute growth, we find that Y remains positive and significant when P is held constant—provided that E (or $E^{1.5}$) is also controlled so that Y does not become a proxy for E. Thus, although a -.77 partial r for $E^{1.5}$ pulls Y down to +.03 when P alone is held constant, Y moves to +.62 if both P and $E^{1.5}$ are partialed out. That is, growth is faster where Y is high relative to P, held constant. If temperature-weighted demand variables are used, it isn't necessary to control E, though it helps; high T partly duplicates low E. For example, when $(T - 9)^2 P$ is held constant, $(T - 9)^2 Y$ still shows a partial r of +.56. When both $(T - 9)^2 P$ and $E^{1.5}$ are controlled, $(T - 9)^2 Y$ climbs to +.75.

The per capita growth findings are especially noteworthy, for per capita growth neutralizes population's influence. Consequently, the demand side of the supply-demand relationship becomes heavily dependent on per capita income. The simple r for Y/P is a paltry +.02, but only because high Y/P coincides with three unfavorable conditions: excess industry (Manufacturing Belt), cold climate (Manufacturing Belt), and high wages (Manufacturing Belt *and* West). Controlling these adverse conditions makes a big difference. A useful variable for controlling industry is E/M—manufacturing employment density (M = square miles). Table 7-1 shows Y/P moving up to +.25 when E/M is held constant. Y/P moves on to +.48 when both E/M and T are controlled (not shown) and to +.58 when E/M and (T - 9)/W—temperature-weighted wages—are controlled (column two). Partial r's aside, the temperature-weighted per capita income variable $(T - 9)^{1.5} \times (Y^{0.8}/P)$ has a simple r of +.59, the highest for any variable correlated with per capita growth.

Percentage growth makes it unanimous: all three types of growth are high where per capita income is high, once the adverse intercorrelations are dealt with. With percentage growth Y/P is again insignificant in its simple r (-.06). But if $\sqrt{E/P}$ (manufacturing employment per capita) is held constant, as shown in table 7-1, Y/P rises to a partial of +.21; if $\sqrt{E/P}$ and T^2 are both controlled, Y/P advances to +.41; and if $\sqrt{E/P}$ and (T - 9)/W are controlled, Y/P hits +.47 (column five). Meanwhile, $(T - 9)^{1.5} \times (Y^{0.8}/P)$ is again significant even in its simple r, which is +.65.

Two alternative measures of consumer demand, CP/P (urban population percentage) and F/P (farm population percentage) are also shown in the table. C/P is high where Y/P is high (+.75 intercorrelation), and F/P is low where Y/P is high (-.75 intercorrelation). Why? Because urban residents have generally higher incomes than farmers. But CP/P and F/P are more than proxies for Y/P. For example, the more urbanized a state is, the more likely it is that the state contains the market centers of gravity for larger marketing regions to be served by various new plants. Thus we find CP/P going higher than Y/P in the first column. And, with percentage growth, both rural-urban variables consistently outperform Y/P. By the way, the negative partials for CP/P in the third and sixth columns do not contradict the importance of demand. In these columns Y/P or F/P is controlled, and CP/P becomes a proxy for industrialization (the Manufacturing Belt).

Relative Supply. Now we come to the most crucial aspect of markets—the relationship between supply and demand. The term "relative supply" is used here to describe this relationship for the simple reason that most of the state-to-state variation in supply-demand ratios comes from the supply side of the relationship. Differences in relative industrialization—E/P or E/M—are much greater than per capita income differences and therefore have greater impact. But since E/P is a supply-demand ratio as well as a measure of industrialization, with E/M being largely a proxy for E/P, we should recognize that demand is still in

Table 7-1
Partial Correlations for Market Variables

	Variables Held Constant					
	Per Capita Growth				Percentage Growth	
	E/M	E/M $(T-9)/w$	Y/P $T-9)/w$	$\sqrt{E/P}$	$\sqrt{E/P}$ $(T-9)/w$	F/P $(T-9)/w$
Demand						
Y/P	+.25	+.58	...	+.21	+.47	+.12
CP/P	+.32	+.41	-.40	+.42	+.49	-.26
F/P	-.35	-.37	+.30	-.48	-.59	...
Supply						
$(E/P)^3$	-.14	-.04	-.58	...	...	...
$(E/Y)^3$	-.21	-.25	-.51	...	...	-.76
$\sqrt{E/P}$	...	...	...	...	...	-.76
$\sqrt{E/Y}$	...	...	...	-.18	-.47	-.75
E/M	...	...	-.65	...	...	...
P/M	+.19	+.10	-.63	...	...	...
log E/M	...	...	...	-.06	-.28	-.77
log P/M	...	...	...	-.06	-.24	-.73
log F/M	...	...	...	-.33	-.56	-.72
Spatial						
Lg	+.18	+.29	+.46	+.22	+.34	+.65
$(50 - \text{Lat}) (\text{Lg} - 65)^3$	+.41	+.43	+.46	+.60	+.63	+.74
West-Metro	+.44	+.49	+.49	+.46	+.50	+.50

Abbreviations: E = Manufacturing Employment, M = Square Miles, T = Temperature, W = Wages, Y = Income, P = Population, F = Farm Population, CP = Urban Population, Lg = Longitude, Lat = Latitude, West-Metro = 6 most developed western states (dummy) the picture. The theory is that economic forces push toward geographic equilibrium between supply and demand: new industry favors states having less than their prorata share of industry when industry is prorated by demand (P or Y). In this way industry minimizes the cost of shipping goods to market and realizes the added marketing advantage of closer contact with consumers and middlemen.

With absolute growth the influence of relative industrialization (or the supply-demand relationship) is tested by examining E, with P or Y held constant. Alternatively, P and Y can be examined with E held constant. The best E variable is $E^{1.5}$. It displays partials of -.77 with P controlled and -.87 with Y controlled. And, as we have already seen, P and Y have respective partials of +.82 and +.89 when $E^{1.5}$ is controlled. Controlling $E^{1.5}$ also results in partials of +.87 for (T - 9)P and +.94 for (T - 9)Y. Interpreting, growth is high where manufacturing is low (demand held constant); alternatively, growth is high where demand is high relative to supply (held constant).

Per capita growth gives the same type of results with the absolute supply and demand variables: E goes to -.49 with Y held constant, and Y reaches +.45 with E held constant. But relative measures of industrialization are now more efficient. There are simple r's of -.46 for $(E/M)^3$ and -.45 for $(E/P)^3$ —compared to one of -.23 for E. These r's would be higher if the adverse effect of relative overindustrialization in the Manufacturing Belt were not offset by high per capita income, and if the westward pull of underindustrialization were not countered by low wages in the Southeast. Table 7-1 demonstrates this: when Y/P and (T - 9)/W are held constant, partials of -.65 for E/M and -.58 for $(E/P)^3$ arise. P/M, which is essentially a proxy for E/M (until the latter is controlled), reaches -.63. The negative signs continue to say that growth is highest where industrialization—relative supply—is lowest.

Percentage growth behaves the same way, both in the sense that the least industrialized states grow fastest and in the sense that relative variables such as E/P best reflect this. Not that the absolute variables become impotent: E has a simple r of -.35 and moves to -.43 when Y is held constant. But the relative industry variables again give higher readings, even higher than with per capita growth. The simple r's include ones of -.60 for $\sqrt{E/P}$, -.61 for $\sqrt{E/Y}$, -.57 for log E/M, -.53 for log P/M, and -.56 for log F/M. (The logarithm of farm population density makes an excellent proxy for manufacturing employment density and is better than the latter on the income side, where a dearth of farmers is tantamount to high per capita income.) Again, better results appear when F/P (substituting for Y/P) and (T - 9)/W are held constant: there are partials of -.76 for $\sqrt{E/P}$, -.75 for $\sqrt{E/Y}$, -.77 for log E/M, -.73 for log P/M, and -.72 for log F/M. Very clearly, industry seeks an industrial vacuum.[1]

Spatial Isolation. The fourth side of markets is spatial isolation. Industry grows best where protected from competition; most of the competition is in the northeastern Manufacturing Belt, extending from Massachusetts and Delaware to Illinois and Wisconsin; the farther a state is from the Manufacturing Belt, the higher the transport cost "tariff" that protects local producers from outside competition. Moreover, the remote states offer substantial transport savings to established firms considering new branch plants: it costs more to ship goods from Indiana to Utah than to Iowa or Nebraska. Isolation is measured mainly by longitude (Lg), which increases east to west. But north-south isolation, measured by latitude (Lat), must also be considered. The so-called contour variables, such as $(50 - \text{Lat}) (\text{Lg} - 65)$, combine east-west and north-south isolation.

Absolute growth gives just a little credit to spatial isolation: population dominates the growth scene and pulls absolute growth toward the East. We do find simple r's of +.26 for Lg and +.54 for $(50 - \text{Lat})^2 \times (\text{Lg} - 65)^2$; but the former is insignificant, and the latter gets considerable support from climate. A +.38 partial r for Lg with P held constant is more convincing. This partial, though, is partly due to lack of industry in the West; Lg is only marginally significant at +.30 when $E^{1.5}$ is controlled along with P. Now the problem is that the residual western growth is concentrated in the more developed states: a "West-Metro" dummy valued at one for the six western states with major metropolitan areas and at zero elsewhere has a +.36 partial, but a "West-Rural" dummy valued at one for the five least developed western states reads only +.20. A more comprehensive set of controls removes most of the uncertainty about the significance of isolation. When six market, labor, and threshold variables—$(T - 9)^2 P$, $(T - 9)^2 Y$, $E^{1.5}$, $(F/M)^4$, $1/W^2$, and West-Rural—are held constant, Lg reaches +.41. This partial exceeds the 1 percent confidence level.

Per capita growth offers simple r's of +.37 for Lg and +.56 for $(60 - \text{Lat}) \times (\text{Lg} - 20)$. But, as shown in table 7-1, Lg moves to +.46 when Y/P and $(T - 9)/W$ are controlled. To a large extent but not entirely, this partial reflects the supply stimulus. Thus if E/M is controlled in addition to Y/P and $(T - 9)/W$, Lg drops to +.10 (not shown). But now the threshold influence is getting in the way: the more developed of the isolated states— those with major metropolitan areas— actually have strong residual growth, while tne least developed ones are dragging down the partial for Lg. The evidence: the West-Rural dummy has a partial of -.26, but the West-Metro dummy reads +.41 (hence Lg's compromise of +.10). Stronger control combinations can restore Lg to its rightful position of significance. A six-variable combination, including $(E/M)^2$ and a threshold variable, puts Lg at +.49. This same combination gives $(50 - \text{Lat}) (\text{Lg} - 65)^3$ a partial r of +.63 (table 5-3).

Percentage growth provides the best evidence of a spatial influence. There are simple r's of +.54 for Lg and +.79 for $(55 - \text{Lat})^2 \times (\text{Lg} - 50)^2$. When F/P and $(T - 9)/W$ are controlled, Lg hits +.65 (table 7-1); and a contour variable gets to +.74. Some of this results from the proxy relationship between industrialization and isolation; hence when $\sqrt{E/P}$ joins the control set—three variables held constant—Lg drops to +.20 (not shown). But the West-Metro dummy, spotlighting the states that combine isolation with adequate development, reads +.33; and $(50 - \text{Lat}) (\text{Lg} - 65)^3$ reads +.44. The latter variable reaches +.60 when six variables, including $\sqrt{E/P}$ and T^2, are held constant (table 6-3). It goes on to +.81 if the nine other variables in the best ten-variable combination (table 6-5) are controlled; Lg reaches +.55. These findings strongly imply that spatial isolation affects growth.

Climate

Climate is safely ensconced in second place. It is, in fact, the only influence except markets that can show simple r's that are statistically significant. These r's, found with all three measures of growth, are not only significant but generally ten points above the 1 percent confidence level. Bolstered by other evidence, they support estimates that climate explains 14 to 28 percent of the variation in absolute growth, 15 to 30 percent of the variation in per capita growth, and 15 to 33 percent of the variation in percentage growth. Like markets, climate has several sides. These are (1) the effect of climate per se, (2) the market-climate interaction effect, and (3) the wage-climate interaction effect.

Climate per se. Climate derives independent significance from its ability to make the colder states unattractive and the warmer states attractive. The disincentives of a cold climate include higher construction and heating costs, the infeasibility of outdoor operations and storage, winter transport breakdowns, winter absenteeism, the unwillingness of executives and professional people to live in regions with harsh winters, and slow market growth resulting from low or negative net migration.

Climate seems to have its least influence—but still quite a bit—with absolute growth. For example, the best simple r for a climate variable under absolute growth is +.45 for T^2. But per capita growth gets to +.47 with T or T^2. Percentage growth gets to +.46 with 50 - Lat; T^2 is back to +.45. The likely reason for climate's being a slightly weaker influence with absolute growth is that cold climates and the Manufacturing Belt overlap. This densely populated region has better absolute growth than per capita or percentage growth; climate is offset by demand. Divorced from the attraction of high income in the Manufacturing Belt (Y held constant), T^2 creeps up to a partial r of +.47 with absolute growth.

Under per capita growth, climate offers many highly significant partial r's that refute proxy theories. Two of the strongest market variables are E/M (manufacturing density, $r = -.45$) and P/M (population density, $r = -.41$). T holds firm at +.47 with E/M held constant and moves to +.49 when P/M substitutes for E/M. A two-variable control combination of P/M and Y/M (income density) indirectly controls per capita income (Y/P) in addition to relative industrialization. This combination gives T a partial r of +.65, adequate to explain 31 percent of the *total* variation in per capita growth. And this isn't because climate is a proxy for the southern labor attraction: the best labor variable is only up to +.39 and, held constant, merely nudges T back from +.65 to +.62. If five market, one threshold, and two labor variables are simultaneously controlled, T goes to +.56 and 50 – Lat reaches +.57.

Percentage growth gives very similar findings. T^2 moves from a simple r of +.45 to a partial of +.54 when the best market variable, $\sqrt{E/Y}$, is held constant. It goes to +.65 when log F/M substitutes for $\sqrt{E/Y}$. The two-variable control combination of log P/M and log Y/M also sends T^2 to +.65. T^2 can now explain 31 percent of the total variation in percentage growth. Here no labor variable is even close to significance; temperature has definitely not become a proxy for the South's low wages and surplus labor. When four market, a threshold, and two labor variables are held constant, there are partials of +.56 for T^2 and +.65 for 50 – Lat.[2]

Market-Climate Interaction. Climate's independent effect is just the beginning. Probably the most remarkable finding of this study is that, beyond its independent effect, climate is variously an inhibitor or a catalyst affecting the market and wage influences. Temperature-weighted variables—market and wage variables—can still explain quite a bit after the independent effects of temperature, markets, and labor have been covered.

The market-climate interaction effect is easily the most important. Many market-oriented firms apparently insist on locations that are not too northerly. The rule: the closer you can get to the market, the better—unless winter gets too rugged. On the positive side, warm climates bring heavy in-migration to certain states. Therefore, whereas an unweighted demand or supply-demand variable can adequately describe initial demand as well as the natural increase in demand (the birth-rate effect), multiplying demand by temperature adds the migration increment, thereby giving a better description of total new demand.

The importance of the market-climate interaction effect is underscored by the fact that all three types of growth bestow their highest r's on temperature-weighted market variables. The market variable responding best to weighting is always income (Y) or an income ratio. What form the income variable takes depends on what growth variable is being used: income and growth take the same denominator, or else (absolute growth) neither takes one. Let us use the notations G, G/P, and G/E to designate absolute, per capita, and percentage growth. The best market variable (when weighted) for G is Y; the best for G/P is Y/P; and the best for G/E is Y/E. These are the basic variables, that is; Y must sometimes be adjusted to allow for curvilinear correlation. Thus Y/P becomes $Y^{0.8}/P$, and Y/E becomes (Y/M)/(E/M) and then $(Y/M)^{0.65}/(E/M)$. Temperature, in turn, is raised to some power to give it an optimal weight.

When these adjustments are made, the three weighted variables with the highest r's vis-à-vis their corresponding growth variables are those shown in table 7-2. The table shows that absolute growth is highest where income is highest, per capita growth highest where per capita income is highest, and percentage

Table 7-2
Best Temperature-Weighted Market Variables

| | | Temperature-Weighted Market Variable | | | Unweighted Market Variable | | | |
| | | | | | | Alone | Combined with T^2 | |
Type of Growth	Variable	r	r^2	Variable	r	R	R^2
G	$(T-9)^{2.5} \times Y$	+.92	.845	Y	+.42	.602	.362
G/P	$(T-9)^{1.5} \times (Y^{0.8}/P)$	+.59	.347	Y/P	+.02	.545	.297
G/E	$(T-9)^{2.5} \times [(Y/M)^{0.65}/(E/M)]$	+.89	.783	$\sqrt{E/Y}$	-.61	.742	.551

Abbreviations: G = Absolute Growth, P = Population, E = Manufacturing Employment, T = Temperature, Y = Income, M = Square Miles

growth highest where the income-employment ratio is highest—provided that climate disparities are allowed for.

It is important to recognize that weighting is not simply a device for adding together two essentially independent effects. If it were, the multiple correlation (R) produced by combining temperature and the unweighted market variable would approximate the r for the temperature-weighted market variable. But in fact one weighted variable is always stronger than two unweighted ones. This can be seen in the table by comparing r (or r^2) for each weighted variable with the R (or R^2) produced by its best unweighted equivalent combined with temperature. With absolute growth the weighted variable, $(T-9)^{2.5} \times Y$, explains well over twice as much of the variance as the two unweighted variables, Y and T^2—85 percent compared to 36 percent.

Wage-Climate Interaction. Market variables are not the only ones that respond to weighting by temperature. The attraction of low wages is measurably enhanced when combined with the attraction of a warm climate, that is, when removed from the hostile environment of a cold climate. It seems that cold states such as Maine and North Dakota, even though they have lower wage levels than some southern states, are not as attractive to labor-oriented industry. Quite possibly, limited supplies of low-cost labor in the northern states contribute to this effect, but then the relative scarcity of labor is at least partly attributable to climate's contribution to the negative net migration rates found in the northern low-wage states.

The wage-climate interaction effect is manifested in better performance by weighted wage variables, such as $(T-9)/W$, than by unweighted ones. (Placing the wage variable in the denominator changes the wage correlation from negative to positive, making it consistent with the positive relationship between temperature and growth.) Temperature-weighted wage variables rather consistently gave higher partial r's than unweighted wage variables, even after temperature itself was held constant. Sometimes not only temperature but a contour (latitude-longitude) and two temperature-weighted market variables were held constant.

No useful comparisons of simple r's for unweighted and weighted wage variables are possible, for (a) the wage influence cannot be seen until two or three market variables are controlled and (b) variables such as $(T - 9)/W$ are essentially reflections of T until the latter is held constant. But when temperature and other obstructing influences are cleared away, we get comparative partial r's such as these (from tables 4-3, 5-3, and 6-3):

	Absolute Growth		Per Capita Growth		Percentage Growth	
	Test A	Test B	Test A	Test B	Test A	Test B
$1/W^2$	+.46	+.40	+.40	+.47	+.38	+.57
$(T - 9^2/W^2$	+.48	+.56	+.59	+.60	+.47	+.71

In some of these tests, the weighted variable is actually $(T - 9)/W$ rather than $(T - 9)^2/W^2$. The "Test A" situations employ three or four control variables; the "Test B" situations use four to six control variables.

Labor

Labor ranks as the third most important regional influence affecting manufacturing location. It accounts for 3 to 9 percent of the variance with absolute growth, 7 to 15 percent with per capita growth, and 3 to 9 percent with percentage growth. It should be understood, however, that these percentages and labor's third-place rank result from grouping under one heading three closely related influences: (1) wages, (2) unionization, and (3) labor supply. (Unionization is actually of doubtful significance and in any case is adequately duplicated by the combined wage and labor supply influences.) A further qualification of great import is that labor can be ranked third only by narrowly defining the labor influence as the effect of labor *on labor-oriented industries.* When the effect of low wages on consumer demand, hence on market-oriented industries, is taken into account, labor appears to have little or no *net* effect on growth.

Wages. The strongest of the labor influences where per capita and percentage growth are concerned is wages. (Absolute growth defers more to labor supply.) Labor-oriented industries—industries in which wages account for a large share of production costs—seek locations offering low wages. Other studies have identified textiles, apparel, and leather goods as the principal industries seeking low wages. Such industries look toward the South, the low-wage region.

The wage influence does not register among the simple r's for any of the three types of growth; no wage variable is even close to significance. The main reason for this is that low wages are unfavorably related to markets. The problem is two-sided. First, low wages help to cause low per capita income. The resulting weakness in consumer demand darkens an otherwise attractive southern setting for market-oriented industries. Second, the supply and spatial isolation facets of markets pull new industry mostly to the West, in opposition to labor's pull to the East (i.e., Southeast). These adverse relationships are reflected in intercorrelations of +.74 between Y/P and W (high wages where per capita income is high) and +.47 between Lg and W (high wages in the West).

Table 7-3 shows what happens when these interfering influences are neutralized. A wage reciprocal, $1/W^2$, has the highest partials among the wage variables but can confuse by changing the sign from negative to positive; $\sqrt{W}$, shown first, has negative r's, assuring us that high growth goes with low wages. With absolute growth Y/P is controlled by separately controlling Y and P, which are weighted by T for improved results; Lg controls the western pull of markets. Now $1/W^2$ is significant at +.51, changing to +.45 when $E^{1.5}$ is also held constant. Under per capita growth, control of Y/P and Lg sends $1/W^2$ to +.30, above the 5 percent confidence level. When the western conflict between high wages (unfavorable) and lack of industry (favorable) is further controlled by also partialing out $(E/M)^3$, $1/W^2$ jumps to +.40—significant above the 1 percent level. Percentage growth gets better results by substituting F/P for Y/P (their intercorrelation is -.75). With F/P and Lg controlled, $1/W^2$ goes to +.41. It stays there when $\sqrt{E/P}$ is added for better control of industrialization.

These partials are not overwhelming, but they do show that wage levels are

Table 7-3
Partial Correlations for Labor Variables

	Variables Held Constant					
	Absolute Growth		Per Capita Growth		Percentage Growth	
	$(T-9)^2 Y$ $(T-9)^2 P$ Lg	$E^{1.5}$ $(T-9)Y$ $(T-9)P$ Lg	Y/P Lg	$(E/M)^3$ Y/P Lg	F/P Lg	$\sqrt{E/P}$ F/P Lg
$\sqrt{W}$	−.47	−.34	−.25	−.38	−.42	−.33
$\sqrt{U}$	−.33	−.17	−.34	−.35	−.54	−.35
$1/W^2$	+.51	+.45	+.30	+.40	+.41	+.41
$1/U^2$	+.41	+.41	+.37	+.37	+.34	+.31
$(F/M)^3$	+.45[a]	+.65[a]	+.34	+.31	+.13	+.39
$F^{1.5}$	+.29	+.59	. . . .	. . . .	. . . .	. . . .

[a]This r is for $(F/M)^4$.

Abbreviations: Lg = Longitude, T = Temperature, P = Population, Y = Income, E = Manufacturing Employment, M = Square Miles, F = Farm Population, W = Wages, U = Unionization significantly correlated with growth. Because the second of each pair of r's has an industry variable held constant, this is not a case of high wages being a proxy for unfavorably high levels of industry in the Manufacturing Belt. Could wages still be a proxy for climate? The use of two temperature-weighted control variables under absolute growth should allay suspicions on that score. If this isn't enough, table 5–3 shows a partial r of +.47 between $1/W^2$ and per capita growth, where six control variables include T, $(T - 9)^{1.5} \times (Y^{0.8}/P)$, and $(50 - Lat)(Lg - 65)^3$. This increases to +.75 when the number of variables held constant is raised to eleven. For its part, percentage growth gives $1/W^2$ a partial of +.57 when T^2, three market-climate variables, and two other variables are held constant (table 6–3).

Unionization. Since unions are in the business of raising wages, and since unions are weakest in the low-wage states of the South, an intercorrelation of +.68 between $\sqrt{U}$ and $\sqrt{W}$ comes as no surprise. If only because of their influence on wages, unions could be suspected of influencing the location of manufacturing. Significant partial r's for $\sqrt{U}$ (negative) and $1/U^2$ (positive) seemingly verify a union influence. But closer analysis indicates that unions may have no independent significance beyond their effect on wages. Instead, unionization appears to combine three advantageous proxy relationships into one factor. These are the relationships between unions and (1) industrialization, (2) wages, and (3) labor supply. Regarding industrialization, the underindustrialized West has high wages but comparatively weak unions (compared to the Manufacturing Belt): there are intercorrelations of +.28 between $\sqrt{U}$ and $\sqrt{E/P}$ (weak unions = lack of industry) but only +.05 between $\sqrt{W}$ and $\sqrt{E/P}$. The labor supply variable $(F/M)^3$ has an intercorrelation of +.52 with $1/U^2$. Think of this as a negative correlation involving U: it says that unions are weak where surplus labor is abundant.

Absolute growth provides the first evidence of the proxy character of unionization. Table 7–3 shows $1/U^2$ becoming significant (+.41) when the controls that make $1/W^2$ significant (+.51) are instituted. But $1/U^2$ lags behind $1/W^2$, suggesting a proxy relationship, with wages as the basic influence. In the second column, where $E^{1.5}$ joins the control set, $1/U^2$ pulls closer to $1/W^2$. Doesn't this deny that unions represent industry (among other things)? Not really. The real explanation is that $(F/M)^3$ has moved up from +.45 to +.65, giving increased support from one sector to offset the loss of support from another. The truth comes out when $(F/M)^3$ is added as a fifth control variable (not shown): $1/W^2$ slips from +.45 to +.39, but $1/U^2$ plunges from +.41 to +.19. In another experiment, eight variables including $E^{1.5}$ were held constant. Here $1/W^2$ led $1/U^2$, +.58 to +.40. But with $(F/M)^3$ used as a ninth control variable, $1/U^2$ trailed +.57 to +.21.

Per capita growth shows similar results. In table 7–3, $1/U^2$ actually leads $1/W^2$ +.37 to +.30 when Lg and Y/P are held constant. But with $(E/M)^3$ –

industrialization—added to the control set, $1/W^2$ moves ahead +.40 to +.37. Although $1/U^2$'s partial stays the same, it now applies to less unexplained growth; variations in industry have explained some of what unionization explained in the first instance. At this point $(F/M)^3$ is too weak (+.31) to give much help to anyone. Still, when $(F/M)^3$ is added to the control set, the best partials become -.40 for $\sqrt{W}$ and -.35 for $\sqrt{U}$; wages' lead increases. A comparable experiment undertaken where $(F/M)^3$ had reached +.61 (table 5-3) was more emphatic: $1/W^2$ went from +.38 to +.40 but $1/U^2$ fell from +.42 to +.24 when $(F/M)^3$ became the seventh variable in a control set. Again, when eleven variables including $(F/M)^3$ and $(E/M)^2$ were held constant, $1/W^2$ held a +.75 to +.31 lead over $1/U^2$.

Percentage growth clinches the point. And, presumably because percentage growth is more sensitive to variations in industrialization, it brings out a very strong relationship between unionization and industrialization. Table 7-3 gives $\sqrt{U}$ (now best) a -.54 to -.42 lead over $\sqrt{W}$ when Lg and F/P are controlled. But $\sqrt{U}$ is heavily dependent on $\sqrt{E/P}$, which also reads -.54 and which is unquestionably significant in its own right (with a simple r of -.60). Thus, when $\sqrt{E/P}$ joins the control set (last column), $\sqrt{U}$ descends from -.54 to -.35. The new leader is $1/W^2$, with a partial of +.41, the same as before $\sqrt{E/P}$ was partialed out. Meanwhile, $(F/M)^3$ is up to +.39, strong enough to support $\sqrt{U}$. When $(F/M)^3$ is made the fourth variable held constant (not shown), $\sqrt{U}$ continues downwards from -.35 to -.28. But $1/W^2$ just goes from +.41 to +.40. An experiment with nine variables held constant, including $\sqrt{E/P}$ and $(F/M)^2$, gave $1/W^2$ a +.47 to +.24 lead over $1/U^2$. Control of $1/W^2$ then sent $1/U^2$ past zero to -.01.

I would not go so far as to conclude that unions have no locational significance whatsoever. At the very least they influence location to the extent that they influence wages. Interview and questionnaire surveys indicate an influence that may go beyond wages. One suspects that firms considering southern locations jointly appraise unionization and wages; no sharp distinction may be made in the locational calculus. But the evidence of the present study makes it clear that the wage influence is much stronger. And wages, labor supply, and industrialization in combination—climate might be included too—can fully duplicate anything that unionization can otherwise explain. Unionization, however, cannot adequately duplicate the others.

Labor Supply. A third labor advantage of the South, if we consider weak unions to be at least a slight advantage, is the region's abundant *supply* of cheap labor. The South has a very high farm population density (it is easily the least urbanized region in the nation) and a high rate of technological displacement in agriculture. These factors combine to produce a steady flow of surplus labor to the cities. (And they provide the rationale for using farm population density—F/M—to measure surplus labor.) Surplus labor is not entirely separable from wages, of course. The theoretical relationship between labor supply and the price of labor suggests as much, and a +.50 intercorrelation between $(F/M)^3$ and $1/W^2$ supports the theory. But abundant labor also has independent advantages. For example, selection standards do not have to be compromised.

Table 7-3 shows partial r's for two labor supply variables—$(F/M)^4$ and $F^{1.5}$—under absolute growth. Raising these variables to a power exaggerates relative differences among the states with the highest values, allowing these states—southern states primarily—to "carry" the correlations. The table shows $(F/M)^4$ achieving partials of +.45 and +.65 when three or four variables are held constant. (Significantly, the control variables are the same ones that worked for wages and unionization, and they work for the same reasons.) For its part, $F^{1.5}$ has partials of +.29 and +.59. The first is low only because $F^{1.5}$ is positively intercorrelated with $E^{1.5}$, which has gone to -.62; this explains the leap to +.59 when $E^{1.5}$ is controlled. Although $(F/M)^4$ is ahead in these examples, $F^{1.5}$ leads just as often. For example, if $(T - 9)^2/W^2$ replaces Lg in the second control combination, there are respective partials of +.73 and +.62 for $F^{1.5}$ and $(F/M)^4$.

Per capita and percentage growth produce significant partials for $(F/M)^3$. Table 7-3 includes one of +.34 under per capita growth and one of +.39 under percentage growth. But $(F/M)^3$ can really go much higher. Under per capita growth, it goes to +.39 when P/M and Y/M are jointly held constant, to +.61 when six variables are controlled (table 5-3), and to +.74 when eleven variables— including $(T - 9)/W$—are held constant. Percentage growth sends $(F/M)^3$ to +.50 with six variables controlled (table 6-3); $(F/M)^2$ reaches +.66 with nine variables including $(T - 9)^2/W^2$ controlled.

To check the interpretation of $(F/M)^{2,3,4}$ and $F^{1.5}$ as labor supply variables, analyses of residual (unexplained) growth were made. These compared residual growth for the forty-eight states before and after the addition of labor supply variables to predictive (multiple regression) equations. The object was to see if the biggest reductions in unexplained growth were in southern states known to have attracted labor-oriented industry. Of particular interest were North and South Carolina, which have led the South in attracting textile firms. Sure enough, the biggest reductions in unexplained growth went to North Carolina, South Carolina, Kentucky, and Tennessee—all of which improved via *increases* in predicted growth. The three states with the biggest textile losses—Massachusetts, Pennsylvania, and Rhode Island—were prominently represented among the states that improved via *decreases* in predicted growth. I would concede the possibility that $F^{1.5}$ records not only surplus labor but the agricultural resource attraction. On the whole, however, the findings are consistent with the labor supply theory.

Labor and Markets. Before leaving the subject of labor, it might be a good idea to elaborate on a matter that deserves emphasis. The labor influence is customarily conceived—and this study so conceives it—as the influence of wages, unions, and labor supply *on labor-oriented firms.* What is often overlooked is that low wages and surplus labor contribute to low per capita income. Cheap labor therefore has an adverse effect *on market-oriented firms,* which are far more numerous than the labor-oriented ones. One type of industry is repelled even while the other is attracted. This probably means that the *net* effect of cheap labor is almost nil. If wage levels in the South were to climb suddenly to the national average, I doubt that manufacturing growth in the South would suffer at all (although the composition would change).

This judgment is supported by many findings. Whereas both wages and per capita income have their primary influence in the South (they are relatively uniform elsewhere), per capita income looks more important than wages. Neither W (or variations thereof) nor Y/P is far from zero in its simple *r*, partly because the two variables neutralize each other. But Y/P does a better job of getting off the ground without having W held constant than W does without control of Y/P. Y/P gets to +.48 under per capita growth with T and E/M controlled and to +.41 under percentage growth with T^2 and $\sqrt{E/P}$ controlled. W, though, simply cannot come up with a significant partial *r* until Y/P, F/P, E/Y, or some other variable reflecting income is held constant.

Since per capita growth is the kindest growth variable toward both Y/P and W, it is a useful testing ground. A fair comparison results when we hold constant four variables: T, $(50 - \text{Lat}) (\text{Lg} - 65)^3$, E/M, and West-Rural × 1/(E/M). The climate variable helps Y/P when controlled, the spatial variable helps W, and the industry and threshold variables help both. (West-Rural × 1/(E/M) is the strongest threshold variable when its three partners are controlled.) Y/P and $1/W^2$ (the best wage variable) can be alternated as an extra control variable to see which goes higher when the other is held constant. Here are the before-and-after partial *r*'s for Y/P, $\sqrt{W}$, and $1/W^2$:

	Simple r	Four Held Constant	After $1/W^2$	After Y/P
Y/P	+.02	+.44	+.60	. . . .
$\sqrt{W}$	+.03	+.03	. . . .	–.44
$1/W^2$	+.03	+.01	. . . .	+.46

With four variables held constant, Y/P reads +.44, safely above the 1 percent confidence level. But $\sqrt{W}$ and $1/W^2$ are close to zero; $\sqrt{W}$ even has the wrong sign, having become a feeble proxy for Y/P. In the "after" situations, Y/P leads $1/W^2$, +.60 to +.46. From all appearances, the income effect of low wages is more damaging on the market side than the cost effect is helpful on the labor side.

Thresholds

The fourth-ranking factor contributing to regional differences in manufacturing growth is the failure of a few states (or their principal cities) to cross a
developmental threshold leading to faster growth. Absolute growth, which would
give very little growth potential to underpopulated states even if there were no
threshold influence, credits thresholds with causing only 1 to 5 percent of the
variance. But 6 to 14 percent of the variation in per capita growth and 2 to 8
percent in the case of percentage growth can be explained by excessive underdevelopment in a few states. A well-rounded view of the threshold influence can
be obtained by separately examining (1) the contrasting growth patterns of
the five least developed and the six most developed western states, (2) the proportionality of growth to development within the least developed group, and (3)
the proportionality of growth to development within the relatively developed
group.

West-Rural vs. West-Metro. "Threshold" refers to the fact that, as an
underdeveloped region grows, more and more places acquire the minimum base
of population and industry needed to support other, more demanding, types
of industry. Although underdevelopment is basically helpful to growth, too
much underdevelopment weakens the advantage. Hence the better-developed
states within the most underdeveloped part of the country—the West— get more
new industry than their strong markets would seem to warrant. These states,
referred to earlier as the West-Metro states, are the six with major metropolitan
areas: Colorado (Denver), Utah (Salt Lake City), Arizona (Phoenix), Washington
(Seattle), Oregon (Portland), and California (Los Angeles, San Francisco). The
other five western states—Montana, Idaho, Wyoming, New Mexico, and Nevada—
come under the West-Rural label.

During the course of the analysis two dummy variables were created to
represent, respectively, the West-Rural and the West-Metro states. A dummy
variable customarily (and as used here) divides all cases (states) into an "in"
group valued at one and an "out" group valued at zero. The West-Rural dummy
was valued at one for the five least developed states; West-Metro gave the
unitary value to the six most developed western states. Since one is high and
zero low, positive correlations with growth represent strong growth for the "in"
group and negative correlations represent weak growth.

The dummy variables give sharply contrasting pictures of growth for
different parts of the eleven-state western region. Here are the simple *r*'s for the
dummies correlated with each growth variable:

	Absolute Growth	*Per Capita Growth*	*Percentage Growth*
West-Rural	–.15	–.06	+.22
West-Metro	+.36	+.47	+.48

Each type of growth gives West-Metro an r that is both positive and significant at the 1 percent confidence level ($\pm$ .36) or better. But West-Rural is negative (weak growth in the least developed states) in two instances and insignificant in the third. The positive r for West-Rural under percentage growth is a reminder that the threshold influence does not imply that the ultra-underdeveloped states are necessarily growing slowly. Rather, they are growing slowly in a relative sense—slowly relative to the high growth potential given to them by the market influence (high per capita income, lack of industry, spatial isolation).

When other influences are held constant, the threshold influence stands out better. Table 7–4 shows two control combinations for each type of growth. The second set of each pair is very much like the first but weights some of the variables by temperature or latitude, making the controls stronger. All six combinations control three market factors—demand (a Y variable), supply (an E variable), and isolation (an Lg variable)—and then add one additional market variable, a climate variable, and a wage variable. Absolute growth shows relatively little contrast between West-Rural and West-Metro, although the stronger control combination has them about forty points apart and opposite in sign. This finding reiterates that the threshold influence is weakest with absolute growth. Per capita and percentage growth, in contrast, show significantly negative partials for West-Rural opposed to significantly positive ones for West-Metro in all four remaining columns. The stronger control set under per capita growth places West-Rural at -.47 and West-Metro at +.45. Meanwhile, a West dummy valued at one for the eleven western states and at zero for the rest stays insignificant (except in the first column): neutrality for the West as a whole hides sharp contrasts within the West.

The next three variables on the left tell the story in a different way. Population density (P/M), urban population density (CP/M), and manufacturing employment density (E/M) are all negatively correlated with growth. Their simple r's are significantly negative with per capita and percentage growth (see table 3–5). That is, growth is inversely proportional to development, and the least developed region—the West—is the fastest growing region. But *within* the West, things are reversed: the least developed states are lowest in growth (for the region), and the most developed states are highest. West $\times$ P/M and its two companions show this. These variables are valued at $1 \times$ P/M = P/M (or CP/M or E/M) in the West and at zero elsewhere. Hence the least developed western states (low P/M) are valued close to the central and eastern states (zero). The result: density becomes positively correlated with growth, which means that the more developed western states have faster residual growth (growth not explained by markets, climate, and wages). At any rate, this is true for absolute and per capita growth.

The West-Rural States. If a threshold influence actually is operating, residual growth is likely to become progressively weaker with increasing underdevelopment in the least-developed states. The best variables for testing for

Table 7-4
Partial Correlations for Threshold Variables

Threshold Variables	Absolute Growth $1/W^2$, T^2, P, Lg, $E^{1.5}$, Y	Absolute Growth $(T-9)/W$, T, $(T-9)P$, Lg, $E^{1.5}$, $(T-9)Y$	Per Capita Growth $1/W^2$, T, NE, Lg, E/M, Y/P	Per Capita Growth $(T-9)/W$, T, $(Y/M)^2$, $Lat \times Lg^3$, $(E/M)^2$, $T(Y^{0.8}/P)$	Percentage Growth $1/W^2$, $50-Lat$, $\log F/M$, Lg, $\sqrt{E/P}$, Y/P	Percentage Growth $(T-9)^2/W^2$, T^2, $(T-9)^2\sqrt{F/M}$, $Lat \times Lg$, $\sqrt{E/P}$, $T(Y^{0.8}/P)$
West-Rural	+.07	−.18	−.34	−.47	−.34	−.41
West-Metro	+.21	+.21	+.47	+.45	+.45	+.33
West	+.33	+.02	+.10	−.06	+.15	−.03
West × P/M	+.60	+.22	+.29[a]	+.46	+.17[a]	+.13[a]
West × CP/M	+.67	+.27	+.29[a]	+.46	+.15[a]	+.13[a]
West × E/M	+.58	+.21	+.25[a]	+.44	+.10[a]	+.10[a]
6/(P/M)	+.09	−.10	−.33	−.61	−.30	−.71
West × 1/(P/M)	+.13	−.05	−.30	−.54	−.25	−.63
West-Rural × 1/(P/M)	+.10	−.10	−.41	−.56	−.40	−.67
1/(P/M)	+.08	−.13	−.32	−.66	−.23	−.67
West × 1/(E/M)	+.10	−.06	−.30	−.60	−.21	−.63
West-Rural × 1/(E/M)	+.08	−.10	−.39	−.59	−.37	−.65
West-Metro × CP	+.77	+.34	....	....	....	....
West-Metro × (CP/P)³	+.58[b]	+.29[b]	+.44	+.60	+.26	+.30
West-Metro × CP/E	....	....	+.53	+.38	+.68	+.52

[a]This r is based on the square root of the density variable on the left.

[b]This r is for West-Metro × (CP/P)⁴.

Abbreviations: Y = Income, E = Manufacturing Employment, Lg = Longitude, P = Population, T = Temperature, W = Wages, M = Square Miles, NE = 16 Northeast states (dummy), $T(Y^{0.8}/P) = (T-9)^{1.5} \times (Y^{0.8}/P)$, Lat = Latitude, $Lat \times Lg^3 = (50 - Lat) (Lg - 65)^3$, F = Farm Population, West-Rural = 5 least developed western states (dummy), West-Metro = 6 most developed western states (dummy), West = 11 western states (dummy), CP = Urban Population progressivity are the reciprocals of the density variables. These reciprocals—$1/(P/M)$, $1/(E/M)$, and so on—have a property that makes them useful for this purpose. If a series of values ranges from around one to some very high number, the reciprocals are practically identical—barely above zero—for all but the lowest of the original numbers. In such instances, the reciprocals vary significantly from case to case only for the lowest numbers, which have the highest reciprocals. Thus $1/(P/M)$ and $1/(E/M)$ effectively differentiate only among the most underdeveloped states, and these states determine the r's. The signs on the r's, of course, are the opposite of those for the original variables: a negative r for a density reciprocal means low density (high reciprocal) = low growth.

With this in mind, we can return to table 7-4. Two density reciprocals—$1/(P/M)$ and $1/(E/M)$—appear on the left. These variables, which are applicable mainly to per capita and percentage growth, show significantly negative partials when the market, climate, and wage influences are held constant: the high reciprocal (low density) states are slowest in residual growth. Under the strongest control sets (the second of each pair), the partials become highly significant: $1/(E/M)$ goes to -.66 under per capita growth, and $1/(P/M)$ reaches -.71 under percentage growth. It appears, then, that residual growth in the least developed states *is* proportional (in nonlinear fashion) to development.

The interpretation of these r's, which says that they are determined by the behavior of the least developed states (not some other states), was tested in several ways. First, analyses of residuals as described in the labor supply discussion were made. When density reciprocals were added to regression equations, the western states ran away with the honors. For example, when $1/(P/M)$ was added to the control combination heading the last column, the three biggest reductions in residual (unexplained) growth went to Nevada, Arizona, and Wyoming; all but two western states gained better predictions; and eight of the thirteen largest reductions went to western states. In general, states that were subsequently designated West-Rural improved via *decreases* in predicted growth (previously overestimated) and the West-Metro states improved via *increases* in predicted growth.

Further tests employed the West-Rural, West-Metro, and West dummies. The fact that the West-Rural states actually had the weak residual growth assumed by the interpretation was verified by significantly negative partials for West-Rural. The significantly positive partials for West-Metro and the neutral partials for the West dummy verified that only the five least developed states were troubled—which is the finding required by the interpretation. Next, $1/(P/M)$ and $1/(E/M)$ were multiplied by West and West-Rural so that all but the western, or else all but the West-Rural, reciprocals would be valued at exactly zero instead of approximately zero. This was done to prove that the reciprocals could not effectively distinguish one of the more developed states from another. If variations within the more developed set of states were actually contributing to the r's, then wiping out these variations (by setting all developed states at zero) should appreciably reduce the r's. As table 7–4 shows, multiplying by West and West-Rural makes very little difference and sometimes raises r. For example, in column five, West-Rural $\times$ 1/(P/M) reads –.40, compared to –.30 for 1/(P/M). In short, the density reciprocals *are* carried by the West-Rural states, and growth *is* proportional to development in the least developed states.

The West-Metro States. Does growth continue to be proportional to development within the West-Metro group? If it does, West-Metro times some appropriate measure of development should yield higher partials than West-Metro alone. Take West-Metro $\times$ CP as an example. This variable is valued at $1 \times CP = CP$ in the six most developed western states and at $0 \times CP = 0$ in all of the other states. The West-Metro states not only have the highest values but these values are proportional to urban population. Assuming that the more developed states in the group have higher residual growth than the least developed West-Metro states, West-Metro $\times$ CP should generate higher partials than West-Metro. By way of reservation, CP is relevant only to absolute growth; relative measures are needed for per capita and percentage growth.

Table 7–4 shows that, sure enough, West-Metro $\times$ CP does have higher partials than West-Metro—+.77 compared to +.21 in the first instance. Unfortunately, this particular test is plagued by ambiguity. Does CP represent consumer demand (markets) or development (thresholds)? A fairly comprehensive set of four market variables has been held constant in each column; Y, P, and $E^{1.5}$, are of particular interest in the first column. Demand, and also the supply-demand relationship, seem well enough controlled. Yet West-Metro $\times$ CP could be describing the dynamic side of demand: faster population growth in the West limits the ability of Y, P, and E to describe markets.

Better evidence comes from per capita growth. Some weighted density variables, such as West-Metro $\times$ CP/M, did marginally better than West-Metro but not enough better to convince. However, when urban population percentage—CP/P—was used to measure development, evidence of proportionality was found: West-Metro $\times$ $(CP/P)^3$ often (but not always) gave substantially higher partials than the dummy. Column four of table 7–4 shows West-Metro $\times$ $(CP/P)^3$ with a partial of +.60, compared to one of +.45 for West-Metro. Since CP/P tends to describe the size of major metropolitan areas, the evidence gives tentative support to the idea that a metropolitan area attraction exists. That is, growth is to a limited extent proportional to the size of metropolitan areas within the West-Metro states.

A pattern is starting to unfold: in the West-Metro group, growth is highest where CP is either highest in absolute terms (absolute growth) or highest relative to the growth-rate base. Per capita growth is G/P, or absolute growth over population, and responds to a CP/P weighting scheme for West-Metro. The comparable variable for percentage growth (G/E) is CP/E. CP/E is a cross between a demand-supply ratio and a rural-urban measure; where high, it describes both strong markets and urbanization. West-Metro X CP/E runs consistently higher—usually much higher—than West-Metro when correlated with percentage growth. (Sometimes it predicts well with per capita growth too, as the table shows.) Each of the last two columns in table 7-4 thus shows West-Metro X CP/E with partial r's (+.68 and +.52) about twenty points above those for West-Metro. Other demand-supply ratios, such as Y/E, do not give comparable results when substituted in the formula. It seems, therefore, that the CP in CP/E measures more than consumer demand and that the more urbanized West-Metro states have an extra advantage.

Other Influences

Thus far we have reviewed four influences identified as the leading determinants of regional manufacturing growth: markets, climate, labor, and thresholds. Markets and climate are the primary influences; labor and thresholds are secondary. Two other influences are significant but must rank as tertiary on the comparative scale. These are resources and the urban attraction. A seventh factor hypothesized as a growth influence—agglomeration—does not register as significant.

Resources. The classification of resources as a tertiary influence is somewhat arbitrary, but resources does fall behind labor and thresholds as the fifth-ranking influence (except that thresholds is behind resources with absolute growth). The estimates for resources are based on indirect evidence and therefore allow relatively wide margins for error. These estimates credit resources with responsibility for 1 to 8 percent of the variation in absolute growth, 1 to 15 percent of the variation in per capita growth, and 1 to 8 percent of the variation in percentage growth.

That there is a resource influence seems well enough established by reliable evidence from other studies, for example, the McLaughlin and Robock study (chapter 1). But how important is it? The best evidence from the present study is the unexplained variances left by the most comprehensive Rs (tables 4-5, 5-6, and 6-5). Two percent of the variance for absolute growth, 7 percent for per capita growth, and 3 percent for percentage growth were not explained by market, climate, labor, threshold, and urban attraction variables. Conclusions drawn from such evidence require caution because of the possibility of duplication—more about this in a moment. Yet the final residuals do not leave much for resources to explain.

Regarding duplication, there is always the possibility that variables left out until the last in a multiple correlation exercise will be partly or even wholly duplicated by the variables given priority. But the popular belief that a variable usually loses some of its explanatory power when given deferred entry simply is not true. Quite to the contrary, a variable is just as likely to *gain* through deferred entry. Except where variables are *favorably* intercorrelated (e.g., wages and temperature), the later a variable enters, the more it adds to R^2; and the effect of late entry is to disparage competing variables entered too early for their own good.

Examples from this study illustrate the point. In column three of table 7–4 there is a –.41 partial r for the best threshold variable, West-Rural $\times$ 1/(P/M). This variable initially explains none of the variance: markets and thresholds push growth in opposite directions. Once the four market variables in the control set are partialed out, however, West-Rural $\times$ 1/(P/M) can add .069 to R^2. When T is also controlled the potential threshold increment drops to .047, because the cold climates of Montana, Idaho, and Wyoming reinforce (duplicate) the threshold influence. But a mild wage advantage in the five subthreshold states causes interference, so that the threshold potential rises to .071 when $1/W^2$ is added in. Similarly, the potential contribution of $1/W^2$ goes from about zero when nothing is held constant to .075 with the four market variables controlled to .054 when T is also controlled to .077 if West-Rural $\times$ 1/(P/M) is controlled sixth. Since there is more interference from than duplication by other variables, both wages and thresholds are better off in last (seventh) place than in first, second, third, fourth, fifth, or sixth. T is exceptional: its potential contribution drops from .216 in the first position to .166 in the seventh. But the four market variables collectively add only .314 to R^2 when entered first compared to .426 when entered last.

The point is that a resource variable might well maximize its contribution by entering last in any of the multiple correlation sets. But this contribution could not exceed the unexplained variance. Indeed, it almost certainly would be less than the unexplained variance, since imperfect measurement of the other influences and maybe even a random element in growth must be allowed for. Even if other variables have explained some of what a resource variable might have explained, the duplication is highly unlikely to amount to more than a few percentage points.

As it is, the estimates give resources the benefit of the doubt and assume some duplication. Percentage transfers have been made from climate to resources to allow for possible duplication of Gulf-state petroleum resources. Under absolute growth another transfer, this time from labor, has been made to cover the possibility that $F^{1.5}$ reflects agricultural resources in addition to surplus labor. The allowances for duplication yield resource estimates equal to two-thirds of the labor estimates (a little more than two-thirds with per capita growth). The two-thirds formula is based on other studies (chapter 1). In brief, these studies have found resources to be a declining influence that is less important than the labor influence.

The Urban Attraction.   Careful definition of the urban attraction is needed to avoid misunderstanding. Rural-urban mix is a congeries of contradictory influences. In general, urban states are characterized by (1) advanced industrial-ization, which hurts growth, (2) high wages, which hurt, (3) above-threshold development, which helps, (4) high per capita income, which helps, and (5) a residual influence, which helps.[3] It is this residual influence, which remains when everything else is held constant, that is being called the urban attraction. Since the link between urbanization and per capita income is very strong, it bears emphasis that the urban attraction is defined as excluding the effect of high per capita income; that is counted under markets. So defined—four things excluded—the urban attraction is estimated to explain 0 to 2 percent of the variance for absolute growth, 2 to 7 percent for per capita growth, and 1 to 3 percent for percentage growth.

To say that the urban attraction is what is left over after other influences are defined away may not be too helpful. Why might urban states be more attractive to industry after their per capita income advantage has been neutral-ized and the threshold influence has explained what it can explain? One factor could be rural poverty—not quite the same thing as per capita income—in some of the southern states. Weak residual growth in Mississippi contributed heavily to some significantly negative partial r's for $(F/P)^4$ —farm population percentage— and made lesser yet still important contributions with some other rural-urban variables. Mississippi has the highest black population percentage and the lowest median family income in the nation. Perhaps there is a qualitative aspect of consumer demand such that the rural poor, especially black families in the South, spend disproportionately low shares of their meager incomes on manu-factured goods. If so, per capita income would not pick this up.

Poverty, though, does not look like the full explanation (if it applies at all). Besides Mississippi, the principal growth-losers were Maine, Vermont, West Virginia, Iowa, the Dakotas, and Oregon. Of these, only West Virginia might be regarded as having an unusually severe poverty problem. The urban states that gained were led by New Hampshire, Georgia, Florida, Minnesota, Missouri, Colorado, and Utah—all of them from outside the Manufacturing Belt. One analysis saw $1/(CP/P)$ giving its three biggest reductions in unexplained growth to Minnesota (previously underestimated) and the neighboring Dakotas (over-estimated). New Hampshire, the most urbanized state in northern New England, seemed to be gaining at the expense of Vermont and Maine, even though New Hampshire is less urbanized than any of the Manufacturing Belt states. Oregon, which is rural only in comparison to California and Washington, was another case where the relative rather than the absolute standard of rural-urban mix was at work. The Manufacturing Belt, which has no potential losers (rural states), had no gainers. The general picture, then, was one of intraregional diversion from regionally rural to regionally urban states in regions outside the Manufac-turing Belt.

Besides having less rural poverty, the urban states are probably more attractive because they (*a*) have faster market growth, the result of migration from rural areas to cities, (*b*) tend to contain the population centers of gravity for multistate marketing regions, (c) can offer a wider variety of urban locations, including metropolitan areas, (d) have disproportionately large numbers of industrial consumers located in metropolitan areas, and (e) can offer services, facilities, and other external economies that are relatively scarce among the rural states. Most of this fits under the heading of markets, but uncertainty as to the relative importance of market and nonmarket items makes separate classification advisable. All of the above factors are probably involved in the threshold influence too; there is no denying that thresholds and the urban attraction are related. But considering the "rural" Oregon is one of the West-Metro states and that all of the rural states with poor residual growth (including the Dakotas) were more densely populated (1950) than the West-Metro states of Utah and Arizona, the urban attraction cannot be described as a matter of thresholds.

Turning now to the evidence that there actually is an urban attraction, we find that it emerges only when markets, climate, labor, and the threshold effect are controlled. But it does emerge. With absolute growth, $(F/P)^4$ develops a partial r of -.49 after nine variables are held constant (table 4-5). Per capita growth is more generous. A dummy CP/P variable valued at one for all states more than 57.7 percent urban goes to +.40 with six variables held constant (table 5-3). This dummy is the ninth variable to enter the best ten-variable combination for per capita growth (table 5-5). It is also in the best twelve-variable combination (table 5-6), although here it plays second fiddle to 1/(CP/P). The latter enters at step 9 with a partial of -.48.

Percentage growth offers tentative and then firm evidence of an urban attraction. The tentative evidence appears when F/P outperforms Y/P with just one or two variables held constant. One finds comparative partials of -.48 for F/P and +.21 for Y/P when $\sqrt{E/P}$ is controlled. When both $\sqrt{E/P}$ and $(T - 9)/W$ are controlled, the partials are -.59 for F/P and +.47 for Y/P. The weak growth in the rural states cannot be purely a matter of low income, or Y/P would have the higher partials. In fact, if Y/P is used as a third control variable, F/P falls only to -.42. A different rural-urban variable, 1/(CP/P), enters eighth in the best nine-variable combination with a partial of -.50 (table 6-5). In the best ten-variable set, F/CP enters last with a partial of -.66. The evidence is too consistent for doubt that an urban attraction is at work.

Agglomeration.   Agglomeration is the term for the tendency of industry to attract industry. The term has been applied primarily to the clustering of industry in the Manufacturing Belt. However, it can be applied to any state with a large metropolitan area where industry is clustered. Such clustering could result from intermediate markets and external economies. Firms are said to congregate in order to buy from, and sell to, each other. At the same time this clustering leads to skilled labor pools, business services, transport facilities, and other economies external to the firm. These external economies attract still more industry.

Many variables potentially able to detect agglomeration were studied. First there were the many manufacturing variables—E, VA (value added), E/M, E/P, and so on. Then there were the MB (Manufacturing Belt) and NE (Northeast) dummies: MB was valued at one for the thirteen MB states and at zero elsewhere, and NE delineated sixteen states by including northern New England. The dummies, in turn, were the bases for many dummy-weighted manufacturing variables, such as MB $\times$ E, MB $\times$ E/M, and MB $\times$ E/P. Five other dummies were created to reach industrial states beyond the Manufacturing Belt. These were E > 145,000, VA > \$1 billion, E/P > 7%, E/P > 6%, and CP/P > 57.7% (where 57.7% is barely low enough to include all MB states).

Significantly positive partial r's for any of these variables might have uncovered an agglomeration attraction. A few such r's were actually found, but agglomeration was not responsible. Industry had already been held constant, and the MB, CP/P, or VA dummy was either (a) acting as a proxy for Y/P or (b) identifying the urban attraction in states outside the Manufacturing Belt. The vast majority of the r's were negative. In effect, the MB and NE variables became market variables describing the negative relationship between the supply of regionally produced goods and growth (high supply, low growth). For example, tables 4-2, 5-2, and 6-2 show respective partials of -.67 between MB $\times$ E and absolute growth, -.62 between MB and per capita growth, and -.48 between MB and percentage growth. As a small surprise, there is even a simple r of -.18 between MB and absolute growth. Industry is decentralizing, not clustering.

Agglomeration appears to be moribund, if not actually dead. Perhaps it never was very important, assuming that we are using agglomeration in a regional sense and not denying that industry clusters in large cities within regions. The agglomeration hypothesis gets most of its support from the Perloff study. There it becomes the main explanation for the Manufacturing Belt's showing only a small decline in relative importance between 1900 and 1957. Two better explanations come to mind. The first recalls the significantly positive r's between absolute growth and population (which r's become very strong after manufacturing is held constant). The most populous states had the highest natural increases in population—and received many immigrants too. New demand led to high absolute growth, even though relative growth was low.[4] The second explanation is that of Chinitz and Vernon, summarized in chapter 1. Briefly, the railroad was king before trucking grew up in the 1930s. Railroads have high terminal costs and low line-haul costs; they are expensive for short-haul transportation. Northeastern manufacturers therefore could not save much on transport costs by setting up branch plants before the highway era: terminal costs were still there. For that matter, many regional markets weren't yet big enough for economies of scale. And air service was not yet available for fast, convenient contact with branch plants.

A reservation must now be expressed. The writing-off of agglomeration is partly conceptual. Intermediate markets and external economies—the forces behind agglomeration—could well be (but are not necessarily) the principal factors behind the threshold influence and the urban attraction. On the other hand, there are good reasons for not calling these other influences agglomeration. Although agglomeration economies were never assumed to be confined to the Manufacturing Belt, the Manufacturing Belt was central to the hypothesis. But the West-Metro states, which hold the equivalent position in the threshold hypothesis, are far removed from the Manufacturing Belt, both spatially and developmentally; while the urban attraction is conspicuously absent in the Manufacturing Belt. Moreover, the threshold concept emphasizes the negative effect of underdevelopment rather than the positive effect of industrialization. There is a positive side to thresholds—the West-Metro side—but here we are not talking about the high levels of development found in the Manufacturing Belt today or even forty years ago. We may not be talking about industrialization at all: the size and centrality of the consumer goods market is probably the most essential feature of thresholds. Thus table 7-4 shows higher r's for West $\times$ CP/M than for West $\times$ E/M, that is, for demand rather than industry.

One more reservation is in order, again conceptual. Intermediate markets are undoubtedly very important locational attractions—for the same reasons that consumer markets are. But in this study intermediate markets are classified under the ultimate attractions. Here a distinction must be made between old and new industry as magnets for supplier industries. The agglomeration hypothesis tacitly emphasizes the attraction of *old* industry by emphasizing the agglomerations of the Manufacturing Belt. The old industry, though, has its suppliers; it can attract few new suppliers to the old agglomerations. New supplier plants will be attracted to the *new* consuming plants, which are located mostly outside the Manufacturing Belt. The consuming plants are chiefly market-oriented; so the intermediate markets will tend to coincide with consumer markets. To this extent, intermediate markets have been counted under markets. Supplier firms selling to and locating near labor-oriented industry have been counted under labor, and so on.

Summary Comparison of Influences

Table 7-5 restates the estimated contributions of the significant locational factors to variations in growth. Both minimum-maximum ranges and central tendencies are given. The central tendencies are of course misleading as to precision but are useful for perspective. Skewed probability distributions are assumed in a few cases where there is more leeway for error on the high side than on the low; not all central tendencies are midpoints of their ranges.

The table forcefully reiterates that markets and climate are the dominant locational influences. Together, these two influences explain about 86 percent of

Table 7-5
Summary Comparison of Manufacturing Location Influences in
Relation to Alternative Measures of Manufacturing Growth

Locational Influence	Absolute Growth	Per Capita Growth	Percentage Growth
Markets:			
Range	55–75%	35–55%	50–70%
Central tendency	(65%)	(45%)	(60%)
Climate			
Range	14–28%	15–30%	15–33%
Central tendency	(21%)	(22%)	(23%)
Labor			
Range	3–9%	7–15%	3–9%
Central tendency	(6%)	(11%)	(6%)
Thresholds			
Range	1–5%	6–14%	2–8%
Central tendency	(3%)	(10%)	(5%)
Resources			
Range	1–8%	1–15%	1–8%
Central tendency	(4%)	(8%)	(4%)
Urban Attraction			
Range	0–2%	2–7%	1–3%
Central tendency	(1%)	(4%)	(2%)

absolute growth, 67 percent of per capita growth, and 83 percent of percentage growth. Labor and thresholds rank as important secondary influences, with wages and labor supply combining to give labor a slight edge. The two secondary influences combined explain 9 percent of absolute growth, 21 percent of per capita growth, and 11 percent of percentage growth. Bringing up the rear as tertiary influences are resources and the urban attraction. These account for 5 percent of absolute growth, 12 percent of per capita growth, and 6 percent of percentage growth.

The three types of growth don't always agree on the relative importance of a particular influence. This is to expected. Much depends on the geographic locus of an influence: an attraction (say, a resource) confined to a few under-populated states could profoundly affect per capita growth despite a relatively small contribution to absolute growth—because small absolute increases in states like Nevada amount to large per capita increases. Similarly, thresholds cannot have much effect on absolute growth, since the underdeveloped states whose growth is cut have population bases too small to support large absolute increases. Yet small cuts in absolute growth can become substantial cuts in per capita or percentage growth.

A unique consideration explains why per capita growth gives appreciably less credit to markets and correspondingly more to secondary and tertiary factors than do absolute and percentage growth. This disagreement is due mainly to per capita growth's treating some of the market influence as a constant: some of the variation in markets is lost, and secondary influences become comparatively more important. Per capita growth, remember, is absolute growth divided by population. This means that if absolute growth were determined entirely by population, per capita growth would not vary from state to state. It would always be $(k \times P)/P = k$, where k was some constant. But absolute growth and percentage growth *would* vary, with this variation being perfectly predictable from market (population) variations. Absolute growth would equal $k \times P$ and could be predicted from P; percentage growth would equal $(k \times P)/E$, or $k \times P/E$, and could be predicted from either P/E or E/P—which would still vary from state to state. Under these conditions, there would be no variation in per capita growth to explain by markets or anything else. But 100 percent of the variation in absolute and percentage growth could be explained by market differences.

The real situation is not this extreme, of course. Population's simple r of +.42 explains only 18 percent of the variation in absolute growth (not counting market-climate interaction). When we get to per capita growth, population's effect on absolute growth is cancelled by population's use as the rate base. There is still a supply-demand ratio effect, comparable to the effect of E on absolute growth when P is held constant, but this should not be mistaken for the effect of population per se. A -.45 partial for $(E/P)^3$ with per capita growth indicates that the supply-demand effect explains 20 percent (r^2) of per capita growth. Percentage growth, or absolute growth divided by E, *is* influenced by population through population's 18 percent effect on absolute growth. This effect *and* the supply-demand effect are now combined in E/P, which should therefore explain something like $18 + 20 = 38$ percent of the variation in percentage growth. Actually, $\sqrt{E/P}$ has an r of -.60 and an r^2 of .36, which is close enough to .38 to illustrate the point. The point is that per capita growth loses around 18 percent of the market influence measured by absolute and percentage growth. This is why markets explains an average of 63 percent of the variance for absolute and percentage growth but only 45 percent (or 63 - 18) for per capita growth.

Policy Implications

The study findings have definite policy implications for governmental programs designed to assist distressed areas (county and multicounty units). Such programs recognize that cities compete with one another for new industry. The more assets (e.g., air service) a city has, the better its chances of securing a new plant desiring to locate in a general region. Agencies concerned with helping distressed areas therefore try to bolster the assets of cities in these areas. The idea is to divert new plants from nondistressed to distressed areas by strengthening urban "infrastructures" in the distressed places.

One implication of the study findings is that this strategy is subject to regional constraints. A new plant's arena of locational competition is normally confined to a particular region of the country: virtually all of the variation in regional growth can be accounted for by *regional* influences. This means that *local* influences merely direct growth to particular cities within preselected regions. (There are exceptions involving the so-called footloose industries, of course, but the findings imply that the exceptional cases have no appreciable effect on disparities in regional growth.)

It follows that the effectiveness of a local infrastructure strategy will be inversely proportional to (*a*) the number of distressed areas in a general region and (*b*) the size of that region. The more distressed areas there are, the greater the likelihood that success in attracting a new plant to a particular area will be offset by a loss in another area in the region—whatever area would have attracted the plant had not the assets of the winning location been strengthened. Similarly, the larger the distressed region, the less likely it is that particular firms able to locate in an area being assisted will have options outside the distressed region. If distress is pervasive within a large region, as with the low-income form of distress in the South, an infrastructure type policy may be only marginally effective.

This points to a related policy implication. In situations where a policy of localized assistance tends to borrow from one distressed area to help another, regional assistance is a possible alternative. A regional policy could be geared to regional influences. Unfortunately, the regional attractions this policy would need to enhance are not easy to manipulate. Markets, climate, wages and labor supply, thresholds, resources, and urbanization are a discouraging set of influences to work with. Even so, one of these influences has possibilities.

That influence is markets. In chapter 1 we noted the possibility of exploiting market forces and asked the question: Is the market influence important enough to be useful? Our subsequent finding that markets is not only the leading influence but a very powerful one provides the answer: Yes.

The market influence, one recalls, has supply, demand, and spatial isolation aspects. We certainly don't want to curtail supply as our means to the end of a stronger market: that would be self-defeating. But demand could be increased through a massive, long-term spending program in a region. The region would have to be large enough to minimize the problem of leakages. Perhaps the only region where such a policy might be appropriate is the South. We have already seen that a potentially strong market attraction in the South is undermined by low per capita income. Thus, in addition to being a large region with a pervasive problem, the South is a logical setting for a demand-generation strategy. Questions of whether a southern market-expansion program is justified and of what public expenditure mix would be most appropriate are beyond the scope of this study. From the narrow standpoint of demand creation, however, the most effective outlays would be ones putting money into the hands of consumers—transfer payments, teacher salary subsidies, and the like. Education programs designed to raise the wage-earning potential of poverty group members—blacks and poor whites—would likewise be relatively effective.

Spatial isolation can also be manipulated— in effect if not in fact. Here we return to the Chinitz-Vernon and Lichtenberg finding (chapter 1) that highways have promoted industrial decentralization. Highways have reduced short-haul transport costs vis-à-vis long haul (rail) costs. This has increased the savings that companies can realize through regional branch plants. New superhighways connecting hinterland manufacturing hubs with relatively nearby cities—markets—might spur further decentralization. The highways would tend to enhance the attractiveness of locations beyond the Manufacturing Belt. They would do this by raising the transport "tariff" (the long-haul-short-haul differential) created by spatial isolation. Again, the question of whether the benefits would justify the program outlays is beyond the scope of this study. What concerns us is that regional influences can play a role in developmental policy.

Notes

Chapter 1
Introduction

1. See Victor R. Fuchs, CHANGES IN THE LOCATION OF MANUFACTUR-
   ING IN THE UNITED STATES SINCE 1929 (New Haven: Yale University
   Press, 1962), esp. pp. 27, 152–164, 259. The other leading study is Harvey
   S. Perloff, Edgar S. Dunn, Jr., Eric E. Lampard, and Richard F. Muth,
   REGIONS, RESOURCES, AND ECONOMIC GROWTH (Baltimore: Johns
   Hopkins Press, 1960); it awards first place to markets.
2. Similar postwar manufacturing employment growth patterns for the periods
   1947–61 and 1950–65 are described in two recent studies: Daniel Creamer,
   CHANGING LOCATION OF MANUFACTURING EMPLOYMENT (New
   York: National Industrial Conference Board, Studies in Business Economics,
   no. 83, 1963), pp. 18–22, 47–49, 94–96; and Advisory Commission on
   Intergovernmental Relations, STATE-LOCAL TAXATION AND INDUS-
   TRIAL LOCATION (Washington: ACIR, report no. A-30, April 1967),
   pp. 8–16.
3. Glenn E. McLaughlin and Stefan Robock, WHY INDUSTRY MOVES
   SOUTH (Washington: National Planning Association, 1949).
4. Wilbur R. Thompson and John M. Mattila, AN ECONOMETRIC MODEL
   OF POSTWAR STATE INDUSTRIAL DEVELOPMENT (Detroit: Wayne
   State University Press, 1959).
5. Ibid., p. 6.
6. The supply-demand ratio aspect of the situation is stronger than it might
   appear. The ratio of employment to population does not vary much from
   state to state; so total employment is proportional to population. The ratio
   of manufacturing employment to total employment (the variable used) is
   therefore closely proportional to the ratio of manufacturing employment
   to population: the former is roughly three times the latter. The –.66
   correlation therefore indicates slow growth where supply is high relative to
   demand.
7. Benjamin Chinitz and Raymond Vernon, "Changing Forces in Industrial
   Location," HARVARD BUSINESS REVIEW 38, no. 1 (January-February
   1960), pp. 126–36.
8. Robert M. Lichtenberg, ONE-TENTH OF A NATION (Cambridge: Harvard
   University Press, 1960).
9. Perloff et al., REGIONS. See also the condensed and updated version:
   Harvey S. Perloff, with Vera W. Dobbs, HOW A REGION GROWS (Washington: Committee for Economic Development, supplementary paper no.
   17, March 1963).

10. Perloff and Dobbs, HOW A REGION GROWS, p. 44; cf. p. 103.
11. Perloff et al., REGIONS, pp. 473, 475; cf. pp. 397, 459.
12. Ibid., p. 398.
13. Ibid., pp. 82, 397.
14. Ibid., pp. 448, 459.
15. Ibid., p. 50.
16. Ibid., pp. 49–50.
17. Ibid., p. 81.
18. Ibid., p. 394.
19. Ibid., p. 393.
20. Fuchs, MANUFACTURING.
21. Ibid., p. 27.
22. Ibid., p. 259.
23. Note that Fuchs treats the furniture industry as labor-oriented, whereas the Perloff study concludes that it is primarily market-oriented.
24. Ibid., pp. 94, 96, 98.
25. Ibid., p. 88.
26. Ibid., pp. 152, 154.
27. Ibid., p. 95.
28. My data give 1947–63 percentage growth correlations of –.53 with the log of population density, –.57 with the log of manufacturing employment density, and –.60 with the square root of manufacturing employment per capita. The fact that population density continues to show the lowest reading, taken in conjunction with its high intercorrelations with the industry variables, strongly suggests that population density is a proxy for industrialization.
29. The Fantus Company, Inc., THE APPALACHIAN LOCATION RESEARCH STUDIES PROGRAM: SUMMARY REPORT AND RECOMMENDATIONS (prepared for the Appalachian Regional Commission, contract no. C-273-66) (New York: December 1966).
30. Ibid., p. 14 (italics in original).
31. Ibid., p. 19.
32. James F. McCarthy, HIGHWAYS, TRUCKS, AND NEW INDUSTRY (Washington: American Trucking Associations, 1963).
33. Edward L. Ullman, "Amenities as a Factor in Regional Growth," GEOGRAPHICAL REVIEW 44, no. 1 (January 1954), pp. 119–32.
34. Edwin J. Cohn, Jr., INDUSTRY IN THE PACIFIC NORTHWEST AND THE LOCATION THEORY (New York: King's Crown Press, Columbia University, 1954).
35. Ibid., pp. 146, 179.
36. Ibid., p. 33.
37. George H. Borts and Jerome L. Stein, ECONOMIC GROWTH IN A FREE MARKET (New York: Columbia University Press, 1964), p. 46.
38. Robert B. Bretzfelder, "Geographic Trends in Personal Income in the 1960's," SURVEY OF CURRENT BUSINESS 50, no. 8 (August 1970), pp. 14–23, esp. chart 10.

39. Advisory Commission on Intergovernmental Relations, TAXATION, pp. 63–68.

40. William V. Williams, "A Measure of the Impact of State and Local Taxes on Industry Location," JOURNAL OF REGIONAL SCIENCE 7, no. 1, pp. 49–59.

Chapter 2
Hypotheses and Methodology

1. A more complete discussion of this point will be found in Robert B. McNee, A PRIMER ON ECONOMIC GEOGRAPHY (New York: Random House, 1971), pp. 135–38.

2. Ibid., p. 139.

3. For a discussion of skilled labor shortages in Pacific Northwest cities of less than 40,000 population, see Edwin J. Cohn, Jr., INDUSTRY IN THE PACIFIC NORTHWEST AND THE LOCATION THEORY (New York: King's Crown Press, Columbia University, 1954), pp. 46–47.

4. The 1967 Census of Manufactures was not published until 1971.

5. The program used was the BMD02R Stepwise Regression program of the Health Sciences Computing Facility, School of Medicine, University of California at Los Angeles.

6. Value added is used to avoid double counting of manufactured inputs. It is the value of shipments less the cost of materials, supplies, fuel, electricity, and contract work (with further adjustments for changes in inventory). Value added includes profits, labor, services, depreciation, maintenance, rent, insurance, and certain taxes.

7. The two-thirds formula passes over the New York study, which classifies 8 percent of the nation's industry as labor-oriented and 8 percent as raw materials-oriented. This classification relates to total industry, not just to relatively new firms. If the study's finding that raw materials are declining in importance is correct, the newer firms would probably have something like 5 to 6 percent of their employment in the raw materials category— which again puts resources at about two-thirds the level of labor.

Chapter 3
Simple Correlations

1. The reason for CP/F's singular performance among the table 3–2 variables is mathematical. Mathematically, CP/F is similar to $(CP/P)^2$; it gives exaggerated weight to the most urbanized states. This is easily seen if we simplify by ignoring the rural nonfarm population—neither CP nor F—and assume that P consists wholly of CP and F. For ten units of population, the possible CP/F ratios are 1/9, 2/8, 3/7, 4/6, 5/5, 6/4, 7/3, 8/2, and 9/1. If these points are plotted above CP/P on a graph, the result is a curve: CP/F rises exponentially as CP/P increases.

Chapter 4
Absolute Growth: Partial and Multiple Correlations

1. Harvey S. Perloff, Edgar S. Dunn, Jr., Eric E. Lampard, and Richard F.
   Muth, REGIONS, RESOURCES, AND ECONOMIC GROWTH (Baltimore:
   Johns Hopkins Press, 1960), p. 417t.
2. Ibid., p. 419, 419n.
3. Ibid., p. 417t.
4. Ibid., p. 485.
5. Ibid., p. 411t.

Chapter 5
Per Capita Growth: Partial and Multiple Correlations

1. Albuquerque, with a 1950 metropolitan area population of 145, 673, might
   be regarded by some as a major metropolitan area. But it certainly is not in
   a class with Salt Lake City (274,895), Phoenix (331,770), Denver (612,128),
   Portland (704,829), and Seattle (844,572)—not to mention some places in
   California.

Chapter 6
Percentage Growth: Partial and Multiple Correlations

1. There is nothing incongruous about having log F/M and $(F/M)^3$ in the same
   combination. They don't duplicate; indeed, they are the two most significant variables. As already explained, logs relatively magnify differences
   among low values by leveling off the high values. Exponents relatively (and
   absolutely) magnify differences among high values. Log F/M is carried to
   significance by the low values—by underdeveloped western states, where
   farm population density is extremely low. But $(F/M)^3$ is carried by high-
   density southern states. Correspondingly, log F/M is negatively correlated
   (low density, high growth) while $(F/M)^3$ is positive when significant.

Chapter 7
Synthesis and Conclusions

1. This applies to regions but not necessarily to localities within them. Local
   attractions are something else. They may even be the opposite of the
   regional attractions: indications are that firms tend to prefer the most
   industrialized cities within regions. Evidence to this effect is presented in
   two papers by the author, "The Effect of Modern Highways on Urban
   Manufacturing Growth" (paper presented at 48th annual meeting of the

Highway Research Board, Washington, D.C., January 1969), pp. 25–29, and "The Effect of Airline Service on Manufacturing Growth in Cities below 40,000 Population" (Washington: Economic Development Administration, 1970), pp. 29–35.

2. In contrast to absolute and per capita growth, percentage growth often gives its best climate r's to latitude rather than temperature. The explanation may lie with New Mexico, where a continental climate produces colder winters than latitude would suggest. (New Mexico's 35 degree January mean temperature compares with Arizona's 50 and Arkansas' 41.) New Mexico has very low absolute growth and below-average per capita growth, which agree more with temperature than latitude. But New Mexico ranks fourth in percentage growth, and its warm latitude is in a better position than its cold temperature to take credit.

3. CP/P (urban population percentage) has intercorrelations of +.69 with $\sqrt{E/M}$, +.63 with E/P, +.50 with W, +.19 with the West-Metro dummy, and +.75 with Y/P. If the right variables are held constant so that a proxy relationship prevails, urbanization can easily be made to appear hostile to growth (see table 7–1).

4. The Perloff study occasionally subsumes the Manufacturing Belt's population attraction under agglomeration. (See Harvey S. Perloff, Edgar S. Dunn, Jr., Eric E. Lampard, and Richard F. Muth, REGIONS, RESOURCES, AND ECONOMIC GROWTH (Baltimore: Johns Hopkins Press, 1960), pp. 448, 459.) In the present study, only the industry-attracts-industry concept of agglomeration is challenged; the population aspect falls under markets.

Index

Absenteeism: 18, 27; and climate, 8, 28, 66
Absolute growth, 2, 8, 49, 52-53, 74, 81-
  114, 184; and agglomeration, 62, 93,
  101, 114; and climate, 85-86, 93, 101,
  113, 114; and demand, 83-84; and
  labor, 96-98, 113; and markets, 95-96,
  113, 114; and population, 3, 184, 210;
  and resources, 113, 203; and spatial
  isolation, 85-86, 125, 188; and threshold, 81, 113, 114; and temperature, 93,
  113; and unions, 86, 91-92, 121, 194;
  and urban attraction, 114; and wages,
  86, 91-92, 98-99
Absolute variables, 32, 51-53, 187
Advertising, 24
Advisory Committee on Intergovernmental
  Relations, 20
Aerospace industry, 28
Agglomeration: 12-13, 21, 23-25, 40-41,
  60-62, 109, 143, 148, 206-8, 217;
  and absolute growth, 93, 101, 114; and
  per capita growth, 122, 128, 136-137;
  and percentage growth, 156, 171; and
  urban attraction, 26; see also Manufac-
  turing Belt
Agricultural resources, 7, 18, 27, 196
Air service, 25, 207
Aircraft industry, 13-14, 28
Alabama, 41, 97, 129, 132
Alaska, 92
Albuquerque, N.M., 136, 216
Aluminum industry, 18
American Trucking Associates, 18
Appalachia, 16-18
Appalachian Regional Commission, 16
Apparel industry, 7, 9, 14, 26, 168
Arizona: 19, 28, 38, 62, 78, 86, 134, 144,
  169, 201; and climate, 84, 153, 167, 217
Arkansas, 217
Atlanta, Ga., 112, 113
Attribution, 47-48
Automobile industry, 7, 109

Birth rate, 84, 184
Blacks, 205
Borts, George, 19-20, 29
Branch plants, 7, 18, 22, 164, 207, 212
Bretzfelder, Robert, 20, 29
Bureau of Census, 2, 57
Bureau of Economic Analysis, 20
Bureau of Public Roads, 32

California: 2, 12, 28, 41, 63, 78, 86, 87,
  134, 144, 155, 205; and climate, 13-14,
  15, 19, 84, 153
"Catching up" hypothesis, 15, 23
Causality, 85
*Changes in the Location of Manufacturing
  in the U.S. Since 1929* (Fuchs), 32
Chemical industry, 7, 19, 27
Cheyenne, Wyo., 136
Chinitz, Benjamin, 10-11, 207, 212
Climate: xi, 2, 8, 13, 14, 19, 28, 44, 49, 58,
  66-67, 69, 79, 106, 161, 189-92, 208-
  9; and absenteeism, 8, 28, 66; and absolute growth, 85-86, 93, 101, 113, 114;
  and consumer demand, 28; and markets, 67, 89, 118, 120, 189-92;
  and per capita growth, 66, 69, 71-74,
  120-21, 127, 136, 147, 148; and percentage growth, 28, 66, 69, 75, 86,
  155-56, 159, 161, 170-71, 180, 182,
  217; and population, 14; and wages, 28,
  69, 85, 86, 98, 120, 129, 155, 191-92;
  see also Temperature
Coal mining, 1
Coefficient of determination, 48
Cohn, Edwin, Jr., 19, 21
College training, 9
Colorado, 38, 62, 89, 110, 134, 145, 146,
  177, 179, 205
Columbia River Basin, 19
Connecticut, 40, 109, 111
Construction costs, 28
Consumer demand: 9, 24, 26, 74, 164,
  184-85; and absolute growth, 91-92;
  and per capita growth, 117, 144; and
  percentage growth, 156-58; rural, 39,
  42, 112; see also Demand
Contour variables: 39, 57-58, 85, 120, 136,
  144, 154, 164; see also Longitude *and*
  Latitude

Decentralization, 11, 212
Delaware, 40, 61, 132, 187
Demand: 53, 69, 79, 183, 211-12; absolute,
  22, 37, 87-89, 184; and absolute
  growth, 83-84; and per capita growth,
  117-18, 123-24, 144, 152, 184; and
  percentage growth, 151-52, 156-58,
  159; and population, 2; relative, 53-55,
  184-85; and spatial isolation, 101; and
  temperature, 84; see also Supply-demand
  ratios
Denver, Colo., 136, 146, 216
Dependent variables, 30-31, 67-68
Depressed areas, 2, 211
Developing nations, 2

About the Author

Leonard F. Wheat is an economist with the Economic Development Administration of the U.S. Department of Commerce. He has also held positions with the Office of Regional Development Planning, the Bureau of the Budget, the Navy Department's Office of Special Projects, and the Minnesota Department of Taxation. He received the B.A. from the University of Minnesota, Duluth, in 1952, the M.A.P.A. (public administration) from the University of Minnesota in 1954, and the Ph.D. in political economy and government from Harvard University in 1958. Dr. Wheat is the author of a philosophical study, *Paul Tillich's Dialectical Humanism*, and of research monographs dealing with the impact of highways and air service on manufacturing growth in small cities. His affiliations include the American Economic Association, the American Society for Public Administration, the Society of Government Economists, and numerous conservation organizations.